STUDIES OF BUDDHISM

STUDIES
OF
BUDDHISM

Edited by
G. PRASAD

BKP

BHARATIYA KALA PRAKASHAN
DELHI (INDIA)

First Published : 2006

Published by **C.P. Gautam**
BHARATIYA KALA PRAKASHAN
3421-A, IInd Floor Narang Colony, Tri Nagar,
Delhi-110035. Phone : 27393083, 32967505

ISBN : 81-8090-070-3

Laser Type Setting by
A-ONE GRAPHICS
JD-18C, IInd Floor, Pitampura, Delhi-110088

Printed By :
BDH Printer at Salasar Imaging Systems
Delhi.

CONTENTS

FOREWORD

The All-India celebrations of the twenty-fifth centenary of the Great Saint Gautama Buddha have served to rouse our consciousness as to the grandeur and excellence of our cultural heritage as also of our ancient cultural link with the eastern countries of Asia. The contributions of Buddhism to Indian culture are varied in the domains of language and literature, art and architecture, and moral and social ideals.

Gautama Buddha lived in an age of iron-cased beliefs and traditions, and he had to overcome an almost insurmountable opposition offered by the deep-rooted orthodoxy of a large section of the people with their long established rituals and ceremonies. His teachings, however, appealed both to the intellectuals and to the masses realizing for the first time that the path of salvation could not be the monopoly of the few. His emphasis on self-reliance, and his exposition of the law of causality were a notable contribution to Indian thought and religion.

PHILOSOPHY : Gautama Buddha was brought up in the Indian traditional faith and doctrines but he had the courage to challenge their efficacy and usefulness in reducing and ultimately eliminating the human sufferings. In pre-Buddha days, many thinkers applied their minds to the quest of the Truth, but their thoughts and beliefs have not come down to us except those found in the *Upaniṣads* and the Jaina literature. In the former, the findings about the Truth and its nature were varied, and it is the monistic conception that found prominence. The highest

Truth, according to this view, is transcendental, and so it can be referred to by negations only of known concepts. Gautama Buddha subscribed to this view but he adhered strictly to negative terms and criticised all attempts at forming any positive concept about the ultimate Truth. It has been expressed in these words by Nāgārjuna:—

अनेकार्थमनानार्थमनुच्छेदमशाश्वतम्।
एतत् तल्लोकनाथानां बुद्धानां शासनामृतम्॥

[It connotes neither one nor many; it is neither annihilation nor eternality—this is the immortal teaching of Buddhas, the leaders of the world.]

His thorough-going view in this respect is due to his firm conviction that the Absolute is perfectly absolute and has no relation whatsoever with the composite universe. It is the *Asaṅkhata* or the unconstituted, and hence uncaused and unconditioned, unoriginated and undecaying, attributeless, one and the same, and it has nothing to do with *Samkhata,* the constituted. He would not admit, even that 'it is',or 'it is not' or it is *both* 'is and is not',or it is not *both*'is and is not'.In the very first Sutta of the *Dīghanikāya* acknowledged as the *Buddhavacana* by all sects of Buddhism, he warned his disciples against any attempt to speculate about the Ultimates, which he said, could only be realised by the Perfect within one's own self (*paccattaṃ veditabbo viññūhi)*. He instructed them to apply their minds to the origin and decay of the constituted world which lacks substantiality and is subject to impermanence and painfulness. It is for this reason that his disciples went to the utmost length to analyse the physical and mental constituents of a being in the Abhidhamma texts. "Buddha's appeal was to logic, reason and experience, his emphasis was on ethics, and his method was one of psychological analysis" says Nehru in his *"Discovery of India"* (1956), P. 109. In course of his analysis of the phenomenal world, Buddha visualised the law of causality or the law of momentary sequence of the dynamic states of worldly beings and objects, and it is by this law that he establishes the non-existence of eternal soul. Of notable importance is his *kṣ aṇikavāda,* which implies that a cause has no duration, and it ceases as soon as the effect is produced; there is not even an infinitesmal interval between the cause and its effect. There is no static cause in a dynamic world and it is by inference only that we say that the cause produces an effect. Bertrand Russell in his *"Mysticism and Logic"* (p.192)) says that cause and effect are mere sequences, and there is no law of causality but mere causal sequences, "*the earlier event is the cause and the later event the effect*", as "night is the cause of day". This interpretation has some affinity with the Buddhist law of causation. A being, according to the Buddhists, is a ceaseless stream of mental and physical constituents (*nāma-rūpa*), which disintegrate and re-integrate almost simultaneously. Such disintegrate and re-integration are in fact invariable sequences and not exactly cause and effect, as there is no substance to maintain the relation of cause and effect, nor is there any interval for the cause to produce an effect.

ETHICS : In pre-Buddha India, there were ethical instructions scattered in the Brahmanic texts but the ethics was subservient to the religious faith. These texts prohibited in a general way the killing of living beings, which was regarded as sin but if the killing took place in a ritual, it was considered proper as also meritorious. It was Gautama Buddha, who presented us for the first time with an elaborate ethical code, which, of course, was meant primarily for the monks and nuns. The code for the laymen was short and simple and was not quite free from a religious bias as it was incumbent upon all lay-devotees to take *Triśaraṇa* and to develop faith in the excellence of the *Triratna.* The rules lie scattered in the Nikāyas, particularly, in the *Dhammapada, Petavatthu, Vimānavatthu* and the *Jātakas.* It was for the fulfilment of the ethical obser-vances that Gautama Buddha introduced the monastic system, hitherto unknown to Indian religion. The monasteries became almost academies for imparting training to the monks and nuns. Some of the monasteries grew into large post-graduate institutions, teaching not only the humanities but also science as it existed then. The later phenomenal development of the monastic institutions started by Buddha on a small scale shows also the organising ability of the Buddhist monks and the laity. It lies to the credit of some of the later masterminds who were not merely recluses and authors but were actively engaged in founding and maintaining magnificent academic institutions, which trained up monks and missionaries, equipped them with sufficient knowledge of the subjects needed for propagating and establishing Buddhism in foreign lands. Apart from the academic aspect, these monasteries led to the development of monumental art and architecture, caityas and stūpas with *bas-reliefs* and images, which are objects of wonder even to the artists and architects of the present day.

BUDDHA'S DISCIPLES : In our enthusiasm for Buddha and his strong personality, we often forget that Buddhism owes much of its greatness to a few generations of his disciples. It is well-known that Buddha's first band of disciples consisted of intellectuals of high class Brahmana and Śreṣṭhī families, and that a substantial portion of the so-called *Buddhavacana* was the composition of his disciples like Sāriputta and Kaccāyana, Upāli and Ānanda. They were followed later by distinguished saintly disciples like Moggaliputta Tissa, Upagupta and Nāgasena. Then there were the galaxies of poets, philosophers and logicians like Maitreyanātha, Aśvaghoṣa, Nāgārjuna, Vasubandhu, Asaṅga, Āryadeva, Śantideva, Diṅnāga, and Dharmakīrti. Some of the terse and learned treatises were commented upon by the authors themselves and they were followed by quite a large number of commentators like Guna-mati, Sthiramati, Candrakīrti, Bhāvaviveka, Śilabhadra, Yaśo-mitra, Kamalaśīla, Dharmottara, Karṅakagomin, Manora-thanandin, all of whom did not confine themselves to mere expositions but introduced fresh food for thought, surpassing in quality and quantity even the original authors. Their contributions to Buddhist logic and philosophy are inestimable. Then there were many authors of Tantrik works, some of which were very deep in their philosophical approach. To these bands of Buddhist intellectuals, we should add the host of translators, who rendered the Buddhist texts, indluding the abstruse ones, into Central Asian dialects, and Chinese, Tibetan and Monogolian. Much of the greatness of the Buddhist cultural movement depended on the literary, spiritual, and cultural activities of the Buddhist teachers covering about a thousand years.

The ancient Indians usually avoided mentioning the names of authors of works, and the Buddhist writers were not an exception to this practice. The works of unknown authors, e.g. the *Lalitavistara, Mahāvastu, Laṅkāvatāra, Prajñāpāramitā* etc. speak highly of the intellectual level of their authors, whose contributions have enriched the Indian literarture. The high-flown lucid and well-knit style of the *Kārikās* and *Kāvyas* shows that there were several Buddhist geniuses, who raised the banner of Buddhism aloft, and wafted the aroma of the religion all around Asia.

Though ostensibly a religious movement, Buddhism rendered an almost unforgettable service to Indian culture in general and covered almost the whole of India from Kashmir to Conjeveram and from Bengal to Bombay , Gujrat and Rajputana. *It behoves* free India to find out how and when this religious *cum* cultural movement developed, casting influence on so many countries of Asia.

The *Indian Historical Quarterly* has been rendering service in its humble way to the unfolding of this ancient Indian culture by bringing together the thoughts of devoted researchers in the field of Buddhism. In order to take a part in the All-India Celebrations, two issues of the *Quarterly* are devoted exclusively to original papers written by distinguished scholars of Buddhist religion, philosophy, art, architecture, history and tradition, and we trust that a collection of such studies will present to our readers important aspects of a movement, of which India should feel proud.

EDITOR

LIST OF PLATES

INTRODUCTION

This compendium on study of Buddhism was earlier published on the great and auspicious occasion on of the twenty-fifth century celebrations organised in the honour of Lord Buddha not only by our grateful nation but also by the world at large. The contributions of Buddhism are varied in the domains of language and literature, art and architecture and moral and social ideas throughout the whole world. The Buddha's teachings inference the religious culture of half of the humanity. It is all due to the fact that the Buddhism moves very easily from one culture to another because its emphasis is on internal practice rather than external forms of religious behaviour. Its emphasis is on the way each practitioner develops his or her mind not on how he dresses, the kind of food he eats, the ways he bears his hair and so forth.

There is no doubt that this collection is comprising of large numbers of topics on various vital and important subjects of which the following are considered to be the rarest ones :

1. Presentation of astronomical examinations of the five dates of Gautam Buddha's life time.
2. The early Bronze Statue of one of the most charming Chinese Buddhas ails from Yunnan. The statue brought to Tali between 788 and 833 A.D. as the construction of the Pagoda was begun in 833 A.D.
3. Hari Varman's theory of cognition. He contended that in case the sense is cognises, it will cognise all things simultaneously. He denied the distribution between primary and secondary elements. He has also done away with the division of thought into mind and mental

properties. Profound Hari Varman was one of the and original thinkers of ancient India.. He taught all his life Paritantric approach to Buddha's preaching, so much so he had to take great pains to weed out the fungi that grew over the master's teachings.

4. A rare type of Bodhisattva images from Sanchi.
5. Buddhist view of re-eternity of Vedas. The theory of momen-tariness is established by Sugata. The question of eternity of Vedas should by dropped by all means.
6. A remarkable view by Professor Paul Nasion Oursel about a fundamental antithesis between the Brahmanical and Buddhist ideas of dharma in their relation to political theory:
   (i) The Brahmanical theory in maintaining a social order based upon the special constitution of each caste does not encourage the appearance of 'a Political sprit' white the Buddhist theory by aiming a low applicable to all mankind makes for unlimited imperialism.
   (ii) While the Brahmanical dharma falls 'short of monarchy' its Buddhist counter part leads to 'world empire'.
   (iii) While the king in the Brahmanical theory continues himself to the preservation of the eternal social order, the king according to the Buddhist theory not only causes the law to reign but also starts and promotes the same.
   (iv) Dharma in the Smritis connotes a above all the comprehensive laws of the social order of which the king himself is the unit, while it signifies in the conception of the Buddhist canonists specially the principle of righteousness.
   (v) In the political aspects the Brahmanical dharma stands particularly for the whole Duty of the king

(Rajadharma) which from the first in conceived is sufficiently the elastic terms to provide for the needs of the kingdom and to permit in Manu and still mire Mahabharata (after Bhisma) the wholesale incorporation of the Arthasastra categories and concepts relations to the branches of the kings internal and external administration. On the other hand the Buddhist dharma in its relation to the king in volues the application of the universal ethics of Buddhism to the state administrations this principle being extended to the somewhat idealistic concept of the world-ruler.

7. The historic importance of Pataliputra including glimpses of its archeological survey and findings pertaining to different periods.

This volume is most interactive and highly educatives informative one and I hope that it will be very useful and popular among scholars, students and readers who are intrested in Buddhism. The wholesome efforts by the different writers will be instrumental in creating interest and generating appreciation and encouragement for spreading over Buddhism in India and western countries in line of the eastern and southern countries of the world.

1

THE MASTER'S LIFE IN STONE[1]

The sixth century before Christ was an era of great spiritual upsurge throughout the ancient East. In India it was marked by birth of Gautama Buddha, the 2500th anniversary of whose *Mahāparinirvāṇa* we are now celebrating.

The epic story of the Master's life,—his miraculous birth under a *Sal* tree, his early mental struggles and renunciation of the world, his sojourn in search of True Knowledge and its attainment, his preachings among men, and demise after a fruitful life of eighty years devoted to the cause of deliverance of all sentient beings, have been told in great detail in the *Buddhacarita*, the *Lalitavistara* and other Buddhist texts. Here it is proposed to place before the reader the life-story of the Master as narrated in sculptures by ancient Indian craftsmen during the first two hundred years or so before and after Christ. These come mainly from places like Bharhut, Sanchi, Gandhara, Mathura, Nagarjunakonda and Amaravati, and have a charmingly simple narrative quality.

It is said that after performing the ten virtues (*Paramitās*) in innumerable previous births, recounted in the *Jātaka* stories, Bodhisattva, destined to be an omniscient Buddha, had been born in Tusita heaven when the gods besought him to be reborn on earth to deliver mankind. Bodhisattva then decided to be born of king Śuddhodana of Kapilavāstu and his queen Mahāmāyā. Māyā had a dream in which she saw the divine Bodhisattva enter her body in the form of a white elephant. This story is narrated in three successive panels in relief sculpture from Amaravati of *circa* 2nd century A.D. (P1.I). The scenes from left to right show the divine Bodhisattva seated on a throne in Tusita heaven while entreated by the gods to be reborn on earth; his descent from heaven in the form of a white elephant carried in a palanquin by the gods with music and dancing; and the queen's dream. The last scene only is depicted in a circular bas-relief on the Bharhut railings of *circa* 2nd century B.C. (P1. II).

When the queen spoke of her dream to the king, he summoned the soothsayers to interpret it. They declared that she had conceived a son, destined to be either a Cakravartī Rājā or a Buddha.

The gods guarded the mother and child during gestation. When her confinement approached, Māyā wished to see her parents at Devahrada, but at Lumbinī Park on the way she was delivered of the child while she stood under a *Sal* tree holding its branch. The child was received by the attending Dikpālas, but he immediately descended on the ground and taking seven lotus steps in all directions exclaimed triumphantly that he was the *foremost* of the world. A Gandhara relief reproduced here (P1. III) shows the divine child coming out of the right side of the body of queen Māyā who stands under a *Sal* tree holding its bending branch. The god Śakra (Indra) receives the child on a piece of cloth while Brahmā looks on from behind, and above, a heavenly being whistles to indicate the rejoicings in heaven. The flywhisk in the panel, a symbol of royalty, suggests the future greatness of the newborn child who is shown as having descended on the ground and standing with his right hand raised in *Abhaya*, about to take the first seven steps.

The child Bodhisattva was then given his first bath, and mother and child were brought back to Kapilavāstu amidst great rejoicings. These scenes are depicted in a Gandhara relief (P1. IV) divided into three panels. The story runs from right to left. The first scene on the right shows the bath, the second in the middle the return of queen Māyā from Lumbinī in a bullock-cart with the child in her arms, and the third on the left, musicians outside the city-gates of Kapilavāstu welcoming mother and child.

Shortly after, the sage Asita visited king Śuddhodana and wished to see the newborn child. When he was brought, the sage bowed respectfully to him for he recognised that the child was a Buddha to be. He was named Siddhārtha. The king then called the astrologers to cast his son's horoscope (Pl. V). They discerned in his body the thirtytwo infallible marks of greatness and declared that he was a Tathāgata who would forsake the world when he had seen four ominous sights.

Māyā having died shortly after childbirth, Siddhārtha was brought up by his aunt and stepmother Mahāprajāpatī Gautamī. Like other Śākya princes he was admitted into a school where he showed himself superior to all others. A relief from Gandhara shows young Sidhārtha seated on a stool writing on a tablet (Pl. VI).

At sixteen Siddhārtha was married to Yaśodharā, daughter of his uncle Suprabuddha. Time passed on and Bodhisattva lived in luxury befitting a prince. His father took great care that none of the ominous sights predicted by the soothsayers should meet his eye, but to no avail. The day came when Siddhārtha driving in his chariot to the pleasure gardens saw the first of the ominous sights—a decrepit old man. He returned home with a heavy heart. On another day he saw a sick man on the road, and on a third, a corpse. His mind was greatly agitated. Then on a fourth occasion he saw a monk whose serene bearing made a deep impression on him, and he longed to be an ascetic. The birth of his son Rāhula at this moment made him decide on renunciation, for he saw that his worldly ties were multiplying. His father re-doubled his efforts to keep him away from such thoughts, and arranged for his nightlong entertainment by the palace dancers and singers. About midnight they became tired and fell asleep. The sight of sleeping women, snoring and in *dishabille*, made Siddhārtha realise the deceptiveness of appearances and the futility of worldly pleasures. A Gandhara relief (Pl. VII) represents the scene in two panels. The upper one shows Siddhārtha reclining on a couch with Yaśodharā seated beside, and female musicians entertaining him. The lower one shows Yasodharā asleep on a couch and the tired musicians dozing in unseemly attitudes. Bodhisattva's mind was filled with disgust and he decided to leave the place at once. He asked his groom Chandaka to bring his horse Kaṇṭhaka. Mounted on his favourite horse and accompanied by his groom, Siddhārtha then left the palace in quest of True Knowledge amidst rejoicings in heaven. The *Mahābhiniṣkramaṇa* or Great Renunciation is illustrated by another Gandhara relief sculpture (Pl. VIII) which shows the prince passing through the city-gates of Kapilavāstu on his horse while his groom holds a parasol over his head and two Yakṣas lift up the hoofs of the horse lest there be noise. Māra, the Evil One, stands in front urging Bodhisattva to abandon his quest.

Travelling far Siddhārtha arrived on the bank of the Anomā where he alighted from his horse and gave up his jewels and ornaments to Chandaka bidding him return to Kapilavāstu with Kaṇṭhaka. Cutting off his long hair he then flung it to the sky where it was received in a golden casket by Śakra for worship in heaven. A bas-relief on the Bharhut railings of *circa* 2nd century B.C. depicts the scene of the worship of Buddha's hair-lock in heaven (Pl. IX). The three-storied building is the Vaijayantī Palace of god Śakra and the building with a domed-roof Sudharmā, the Assembly Hall of the gods. The panel shows Buddha's hair-lock placed on a throne and nymphs dancing around to the accompaniment of music.

Wandering from place to place in search of True Knowledge Siddhārtha Gautama came upon Ālāra Kālāma of Vaiśālī and Rudraka Rāmaputra of Rājagṛha, and became their disciple. But their teachings did not satisfy him, and he resolved to apply himself to the severest austerities (*Mahāpadhāna* or the Great Effort) at Uruvilva near Gaya. For six years he performed the most severe penance and became as thin as skeleton (Pl. X).

But the Truth still eluded him. He realised that self-mortification was not the way to Enlightenment and gave up the practice of austerities. At daybreak on the fullmoon day of Vaiśākha Bodhisattva took his seat under a big pipal tree on the bank of the Nairañjanā, when Sujātā the village headman's daughter came to make her offering to the holy tree. Seeing Bodhisattva seated under the tree shining in his own effulgence she took him to be the tree-god come to life, and offered him the food. Nourished by her food Bodhisattva resumed his meditation resolved on attaining *samyaksambodhi*. He obtained from a grass-cutter a bundle of soft green grass, spread it at the foot of the pipal tree and thereon took his seat. A Gandhara relief (Pl. XI) shows Gautama approaching the seat under the Bodhi tree on which grass has been spread. Behind him is Māra carrying a sword.

Māra thought that his authority over the temporal world would end if Bodhisattva attained supreme knowledge. He was, therefore, determined to use all his powers to prevent Bodhisattva from attaining *samyaksambodhi*. He tempted, threatened and entreated Bodhisattva, but when all his efforts failed Māra attacked him with his hosts. But Bodhisattva remained unmoved in his seat and overcame Māra and passed on to Buddhahood. A fragmentary relief sculpture from Gandhara (Pl. XII) shows below seated Buddha (broken) two of Māra's soldiers with sword and shield tumbling down in defeat.

After his attaianment of Bodhi the gods entreated Gautama Buddha to preach his new Dharma for the benefit of mankind. Buddha yielded to their entreaties and proceeded to Riṣipattana Mṛgadāva (Sarnath) near Vārāṇasī to preach his new gospel. Here he delivered his First Sermon known as the "Turning of the Wheel of Law" (*Dharmacakrapravartana*) to the five Brahman ascetics *(Bhadravargīyas)* who had earlier deserted him at Gaya for giving up the practice of austerities. A Gandhara relief (Pl. XIII) shows Buddha seated under a tree surrounded by a number of devotees among whom may be recognised his first five disciples with their shaven heads.

Some time later Buddha again proceeded to Uruvilva near Gaya to convert Kāśyapa's and his brothers who were fire-worshipping Jatilas. In Kāśyapa's fire-temple lived a fierce serpent. Buddha spent a night in this temple and subdued the serpent with his own effulgence. A relief panel (P1. XIV) on the Eastern Gateway of the Great Stūpa at Sanchi shows the scene of this Miracle of the Fire Temple. The temple is shown with an altar in front, a throne indicating the presence of Buddha, the five-hooded serpent, the Brahman ascetic Kāśyapa and his brothers, as also the Nairañjanā river. After the miracle at the fire-temple Kāśyapa and his brothers arranged a sacrifice. But Buddha spread a spell over them so that wood could not be split, fire could not be lit, and sacrifice could not be offered until Buddha consented. Another relief panel from the Eastern Gateway of the same Stūpa at Sanchi illustrates this second miracle (P1. XV).

When news of Gautama's attainment of Buddhahood had reached king Śuddhodana he sent repeated messages to his son to return to Kapilavāstu. Buddha finally consented to visit his home town. But the proud Śākyas were at first unwilling to show due respect to him. Buddha won them over by walking miraculously through mid-air and performing many other wonders. A relief panel on the Eastern Gateway of the Great Stūpa at Sanchi shows at the bottom the aerial pathway, while the scene of Māyā's dream incised at the top indicates that the scene is the Miracle of Kapilavāstu (P1. XVI).

Anāthapindika, a rich merchant of Śrāvastī, became a follower of Buddha and presented prince Jeta's Park at Śrāvastī to the Lord for constructing monastery. Prince Jeta agreed to sell the park for as many gold Kārṣāpana coins as would cover the ground. A relief medallion on the Bharhut railings (P1. XVII) shows a bullock-cart bringing the coins to the garden and two persons engaged in spreading them. Anāthapiṇḍika is shown as carrying a waterpot for consecrating the gift by pouring water.

While at Śrāvastī king Praesenajit of Kośala visited Buddha, and the latter performed one of his great miracles to convince people of his superiority over the heretical teachers, Pūrṇa Kāśyapa and others. At his bidding an immense pathway appeared in the sky from east to west, and there were many wondrous lights. He made water and fire issue from his body, then seated on a lotus he multiplied himself in all directions. A Gandhara sculpture (P1. XVIII) shows the pavilion of the Miracle at Śrāvastī where the contest was held. Buddha is seated in the centre on a lotus flanked by Śakra and Brahmā on either side, while women peep from windows above.

It is said that Buddha went up to the heaven of the Thirty three gods *(Trayastriṁśa)* to expound his *Dharma* to his mother, who was reborn there. When he was about to descend a triple ladder appeared in the sky at Śakra's command, and accompanied by Brahmā and Śakra, Buddha came down it near Sāṇkāsya. A relief panel on the *stūpa* railings from Bharhut (P1. XIX) shows the triple ladder, a throne under a tree, two flying deities and devotees waiting. A footprint on the top and lowermost rungs of the middle ladder indicates the descent.

Once when Buddha was at Kauśāmbi a monkey offered him honey in bowl and then drowned itself in a nearby tank. A relief panel from the Northern Gateway of the Great Stūpa at Sanchi shows this scene (P1. XX).

In the course of his journeys in Magadha, Buddha lived for some time in the Indraśāla cave on Vediyaka hill near Rājagṛha where Śakra visited him to discuss some philosophical problems. He was accompanied by his Gandharva musician Pañcaśikha. The scene is depicted in relief sculpture from Mathura of *circa* 2nd century A.D. (P1. XXI).

Devadatta, the jealous cousin of Buddha, made several attempts to destroy him. Once he hired some assassins and waylaid Buddha. But eventually the assassins confesed their guilt and were converted. A relief panel from Gandhara shows the assassins assembled behind a wall, while one of them bows down at the feet of Buddha (P1. XXII).

Buddha died at the ripe old age of eighty in the *Sal* grove at Kuśīnārā, between twin *Sal* trees. It is said that when he reached the *Sal grove at* Kuśīnārā Buddha was too ill to proceed. Ānanda then spread a couch for him between the twin *Sal* trees. Buddha laid himself down on his right side with his head to the north and finally breathed his last. The Gandhara relief reproduced here (P1. XXIII) is an elaborate representation of the Great Decease. In the centre of the panel Buddha's body rests on a cot between two *Sal* trees. In the uppermost row are flying deities, while the next two lower ones show a number of princely figures who are possibly the Malla chieftains, some of whom are throwing flowers on Buddha's body while others are grieving. The monk nearest Buddha's head holding a flywhisk is possibly his disciple Ānanda, while the nude figure standing second from the left is an Ājīvika ascetic. The monk standing next to the Ājīvika ascetic is possibly Buddha's principal disciple Mahākāśyapa who is said to have arrived on the scene just after Buddha had passed away. According to the story he got the news from an Ājīvika ascetic.

It is said that the dead body of the Master was placed in a coffin before it was consecrated to the flames. A Gandhara relief (P1. XXIV) reproduced here shows the coffin between twin *Sal* trees attended by five persons, namely, Vajrapāṇī, three monks of whom the one carrying a staff is possibly Mahākāśyapa, shows the Great Decease and the cremation at Makuṭ abandhana near Kuśīnara. Beside the funeral pyre are two Malla chieftains extinguishing the flames by pouring milk from vessels tried to long poles.

After the cremation there was a scramble for the relics. Finally these were divided among eight claimants which included King Ajātaśatru of Magadha, the Licchavis of Vaiśālī, the Śākyas of Kapilavāstu, the Bulis of Allakappa, the Koliyas of Rāmagrāma, the Mallas of Pāvā and a Brahman of Veṭhadvīpa. A relief on one of the entrance pillars of the Bharhut *toraṇa* shows a royal personage riding on an elephant carrying relic casket.

Stūpas were built over the relics of the Master and worshipped by the devout. Thus said the Lord to Ānanda when the latter wanted to know how they should treat his remains after his death : The remains are to be burnt and the bones put in golden caskets, and at the cross roads *caityas* are to be built over these and venerated with flags and streamers, and perfumes and garlands. This is shown in a Bharhut relief panel (P1. XXVI).

R. C. Kar

FOOTNOTES

1. The article is based on an illustrated talk delivered by the author at the Indian Museum in July, 1956. The illustrations are of exhibits in the Indian Museum, Calcutta, copyright reserved by the Department of Archaeology, Government of India.

2

DATES OF PRINCIPAL EVENTS IN THE BUDDHA'S LIFE

It has been very widely circulated in the press that the Buddhists of Ceylon and Burma have declared that in this year of 1956 A. D. on May 24,2500 years will be completed from the date of the Buddha's *Mahāparinirvāṇa*. About the date of this great world event, there are current the Ceylon and Burma traditions, according to which the date is 544 B.C.

In the *Saṁyutta Nikāya* (I, p. 50-51) there is a veiled reference to two eclipses, first the lunar and the second the solar, both in the month of lunar *Māgha* and the events were in this order:[1]

(1) Coming of the month of Māgha

(2) The lunar eclipse which happened on Dec. 29—559 A.C. (560 B.C.)

(3) The solar eclipse of Jan. 14,—558 A.C. (or, 559 B.C.)

I have also shown[2] that in the year on Dec. 27, 576 B.C. (—575 A.C.) at G.M. Noon,

True Sun=270° 17'
True Moon=95° 57' } δ Cancrae=93° nearly

The full-moon happened about 5-12 A.M., I.S.T.

Hence the true Winter Solstice day was at this period of eclipses, 27th of Dec. This date of December 27, shows that the month of *Māgha* began with the Pauṣa full-moon on the W.S. day and the months were full-moon ending.

On examination of the great work, "*Canon der Finsternesse*" by Oppolzer for the period of time from, —580 A.C. to —483 A.C. I found that the only eclipses first of the Moon and then of the Sun at an interval of fortnight, of which the solar eclipse happened at the middle of the month of Māgha and both the eclipses were visible from Śrāvasti. The dates of the two eclipses have been stated above.

If we accept that the Buddha's Nirvāṇa happened in,—544 A.C. the eclipses referred to in the *Saṁyutta Nikāya,* happened about 16 years before. The other view of the *Nirvāṇa,* viz., 483 B.C. about 76 years later than the year of the eclipses (560-559 B.C.) is not correct.

There can thus be no doubt that the Nirvāṇa of the Buddha happened in the year,—544 A.C. (i.e. 545 B.C.). With this basis as a certainty it has been possible to find out five dates of principal events in the Buddha's life-time, as we shall see presently.

It is generally known that the Buddha passed away exactly after completing 80 years in luni-solar reckoning. It is generally known that the moon's phases near to the fixed stars repeat in 19 years. Hence on completion of 76 years or 4 times 19 years, the lunar phase of his birth day would be repeated approximately. In the remaining four years of the Buddha's life the birth day in the Julian calendar would very nearly present a new-moon day instead of a full-moon day and *vice versa*. The same birth day lunar phase would come about half a lunation later. This point cannot or should not be lost sight of by any scientific researcher.

Observations: — We take that the Buddha's Nirvāṇa happened in, —544 A.C. This year and date are similar to May 21, 1951 A.D. The actual date has come out as April 22,—544 A.C. (J.D.=1522474).

Again on completion of 76 years, the year and date are similar to May 4,1947 A.D. The actual date year becomes April 7,—558 A.C (J.D.=1520997).

Here by the difference of the J.D. Nos. viz., 1477 days we have 4 years of 365.25 days + 16 days.

In the last four years of the Buddha's life there must have been 50 lunations.

The dates as correctly found out are serially presented:—

1. Siddhārtha's Birth Day

April 6,—624 A.C. (J.D. = 1493238) at G.M. Noon or I.S.T. 5-30 P.M.

Long. of—	Long. of—
Mean Sun = 7° 55' 19" .44	Libra = 186° 45' 33"
Mean Moon = 186 20 19 .61	True Sun = 9 34 44.44
Lunar Perigee = 237°38'52".31	True Moon = 182 18 11
A. Node = 112° 21' 44" .55	Full Moon next day *about* 8 A.M. Moon, conjoined with & *Libra* the chief star of the *Viśākhās*.

II. Prince's Renunciation

December 18,—596 A.C. at G. M. N. or I. S. T. 5-30 P. M., J.D. 1503722.

Long. of—	Long. of—
Mean sun = 261° 25' 55".36	True Sun = 262° 12' 50"
Mean Moon = 87 36 20.26	True Moon = 91 25 25
Lunar Perigee = 323 5 25	α *Cancri* = 92 24 26
A. Node = 6 11 36.05	F.M. about 18 hrs. before, i e. on the previous day.

This date of Dec. 18,—596 A.C. was the day of the moon's conjunction at night with *Puṣyā nakṣatra* of which δ *Cancri* is the "junction star". Gautama summoned his attendant Chandaka and with him left his father's palace at midnight when all the citizens were fast asleep.[3]

III. Siddhārtha becoming the Buddha

April 10,—589 A.C.J.D.=1506025, at G.M. Noon or I.S.T.5-30 P.M.

Long. of—	Long. of—
Mean Sun = 11° 22' 40".35	True Sun = 12° 57' 11".95
Mean Moon = 192 50 51.02	True Moon = 189 54 20.00
Lunar Perigee = 224 36 16	F. M. about 6 hrs. later.
A.Node= 245 14 26.07	Long. of α *Libra* = 190° 14' 43"

IV. Buddha at the age of 76 years

April 7,—548 A.C. (J.D. = 1520997) at G.M.N. or I.S.T. 5-30 P.M.

Long. of—	Long. of—
Mean Sun = 8° 29' 22".22	True Sun = 9° 47' 46".88
Mean Moon = 189 51 33.52	True Moon = 190 34 2.19
Lunar Perigee = 184 12 21.84	α *Libra* = 190 48 53
A. Node = 82 24 51.94	F.M. and conjunction with α *Libra*, at this time of 5-30 P.M. I.S.T.

V. Buddha's Nirvāṇa

Date April 22,—544 A.C., G.M.T. x o^h or I.S.T. 5-30 A.M. J.D. = 1522474.

Long. of—	Long. of—
Mean Sun =23° 47' 52".06	α *Libra* = 190° 52' 13''
Mean Moon = 204 48 32.82	*Libra* = 196 47
Lunar Perigee = 254 41 29.36	F.M. at about 8-30 P.M. I.S.T.
A. Node = 4 13 40.81	True Sun =24° 55' 35".50
	True Moon = 201 2 34

Over and above the five dates of Gautama Buddha's life-time it is possible to present below the planetary positions on Gautama Buddha's birthday.

Date, April, 6,—624 A.C. at G.M. Noon or I.S.T. 5-30 P.M. (J.D.=1493238).

Tropical longitude of—

True Sun=	9°	34'	49" 44	Full-moon about 6 A.M. next day.
Moon=	182	18	11	
Mercury=	356	23	44	Mercury stood at 13° from Sun
Venus=	329	21	43	Venus ,, ,, 40 ,, ,,
Mars=	354	2	51	Mars ,, ,, 15.5 ,, ,,
Jupiter=	298	32	32	Jupiter ,, ,, 71 ,, ,,
Saturn=	345	31	59	Saturn ,, ,, 24 ,, ,,

These "star planets" were all visible by the naked eye, as morning stars and could be seen before some hours of the Buddha's nativity. Buddha might have been born on the 7th April of,—624 A.C. about 3 A.M. This procession of the planets was something extraodinary.

Concludidng Observations—

The astronomical exmination presented above shows conclusively that the Ceylon-Burma tradition as to the Mahāparinirvāṇa of Gautama Buddha is the most accurate a tradition that has been faithfully and wonderfully recorded. I have seen the work of Geiger; his conclusions as this date of the Nirvāna are indefinite and confusing.

I began the writing of this note and on the request Mr. Nirmal Chandra Lahiri, now in-charge of the Office of the Indian Ephemeris and Nautical Almanac in Calcutta, who has very kindly helped me in revising the calculations.

The moon has been corrected by four of five principal equations. The most important in my findings is the procession of planets" as morning stars which led the astrologers at the birth of Gautama—624 A.C. would either be an Emperor of the World or a holy man who would be a mendicant pure and simple. His teachings influenced the religious culture of half the humanity.

The Buddhists always record the Mahāparinirvāṇa era and never the birth-day of Gautama Buddha.

P. C. Sengupta

FOOTNOTES

1. P. C. Sengupta, *Ancient Indian Chronology,* pp. 220, 221.
2. *Ibid.*, p. 220n.
3. *Lalita Vistara,* R. L. Mitra's edn., pp. 265-266. Bodhisattvaḥ sarvaṃ nagarajanaṁ prasuptaṁ viditvārātrisamayaṁ copasthitaṁ jñātvā Puṣyañca nakṣatrādhipatiṁ yuktaṁ jñātvā sāmpratam niṣ-kramanakālamiti jñātvā Chandakamamantrayate sma,

3
THE BUDDHA AND LANGUAGE

Language is one of the most fundamental features of human culture; some would say *the* most fundamentally important. The use of language distinguishes man, as a biological genus, from other animals. No other animals have yet been shown to possess articulate speech as we know it in men; no doubt many animals succeed in communicating with each other in limited ways by the use of vocal sound, but in spite of the efforts of many able biologists, no one has yet proved that such communication approaches the elaborate conventionalized systems which characterize all known human speech. And conversely, no human group has ever been found which lacked a language in this sense.

In one way, then, language may be said to be a unitary feature characterizing all men. But in another sense, which is socially much more important, language divides man from man. For no two languages, no two dialects of the same language even, are exactly alike. And language differences are very noticeable. The most naive human being quickly becomes aware of them, and if pressed, he would often find it hard to do so. If he hears speech in a language so remote from his experience that he cannot understand it, his first reaction may be that the alien speaker cannot really talk at all. The Russian word for Germans means literally "dumb; people who can't talk" — that is, can't talk Russian. There are many similar instances. If the alien speaker uses a dialect closely related to the hearer's own, then, while the hearer may understand perfectly or nearly so, he may be more or less surprised, and his surprise may be tinged with amusement or scorn; the speaker may seem to him to be strangely ignorant of the "proper" way of talking.

There are countries where only one language is spoken, but where in the course of time strikingly different dialects of that language have developed. It often happens then that one such dialect acquires superior social prestige, most commonly for political reasons; it is often the language of the capital. This becomes the "standard" language of the country, like standard Southern British, or standard French (originally local to Paris), and all members of the politically or culturally dominant class speak it; but often many of them can also speak the dialects of their original homes.

A peculiar variant of this situation occurs when the "upper" classes adopt a language of culture which is noṭ the same as any dialect actually spoken (by the uneducated) in the country. It may be a language quite unrelated to any of the country's living dialects; Latin occupied this position in Hungary for centuries; until 1825 Latin was the only language allowed to be spoken in the Hungarian parliament. In the Roman Catholic Church, wherever it flourished, Latin even now has a certain vogue, in writing and speech. It is thus used especially when Roman Catholic priests need to communicate with each other but cannot speak or understand each other's vernaculars; for example when a German and a Spanish priest have occasion to write or speak to one another. A very similar situation exists in India. Most Indians know that when a South Indian pandit, whose native language is Dravidian, communicaties with a North Indian Paṇḍit, both will naturally write or speak in Sanskrit, which is ordinarily the only language known to both.

With this we draw near to the main topic of this paper. The general historic position in India of Sanskrit as a literary and religious language is so well known to Indian readers, and to most others who are likely to see this article, that I shall not discuss it. What interests me here is its relation and the relation of linguistic usage in general, to Buddhism, and to the Buddha himself.

I begin with a somewhat abbreviated translation of passage from the Pali canon (*Cullavagga* 5.33; *Vinaya Piṭaka,* PTS. ed., ii. 139. 1ff.):

Two monks, brothers, of fine (cultivated) language and fine (eloquent) speech, came to the Buddha and said: Lord, here monks of miscellaneous origin (literally, of various names, clan-names, races or castes, and families) are corrupting the Buddha's words by (repeating them in) their own dialects; let us put them into Vedic (*chandaso āropema*). The Lord Buddha rebuked them: Deluded men, how can you say this? This will not lead to the conversion of the unconverted ... ... And he delivered a sermon and commanded (all) the monks: You are not to put the Buddha's words into Vedic. Who does so would commit a sin. I authorize you, monks, to learn the Buddha's words each in his own dialect.

This incident is certainly a part of the oldest Buddhist tradition, for very similar accounts are found in a number of Chinese translations of the Buddhist canonical works. They are fully presented in French translations by Lin Li-kouang, *L'aide-memoire de la vraie loi* (Paris, 1949), 218ff. I have given excerpts from the most important parts in English (based on Lin's French) in my Buddhist Hybrid Sanskrit Grammar (New Haven, 1953) 1.10-12 (see also the adjoining sections). These will not be repeated here, but should be consulted by any one who wishes fully to understand the reasons for the inferences I am about to draw.

Several facts of considerable interest emerge from a study of the various forms of this ancient passage.

First: dialect differences were clearly and easily preceptible in the speech of the monks who attended the Buddha. It is said, in a Chinese translation, that "their pronunciations are not the same."

Second: many, doubtless most of these monks spoke Middle Indic dialects. There were some, particularly born brahmans, who knew and could use the sacred language of brahmanism; but it may perhaps be assumed that even they, when not speaking to one another, made use of Middle Indic. In one of the Chinese translations the two originally brahman monks complain that their fellow-monks "do not know mascu-line and feminine gender, nor singular and plural, nor present, past, and future, nor long and short vowels, nor metri-cally light and heavy syllables." Such traits of language, which seemed errors to the brahmans, characterize some Middle Indic dialects as they would appear from the standpoint of Sanskrit,. when compared with it'.

Third: when proposing to codify the Buddha's teachings in their own "cultured" language, the two brahman monks say *chandaso āropema*, which certainly means "let us put (them) into Vedic." Some have understood, "into verse". But this makes no sense in the context; it is clearly not verse as contrasted with with prose, but a different *language*, which they wish to use. The word *chandas* is regularly used by Pāṇini when he notes a Vedic usage that differs from his own Sanskrit; he always says *chandasi*,"in the Veda" (such and such a form is used).This use of *chandas* is also familiar in epic and classical Sanskrit literaturre (Boethlingk and Roth, Sanskrit-Worterbuch, II. 1080, s. v. *chandas* 3; V. S. Apte, The Student's Sanskrit-English Dictionary, Bombay, 1922, p.212, s. v. *chandas* 5). Here *chandas* need not refer to the poetic parts of the Veda alone, and it is not at all likely that it was so intended. The Brāhmaṇas and Upaniṣads, which are mainly prose, are classed as parts of the Veda, that is *chandas*. The language of the Upaniṣads, even the oldest of them like *Bṛhadāraṇyaka* and *chāndogya*, is fairly close to classical Sanskrit, but it could still be called linguistically *chandas* "Vedic". It was probably something like this language that the brahman monks wanted to use. It may, of course, have been even closer to Pāṇinean Sanskrit. We have no way of telling. But no such term as "Sanskrit" is used in the Pali text, nor even in the commentaries on it; indeed, the Pali equivalent (Saṃkhata) of the word Saṃskṛta seems never to be used in a linguistic sense. Nor do the Chinese translators use any word which proves that their Indic originals used that word. Pāṇini's date is still uncertain, and it is at least possible that he was later than the Buddha. In any event, the use of the word Saṃskṛta of the Sanskrit language seems to be relatively late. The high, cultivated language of brahmans, into which the two monks wanted to translate the Buddha's teachings was known to them as "Vedic" *(chandas)*, in contrast with the Middle Indic dialects which were used by most of their brother-monks; some Middle Indic dialect was doubtless used by the Buddha himself.

Fourth: the Buddha emphatically rejected the proposal of the brahman monks, and gave orders that all monks should learn and repeat his teachings in their own several dialects. This clearly implies that when the Buddhist gospel was carried by missionaries into new regions, the coverts were to exercize the same privilege. They were to learn and recite the teachings in their own local dialects. This is very definitely stated in several of the Chinese translations, which command use of "the popular language" of the various regions or countries. And all versions of this passage, northern and southern, make very clear and Buddha's reason for this injunction. He was preaching a gospel for all men, not for a select elite. He wanted to be sure that every human being could understand his message. He felt that his aim would be defeated if his words were codified in a learned, literary language (Vedic) which only the upper classes could understand.

At first, it seems clear that Buddhist monks and missionaries obeyed this injunction. Early Buddhist inscriptions, like those of Bharhut, give evidence of this. Wherever Buddhist communities were established, versions of the sacred texts, or some of them, were recited in the local vernaculars. In one or two cases, extensive local cannons of this sort, or parts of them, in Middle Indic vernaculars, have survived to this day. The best known is the Pali canon; it originated somewhere in west-central India. We may be certain that there were many others, but most of them have been lost.

As long as Buddhism spread only in the northern parts of India the use of local vernaculars can hardly have involved anything like what we should call "translation". In the Buddha's time, the popular dialects of those regions were almost exclusively Indo-Aryan, and chiefly in the Middle Indic stage. They must also at that time have been so close to each other as to be mutually intelligible. (Even some centuries later, the edicts of Aśoka suggest that this may still have been true). A Buddhist missionary could recite the texts in his own vernacular, and his hearers would repeat them in theirs, perhaps without even clearly apprehending the linguistic differences. (But it is quite possible, also, that the dialect of the missionary may at times have been imitated, to some extent, by the local converts, consciously or unconsciously.) Translation cannot have become a serious problem until Buddhism spread to Dravidian-speaking regions in the south, and to extra-Indian counties like Chinese Turkestan, Tibet and China.

However, after a few centuries the Buddha's followers in India, and in some adjoining countries, began to ignore his injunction to clothe his teachings only in genuine, popular vernacular. Instead they began to make use of canons composed in learned languages, which were not, no longer, the native dialects of any people. Pali itself was originally based on a north Indian vernacular; but after Buddhist monks carried the Pali canon to Ceylon, Burma, Siam, and Cambodia, it came to be a church language, like Latin in Europe. It had to be learned in school, and is still so learned in southern Buddhist countries. In short, it came to have a position in those regions similar to Sanskrit in branmanical India.

In India itself, or in some part of it, what happened was different. The great social prestige of Sanskrit, as a language of literature and culture among brahmanical Hindus, began to influence their Buddhist neighbours and associates. Like the two learned monks in the old Vinaya story, later Buddhists felt that it would be more dignified if they imitated the brahmans and Sanskritized their compositions. Some of them—the poet

Aśvaghoṣa is an example—frankly abandoned the use of vernaculars in literary works, and used standard Sanskrit as a vehicle. Aśvaghoṣa believed to have been a brahman himself originally, and to have undergone the usual brahmanical Sanskrit education in his youth.

A different and a very curious course was adopted by one group of Buddhists. Instead of completely giving up the literary use of vernaculars, they took an old Middle Indic dialect (its original locale is unknown to us) in which Buddhist texts existed, and partially Sanskritized it, but so imperfectly that the underlying Middle Indic still showed through the half-veneer of Sanskrit. Thus arose what I have called Buddhist Hybrid Sanskrit (it could have been called, perhaps, Hybrid Middle Indic), a strange language in which for centuries most North Indian Buddhist texts (so far as we know them) were composed. It has often been described as a corrupt or bad Sanskrit, but this distorts the truth. It is a blend of Middle Indic with Sanskrit, but this distorts the truth. It is a blend of Middle Indic with Sanskrit, but its basis, or substratum, is Middle Indic; the Sanskrit features are secondarily and superficially laid on.

To be sure, as time went on this Sanskritizing process was carried further and further. In the oldest texts preserved to us, notably the *Mahāvastu,* Middle Indic or hybridized phonology and grammatical forms are still very abundant, though genuine Sanskrit forms are perhaps equally so. In later times, more and more regular Sanskrit forms appear. Often these replace original Middle Indic or hybrid forms in later versions of the same passages, so that we can see the process of Sanskritization going on before our eyes. The latest works of this tradition came to look superficially like almost standard Sanskrit, though careful study will always reveal some Middle Indic forms. But even the latest Buddhist Hybrid Sanskrit texts still retain numerous *words*, lexical items, which show their vernacular origin. Though they may be made to look like Sanskrit, though their phonetic shape and grammatical formations may be perfectly standard Sanskrit, these items of vocabulary never occur in Sanskrit, or never in the same meanings, whereas they do occur (for the most part) in Middle Indic dialects, especially Pali. They thus prove that they belong to the Hybrid tradition, going back ultimately to Middle Indic, in spite of their seeming Sanskrit guise.

Thus the Buddha's desire that his teachings be couched in the native dialects of all peoples was frustrated, at least in his native land. It would not have consoled him to know it, but there ensued one result of interest to linguists—the development of a strange, artificial, literary language, perhaps unique in its nature—Buddhist Hybrid Sanskrit.

Franklin Edgerton

4

PHONETIC CONVERGENCE IN PĀLI

In his Preface to the Pāli Dictionary, p. xvi, Childers has compiled a short list of Pāli words, origin of which is traced to one or more Sanskrit words. He has just listed the words without indicating any lines on which depends the trend of these changes.

I propose to label the process of transforming two or more Sanskrit words into one Pāli word as 'Phonetic Convergence', since in it we notice actually two or more Sanskrit words giving rise to one Pāli word only. The changes have been carried on so far that at times five or six words have originated one word, i.e., five or more words have been converged into one word, e.g., sattha from Śastra, śāstra, sārtha, śakta, śasta etc.

The changes that normally take place are due to the working of the laws of assimilation. In assimilation we see that *rt, tra, rth* etc. are changed to *tth* and if any word contains any one of the above combinations, it is natural that it will converge into one phonotype. In the process of change, meanings of the words are to be taken into consideration, and it is only the context which determines what meaning is to be attached to that particular word in question.

There are many other factors that generally lead to such convergences. It may be due to a dialectal pecularity or to the operation of the various laws of phonetic changes. The following is a list of words where such convergences take place.

Thus Skt. doṣa 'fault' and dveṣa 'hatred' give rise to Pāli (henceforth abbreviated as P.) dosa, the phono-type preserving both the meanings in different contexts. The first meaning dosa 'fault' is found usually with dosakhetta 'blight of the field' (Miln. 360), dosatiṇa 'spoilt by weeds' (Dh.356). The second is not very often distinct in meaning from the first. In most frequent combination dosa appears with either rāga (lust), and moha (delusion), or lobha (greed) to denote three main blemishes of character;

P. oṭṭha may be derived from Ved. oṣṭha, 'lip' (J.11.264) or from Ved. ṣuṭra 'bison'.In Cl. Skt, it means a camel. It is mentioned in two lists of domestic animals (J.111.385);

P. bhusd 'chaff, husk' (Dh.252) or 'strong' (J.v.361) is either from Ved. busa 'chaff' (nt.) and buśa (m) or Ved. bhṛśa 'strong';

P. puṭṭha 'nourished' (J. 111.467) or asked (Sn.84) is either from Ved. puṣṭa 'nourished' or pṛṣṭa 'asked';

P. hasita 'laughing, merry' (A.1.261) either from Skt. hasita or hṛṣṭa; hāsa 'laughter' either from Sk. hāsa or harṣa;

P. sukka 'planet, star (Nett. 150) or white (Dh. 87) is either from Ved. śukra or śukla 'white'; P. sutta 'asleep' (Dh-47) or 'a thread, string' (J.1.52) either from Skt. supta or sūtra; P. sutti 'pearl-shell',a perfume Kuruvindakasutti, a powder for rubbing the body (Vin.11.107) or a good speech (Sdhp-340) is either from Skt. śukti or sūkti;

P. kiṇṇa 'ferment, yeast' (Vin.11.116) or scattered is either from Skt. kiṇva 'strewn' or pp. of kirati;

P. appamatta 'little, slight' (J.1.242) or diligent, careful (Sn.223) is either from Skt, alpamātra or apramatta;

P. accha 'bear' (J.iv.5O7) or clear, not covered, not shaded either from Ved. ṛksa or Skt. accha;

P. sarati 'remembers' (J.1.1.29) or moves, flows (J.1. 11.95) is either from √smṛ, 'to remember',or √stu 'to flow';

P. sattu 'ememy' (J.v.94) or barley-meal, flour (J.111.343) is either from Skt. śatru or śaktu;

P. adda 'ginger' (J.1.244) or to melt (J.iv.353) is either from Skt. ādraka or ādra (<,ṛdati) or ardati;

P. diṭṭha 'seen' (Sn. 147) or an enemy (J.1.280) is either from Skt, dṛṣṭa or dviṣṭa;

P. icchati, desires, asks (Sn. 127) or to go (J.111.462), cf. aticchati (<ati+ṛ) is either from Skt. icchati or ṛcchati;

P. asita 'having eaten' (J.vi-555) or not clinging to or unattached (J.11.247) is either from pp. of asati or aśrita <a+sita, pp. of *śri;

P. assa 'horse' (Sn. 769) or corner only in comp*ou*nds 'caturassa',fo*ur*-cornered (J.iv.46) is either from Skt. aśva or aśra;

P. assattha, the holy fig-tree, Ficus Religiosa (J.1.16) or a species of antelope in phrases issammiga = issāmiga (J.v.41o) is either from Skt, īrṣyā or ṛṣya-(mṛga);

P. agga 'foremost' (J.1.52) or a small house, hut (J.1.123) is either from Skt. agra or a contracted form of agāra, a small house;

P. patta 'wing of a bird, feather (V in iv.259) or a bowl, specially the alms-bowl of a bhikkhu (J.1.52) is either from Ved. patra or patra;

P. juti 'splendour' (J.11.353) is either from Skt. dyuti or jyuti;

P. muddha infatuated (J.v. 436) or head (Sn. 983) is either from Skt. mugdha or Ved. mūrdhan;

P. muddikā, a seal-ring, signet-ring (J.1.134) or a vine or bush of grapes (J.VI.529) is either from mudṛkā or *mṛdvīkā;

P. jhāyati 'meditates (Sn. 165) or burns (J.1.61) is either from Skt. dhyāyati <√dha 'to meditate' or kṣāyati <√kṣāy and kṣī (cf. khara and charikā) to burn, to be on fire, fig. to be consumed;

P. vassati 'rains' (Sn. 30) or to bellow, to crow, to utter a cry 'of animals' (J.1.436) of a cock is either from Skt. varṣati <√*vṛṣ*, I.E. Werś 'to wet' or vāsyati <√vāś to bellow, Ved. vāsyate;

P. aṭṭa, law suit, case (J.11.2) or distressed (Sn.694) is either from Skt. artha or ārta 'distressed',cf. Skt. ādra (P. adda and alla) ;

P. aññāta, known (S.699) or unknown. (Vin. 1.209) is either from pp. of ajānāti or ājñāta;

P. rukkha 'tree' (J.111.327) is either from Ved. ruksa or Skt. vṛkṣa, cf. also P. rakkha;

P. hiṃsati, injures (Sn. 515) is either from Skt. hiṃsati or hinasti;

P. pubba, pus (J.1. 1.18) or before (J.1 11.200) is either from Ved. pūya > √pūva >' √puvva > pubba, cf. pūyati, to small rotten, b. pūs = E. pus or from Ved. pūrva, Gr. promos. Goth. fruma, Av. pourvõ, Skt. pūrvya;

P. satta, living being (Vin. 1.5) or curse (J.111.460) or attached to (J.1.376) or seven (Sn.446) is either from Skt. satva or sapta or sakta;

P. sattha, a weapon, knife (J.1.72) or a science, art (Miln.3) or a caravan (Vin.1.152) or able, competent (J.111.173) or breathed (Vin.1.87) is either from Skt. śastra or śāstra or sārtha or śakta or śvasta <√*svas* 'to breathe';

P. aṭṭha, eight (J.1 1.86) or meaning (Sn.331) is either from Ved. aṣṭau or artha; attha, .meaning (Sn.331) or disappearance, setting (J.1.175) is either from Skt. artha or Ved. asta (of unknown etymology);

P. aḍḍha, half (Sn. 721, usually in combination wit*h* diyaḍ*h*a 1½ or thrive, rich (D.1.115) is either from Skt. ardha or aḍhya.

Madhusudan Mallik

5

PALI 'MĀRAJI': SANSKRIT 'SMARAJIT'

Gautama Śākya became 'Buddha' (The Awakened) after having defeated Mara and his host. In Buddhist literature and tradition Mara is the demigod of temptation and evil and therefore of Death. The word is generally accepted as a derivation of the root *mṛ* 'to die'.This appears to be only folketymology as Mara does not strictly conform to the Indian idea of the god or the demon of Death.

Māra is essentially a tempter, and the most powerful of his host are the nymphs that excite passion which is fatal to the meditation of a man on the spiritual path. The most obvious derivation is from the root s*mṛ* 'to remember, to remember longingly, to desire company, to desire lustfully'.'Māra' therefore comes from an older form **smāra* (for the loss of the initial sibilant compare Middle Indo-Aryan 'neha' from *sneha,* and Sanskrit *candra, tāyu, tārā, paśyati* from historical *scandra, *stāyu, *stārā, *spaśyati* respectively) which is a close cognate of Sanskrit *smara* 'sexual love (abstract or personified), god of love'.*Smara* first occurs in *Atharvaveda* where three hymns (6.130-132) are devoted to sexual love personified. The first verse of the first of these hymns is quoted below. It shows that 'Smara' of Atharvaveda not only is akin to both 'Māra' of Buddhist literature and 'Smara' of Sanskrit literature but appears to be their source.

rathajitām rathajiteyīnām apsarasām smaraḥ/
devāḥ pra hiouta smaram asau mām anu śocatu//

'This is Sexual Love *(smara)* of the *Rathajits* (Conquerors of Chariot-riding Warriors, or Fighters Riding Chariots) and of the nymphs belonging to the *Rathajits*. O Gods, send Sexual Love to that man *(so* that) he would long for *me'*.

The word *māra* signifying 'physical love' and 'god of love' is not unknown in Sanskrit literature. The earliest occurrence is in *Harivaṃśa (vide* Monier-Williams' Dictionary).

As conquers of physical love and temptation there is a close agreement between the Buddha and Siva. Both were the targets of Māra/Smara when engaged in meditation and penance. Gautama Śākya remained unmoved and he ultimately emerged as the vigilant or awakened *(buddha, prabuddha* or *pratibuddha)* conqueror of Māra. Śiva was moved only for a moment and his wrath put Smara to ashes.

It is not unlikely that the two stories are ultimately connected. There is a basic connection between spiritual penance *(tapasyā)* and subjugation of passion. At least there is no possibility of the story of Siva having been modelled after the story of the Buddha or *vice versa*.

The story of the destruction of the god of love (*Smara, Madana*) by Śiva ultimately goes back to a Vedic origin, *Śatapatha Brāhmaṇa* (1.7.4.1-3) narrates a story which tells us of Rudra's terrible anger against Prajāpati when the latter had contemplated incest with his daughter.

prajāpatir ha vai svaṃ duhitaram abhidadhyau divaṃ
voṣasaṃ vā mithunyenayā syām iti tārn saṃbabhūva
tad vai devanam aga asa ya ittham svāṃ duhitaram
asmakam svasāraṃ karotīti. te ha devā ūcuīḥ
yo' yaṃ devaḥ paśūnam īṣṭe 'tisaṃdham vāyaṃ
carati ya ittham svāṃ duhitaram asmākaṃ karoti
vidhyemam iti. taṃ rudro 'bhyāyatya vivyādha...

'The creator had desire for his own daughter, Day or Dawn, I would pair with her,and he paired with her. This appeared as a sin to the gods (who thought,) He is thus behaving with his own daughter, our sister! The gods spoke to the god that ruled over the beats, He is committing an act of transgre-ssion as he is behaving thus with his own daughter, and our sister. Do smite him. Rudra charged and smote him.

Sukumar Sen

6

THE BUDDHIST SOCIAL IDEALS

The social and political world in which Early Buddhism arose was characterized by an element of intense crisis. In its homeland of Magadha there was arising an imperial state which was threatening the very existence of a number of other states both monarchical and oligarchic-republican. Kāsi, Aṅga, Kośala, Avantī, the Vajjis, Mallas, Śakyas, all these 'and many more, were soon to feel the compelling impact of the rulers of Magadha. Economic life was experiencing a virtual revolution with the development of currency as a medium of exchange and the consequent growth of trade and commerce. Out of this revolution was emerging a new class, the *Gahapati* and *Seṭṭhi,* whose economic influence and political prestige could no longer be ignored. The story narrating how Anāthapiṇḍika bought a plot of land belonging to Prince Jeta is indicative of the position of this new class. Large standing armies replacing the old tribal levies, a new class of professional bureaucrats and a new powerful class of bankers and merchants, these were the characters in the drama of the new society that was in the making. The conflict of ideas was paralleled by a clash of classes and in this time of troubles the old norms and values developed by the tribal culture of the invading Aryans were successfully challenged. The new age that was dawning demanded new forms of political organization and a revaluation of norms of social behaviour and formulation of new social goals. The history of Early Buddhism reflects the elements of crisis as also the attempts made to crystalize and express the new social outlook.

The traditional accounts tell us that Slddhārtha saw the four signs prior to his Great Renunciation. These are significantly described as an old man, an ailing man, a dead body and a recluse. It is possible to interpret these as symbols not only of the different phases of an individual's life but also as those of the changing social scene. The first three may be taken as portents of the sense of anxiety from which the old society, now on the verge of a transformation, was suffering while the figure of the Recluse was the traditional answer to the challenge of the times. Siddhārtha himself became a Recluse and practised severe austerities.[1] The Bodhisatta gave up austerities as futile but continued to pursue the phase of withdrawal from the world. With the Enlightenment and the *Dhammacakkapavattana*, however, came the culmination. Indeed the *Mahābhinikkhamaṇa* can be properly understood only in the context of the *Dhammacakka-pavattana* for the two are organic parts of the single process of the making of the Buddha. The Turning of the wheel of Law and the foundation of the Saṅgha were events of great social significance.[2] The whole episode of the Buddha's reluctance to preach the Doctrine and the successful intervention of Brahma Sahampati is significant in its social content. It is the dramatization of the profound conflict between the claims of the traditional ascetic and the demands of the New Man whose ideals and aspirations were to be reflected in Early Buddhism. And the portals were thrown open and Buddhism began its career.

This Early Buddhist movement had to pass through three distinct phases before it could achieve its ultimate social fulfilment. These phases may be described as isolation, association and transformation. The phase of isolation may be called the *Khaggavisāṇa* phase.[3] This was the phase of wandering alone "like the horn of a rhinoceros." This phase persists throughout the history of Early Buddhism as phrases like "a hole-and-corner life is all a home can give, whereas Pilgrimage is in the open, it is hard for a house-keeping man to live the higher life in all its full completeness and full perfection and purity"[4] is almost a stock-phrase in the *Nikāyas*. To a certain extent it also expressed the antagonistic claims of the temporal realm and the realm of the spirit, a sentiment which is common to all great religions of the world. As the *Dhammapada* puts it *anna hi lābhūpanisā, anna nibbāṇa-gāminī—the* Path of gain and the path of Nibbāna are totally different (Verse 75). This early phase, then, was preoccupied with renunciation and seclusion, the phase when monks lived away from all social contacts beyond the most rudimentary and restricted to the receiving of alms. But mere renunciation and seclusion were but a part of the New Way of Life preached by the Buddha. And the social consequences of a large scale renunciation were not slow in making themselves manifest as the *Mahāvagga* story indicates. Seeing a large number of their men folk adopting the garb of the homeless wanderer the people cried : *vedhavyāya āgato samaṇo Gotamo—sabbe Sañjaye netvan kimsū dāni nay is sati* (the ascetic Gotama has come to deprive our women of their husbands—after having taken away all the Sañjayas, whom shall he take away now?[5]) It also led to an incipient clash with the State when men of the royal service, debtors and others who had social, economic and political obligations to discharge came to be admitted and the Buddha promptly laid down rules forbidding such ordinations.[6]

In the meanwhile a transformation was going on within the body of the Sangha itself. Devadatta's Five Demands, whatever the motive behind their presentation, represent the last stand of the old phase. These related to life-long practice of living in the woods, on alms, dressing themselves in cast-off rags, living under trees and abstaining from eating fish or flesh.[7] Demands like these were rightly rejected for they would have isolated the community from the broad surface of popular life. Now the ideal of *khaggavīsana* was being slowly replaced, in the matter of emphasis, by that of *sukhā samghassa sāhmaggī, samaggānam tapo sukho*—blessed is the unity of the Saṅgha, blessed is the exertion of the united *(Dhammapada,* verse 194).

This change was due, in part, to the development of the Buddhists as a distinct religious community. The insistence on sā*maggī* may be adequately explained in the changed social composition of the Saṅgha and the change in its social role. Now had begun the phase of the association of the Saṅgha with the society at large and this created the problems of adjustment. The Sangha had to define its own social relations and also influence the social ideals of the society at large. The members of the Saṅgha were now in sustained social contact with the aristocracy as well as the common people. This social orientation is indicated by the fact that among the categories of proficiencies acquired by certain outstanding monks, such as in the knowledge of the *Suttanta, Vinaya* and *Dhamma,* there is also mentioned one of wisdom in worldly lore.[8] And among all the foremost disciples the Venerable Ananda was the one who had shown the greatest proficiency in maintaining excellent and intimate relations with members of the society at large. Oldenberg explains it in material terms as "the external existence of the Church even demanded, that regular relations be maintained between it and the worldly circles, which were favourably disposed to the interests of the Order. Without a laity......an order of mendicants could not be thought of, and the religious movement of Buddhism would have been shut out from contact with the broad surface of popular life".[9] But to describe the association of the Saṅgha with society at large in purely utilitarian and material terms would be to state only a part of the process. For Buddhism had now begun to distinguish the believers from the non-believers in the lay society indicating thereby that the process of the creation of a Buddhist society was already at work. Thus when a monk spent his *Vassa* in a village and if the people of the village had to migrate during that time the monk was required to go with those who were believers whatever their number.[10] The importance of this emergent Buddhist society was duly recognized by giving the laity the right to scrutinize the intellectual accomplishments and moral earnestness of a monk supported on their devoted charity.[11] Certain influential laymen successfully mediated between the Buddha and those monks with whom the Master was displeased;[12] the moral and social pressure of the lay society was duly enlisted in the task of disciplining quarrelsome and recalcitrant groups of monks like the Kosambaka bhikkhus[13]; and an attempt was made to curb the evil schismatic activities of Devadatta by carrying out an act of public denunciation in Rājagaha.[14] Incidents like these, and they are numerous, bring out the increased importance of the society at large in the affairs of the Saṅgha, This awareness of social ties also led to the formulation of such rules whereby the Saṅgha was required to expel one of its members when, in the opinion of the congregation, his conduct was likely to lead the laity astray.[15] This close identification of spiritual and social interests between the Saṅgha and the laity is very succinctly expressed by Nāgasena when he enumerates the ten qualities of an ideal layman. The ideal layman, according to Nāgasena, "suffers like pain and feels like joy as the Order does".[16] With the state-ment of such views the process of association was completed and that of transformation was already underway.

This process of transformation in the role of Buddhism and its Sangha was closely associated with the Buddhist view of society. It was readily recognized that society was constantly preoccupied with things *(papañcābhiratā pajā);*[17] that this acquisitive instinct led to conditions of strife, conflict and imbalance.[18] The situation was further complicated by the existence of hierarchies of power, wealth and prestige. By the laws of its own being and nature Buddhism, as an organized way of spiritual life, could not directly initiate a social revolution for then it would have projected itself into the social and economic problems of the times. It has often been argued that the Buddha was no social reformer.[19] In such arguments the Buddha's views about the irrelevance of caste distinction is explained away as doctrinaire discussion. But suttas like *Vasala* in the *Sutta Nipāta* and *Madhara, Assalāyana* and *Canki* in the *Majjhima Nikāya* are not just doctrinaire dissertations but have a most direct social content. It is readily agreed that the Saṅgha knew of no caste distinctions but it is parenthetically added that this castelessness of the Sangha living in close association with the lay community had no effect on that lay community. This is a proposition difficult to accept. The Buddhist position was made quite clear in the many utterances of the Buddha and in the composition of the Order itself and it was that caste as an institution was unacceptable to the Buddhist community. In fact the whole trend of Buddhist teachings was to create an equalitarian ethos which would cut across tribal lines and the distinctions of caste and race. The Buddha had said : "I assert that lineage does not enter into a man's being either good or bad; nor do good looks or wealth."[20] He had challenged the extravagant claims put forward by the priesthood. During its third phase of becoming an instrument of social transformation Buddhism had postulated certain new norms and goals of social behaviour. The ideal put forward before society now was the creation of a *sappurisa* or an *uttamapurisa.* [21] The basis of this new society were *vissāsa* (mutual trust, co-operation in the place of conflict and acquisitiveness),[22] *asāhasa* (non-violence), *samaṭā* (basic equality of all human beings) and *dhamma* (righteousness as an ultimate value) In fact the four pillars of this society were declared to be *sacca* (truth, homogenity, unity through an absence of invidious distinctions based on birth, wealth or family in the matter of social evaluation,) *dhamma* (righteousness, goodness, morality) *dāna* (charity as a way of life rather than a specific set of isolated acts) *asāhasa* (non-violence, violence being the negation of righteousness.)[23] The rule of *dhamma* was to be looked upon as of all-pervasive force, valid as much in the home as in the market-place as indicated in *dhammena mātāpitaro bhareyya, payojaye dhammikam so vaṇijjam* (righteously he should support his parents and righteously he should carry on his trade.)[24] The Five commandments for the laymen namely, abstinence from violence, stealing, falsehood, immorality and drinking intoxicating liquors, were a simple formalization of the four pillars of society and became the basis of Buddhist social ethics. When to these were added Faith in the Buddha, Dhamma and Saṅgha, respect for elders and women,[25] disciplining of the mind in the way of righteousness, the formulation of the Buddhist social ethics was completed. These ideals were postulated as a middle way between the two extremes of aggressiveness resulting in constant preoccupation with acquisitiveness to the exclusion of all other considerations and indulgence leading to dissipation and degradation. Reason, moderation, harmony, a constant awareness of the primacy of righteousness, the ennobling nature of charity as a way of life, compassion and wisdom were the norms which were now constantly put before society. This society was conceived of as a "universal" as distinguished from a tribal society; it was the community of the righteous anywhere and everywhere unencumbered by rules of tribal, regional or caste affiliations.

These were the social ideals that Early Buddhism espoused and put before the society of its times. The role of the Saṅgha was now that of the custodian of the moral and spiritual values of society. The Saṅgha now, in this final phase, became the spiritual preceptor, the personal counsellor and the educator of the society within which it lived. It functioned within society though it was not of it. The *Dhamma* had now become both a spiritual and social force. It became an instrument dedicated to the creation of certain values like *samatā,* (cf. Aśoka's insistence on *daṇḍasamatā* and *vyavahārasamatā), dāna sacca* and *dhamma.* These social ideals were of general applicability and cut across divisive lines of caste, tribe and race and thus provided the social cement to fuse the diverse ethnic and cultural elements into a harmonious social group based on certain basic postulates.

B. G. Gokhale

FOOTNOTES

1. See *Majjhima Nikāya,* I, pp. 162-163

2. See Arnold Toynbee, *A Study of History,* III, pp. 270-271. It is difficult to agree with all that Toynbee has to say especially when he describes the mental content of Buddha's Enlightenment as nothing short of ''spiritual self-annihilation".
3. As in *eko care khaggavisāṇakappo, Sutta Nipata.* Verse 35ff.
4. *M. N.* I, p. 240, Chalmers, *Further Dialogues of the Buddha,* I, p. 173
5. *Mahā Vagga,* I, 24, 5
6. See *Ibid.,* I, 40ff.
7. *Culla Vagga,* VII, 3, 15
8. *Ibid.,* IV, 4, 4
9. *Buddha,* p. 382
10. *M. V.,* III, 10
11. *M. N.,* II, p. 172
12. *Ibid.,* I, p. 458
13. *Ibid.,* II, p. 172
14 . M. V., X, 5, 1.
15. C. *V.,* I, 13, 7.
16. *Milinda Pañha,* pp. 94-95
17. *Dhammapada,* verse 254
18. *M. N.,* II, p. 120
19. See Oldenberg, *Op. cit.,* p. 153. Fick, *Social Organization in North-East India, in Buddha's Time* (Trans, by Maitra), p. 32
20. *M. N.,* II, p. 179
21. Dhp., Verse 54
22. *Ibid..* Verse 204
23. See *Dhp.,* Verses 84, 129, 142, 223, 256, 257
24. *Sutta Nipāta,* Verse 404
25. Cf. the seven conditions of stability as preached to the Vajjis by the Buddha, *Mahāparinibbāṇa Sutta, Dīgha Nikāya,* S. B. E., XI, pp. 3-5.

7

BUDDHIST CONTROVERSY OVER THE FIVE PROPOSITIONS

At an ancient time to which we refer, five propositions derogatory to the dignity of Arhats were discussed in the Buddhist Communities of Ceylon as well as of the Indian continent[1]. They are explained both in the Abhidharma of Sarvāstivādins *(Jñānaprasthāna* of the IIIrd century after the Nirv., T. 1543, k. 10, p. 819 b; T. 1544, k. 7, p. 956b)[2] and the Ceylonese Abhidhamma *(Kathāvatthu,* II. 1-5, pp. 163-203). They were taken up later again and discussed in the *Vibhāṣā* (T. 1545, k. 99, p. 510 c), *Kośa* (I. p. 2), the glosses of Paramārtha and the Treatise of Ki-tsang on the sects[8]. In these are found the enunciation of those propositions and the references furnished by the authors 'and in the ancient sources to the date of their invention and the name of their inventor. On the whole the references are not concordant.

In the sources enumerated above, the five propositions (*Pañcavastu*) are formulated in the following manner:

(a) The Arhat can be seduced by others and may have seminal losses while asleep.

(b) Though they are freed from sullied ignorance *(kliṣṭa-avidyā)* they remain meanwhile subject to unsullied ignorance *(aklista ajñāna),* the residue of their old impurities.

(c) Though free from doubt with regard to the three doors

of deliverance *(vimokṣamukha}* they remain subject to doubt with regard to the external things, and even the four holy truths.

(d) They can be taught by others and owe them their salvation.

(e) The exclamation: "Oh sorrow" may be regarded as a means destined to initiate the appearance of the Way.

These propositions aim at nothing less than dethronement of the Arhat from the enviable position enjoyed by them from the very beginning. These appear to be the characteristics of the commoners *(pṛthagjana)* instead of the perfects *(ārya = arhat),* of laxity in place of austerity, nay, in fact, the laymen sought equality with the religieux in spiritual attainments. The heresy, if there be any, endured for a long time and served within the community as a mischievous leaven: it is concerning this that the Buddhist schools were set against one another and became divided among themselves.

When did the heresy appear and who was its inventor? Here are the answers given in the sources:

1. Vasumitra: In 116 PN during the reign of Aśoka, among-the Nāgas and their partisans.
2. Vibhāṣā and Mahāyānist authors supporters of the Vibhāṣ ā: During the reign of Asoka as a result of the activities of Mahādeva.
3. Sammitīya tradition: In 137 PN, among the Sthaviras Nāga and Sāramati, and the Bahuśrutas,
4. Bhavya: In 160 PN, during the reign of Asoka.

VASUMITRA: Vasumitra, a Sarvāstivādin teacher, who lived 400 years after Parinirvāṇa and who was posterior by a century to Kātyāyanīputra, author of the Jñānaprasthāna, wrote a book on the Buddhist sects entitled Samayabhedoparacanacakra[4]. The book was translated into Chinese by Kumārajīva between 385 and 431 (T. 2032), by Paramārtha between 557 and 569 (T. 2033) and by Hiuan-tsang in 662 (T. 2031); it is commented in Chinese by K'ouei-ki in 662 (TKS.A. LXXXIII, 3) and translated into

Tibetan in the IXth century by Dharmākara (Tanjur, Mdo. XC,11).

The book opens with a reference to the five propositions (T. 2032, p. 18 a 9-14; T. 2033, p. 20 a 15-25; T. 2031, p. 15 a 15-23): "One hundred and sixteen years after Parinirvāṇa of Buddha, there was a town called Pāṭaliputra. Then king Asoka reigned over Jambudvīpa, ruling over the universe. At that time the Great Community *(mahāsaṃgha)* was divided into schools and made variations in the law. There were then the bhikṣus: (1) the first called *Neng,* Naga (variant: *Ta-Kouo,* Mahārāṣṭra; *Long-kia,* Nāga); (2) the second called *Yin Yuan,* Pratyaya (variant: *Wai-pien,* Prācya; *Pien-pi,* Pratyantika); (3) the third called *To-wen,* Bahuśruta; (4) the fourth called *Ta-to,* Sthavira. They discussed the five propositions *(pañcavastu)* instituted by the heretics. It is in this way that for the first time after Buddha, two schools came into being, one called Mahāsānghika and the other Sthavira."

Among the translators, Hiuan-tsang alone precisely states that the originator of the Five Propositions was Mahādeva, the information being taken from the Vibhāṣā. According to Vasumitra and his first translators, names of the heretics were yet unknown. The comparison of the versions clearly reveals that the Pancavastu was criticised by the Sthaviras but adopted by these Sanghas of the Nagas, of the Pracyas or Pratyantikas, lastly of the Bahusrutas. We may ignore entirely the first two Saṅghas, According to the comments of K'ouei-ki (l.c), the Nagas whose name implies an irresistible power and an obdurate obstinacy, were the chief organisers of the dispute and of the schism that followed; the Prayantikas sided with the heretics, and without being the originators of the disputes not possessing the irresistible power, followed and supported the heresy; lastly the Bahusrutas comprised the commoners *(pṛthagjana)* still occupied with study *(śaikṣa),* but observing the prohibitions and acquiring vast knowledge.

Personally in the first two names we notice ethnical: heresy originated with the Nagas whose primitive habitat was, according to the tradition of the purāṇas, the region of Narmadā, a tributary of Maharasṭra to which the version of Paramartha refers; thence it was extended to the neighbouring regions designated by Vasumitra under the vague denomination of "Frontier Regions" (Pratyantika).

As far as the riverine residents of the Gangetic basin and of Yamuna are concerned, the Maraṭha country was situated in Southern India. Now, according to the Aśokāvadāna (T. 2042 k. 5, p. 120 c 11-121 b 1; T. 2043, k. 9, p. 162 a 1-162 c 8)[5], the Sarvāstivādin community of Mathura under the leadership of the famous patriarch Upagupta at the time of Aśoka, was put in a flutter by the visit of a monk who hailed from Southern India, but no notice is taken of his name. Before his admission into the religion,' this monk committed fornication with a woman of another family. He killed his mother for having reproached him for his conduct. He then sought the hand of his beloved. Being repulsed by her he retired from the worldly life, learnt by heart the text of the Tripiṭaka and gathered around him a number of disciples. He then betook himself to Mathura to discuss with Upagupta, but the latter being aware of what crime he had been guilty, refused to have a discussion with him and so the monk returned to his native country taking with him the band of his disciples.

It would be tempting to find in that religious person a champion of heresy of the Five Propositions which the holy patriarch Upagupta, chief of a school of Arhats, could only condemn. But the religious man had already exercised an ominous influence over those disciples of Upagupta, who remained still in the stage of commoners *(pṛthagjana)*. They remonstrated with their master for his impoliteness to a foreigner and Upagupta, in order to appease those critics, was compelled to appeal to his master Śāṇavāsa.

This anecdote referred to in the Aśokāvadāna bears remarkable resemblance to the version of the Vibhāṣā.

The Vibhasa: This great book on the Abhidharma of the Sarvāstivādin compiled in the 2nd century of our era by the Kashmirian Arhats, devotes quite a chapter (T. 1545, k. 99, p. 510 c. 23-512 a 19) to the heresy of the Five Propositions. It attributes the invention to a certain Mahādeva about whom it narrates a long story though less edifying and tries to paint his character in a black manner.

Mahādeva was the son of a merchant of Mathurā. His father went abroad, leaving his son at home. At the age of twenty, the son became fine in appearance; and his mother fell in love with him and had secretly intercourse with him. During more than six years, the son did not know that his mistress was his own mother, then though he came to know of it, he did not give up his passion. The father came back from abroad, having acquired great wealth; little before his arrival, the mother being afraid of his getting scent of this affair persuaded her son to administer poison to him. Mahādeva administered the poison and killed his father; then he secured his wealth and continued to live with his mother. But in the long run, when he was found out, he felt ashamed and ran away and concealed himself with his mother in Pāṭaliputra. He met there the Arhat monks whom he had previously revered in his own country, and he murdered them also lest they might betray him. Then he killed his own mother finding that she played false with him. Having thus committed three *ānantarya-sins,* he realised the evils and felt deep remorse; and in order to wash out those sins he gave up his family life. He then entered into the monastery of the Kukkuṭārāma where he heard a monk recite a stanza on the redemption of sinners by good conduct; this monk ordained him by giving him *pravrajyā*.

Mahādeva listened to and studied the Tripiṭaka and collected several followers. The king of Pāṭaliputra (whose name is not given) when got to know of this, invited him to his palace and bestowed on him his offerings. Returned to the monastery, Mahādeva formulated by turn the five heretical propositions explained above. On account of the controversies which the heresies raised, the king sought advice of Mahādeva to settle the dispute. The latter told him that, according to the Vinaya, it was the majority that decided the controversies. The king then put two parties in two sides, and as the party of Mahādeva was greater in number, he decided in his favour and condemned his adversaries. It is thus that the religious people of the Kukkuṭārāma were divided into two schools: the school of the Sthaviras and the school of the Mahāsāṃghikas.

The Sthaviras however wanted then to quit the monastery. Being apprised of their intention, the king ordered to put the Sthaviras on a rotten boat and to throw them into the river Ganges, and then it would be known who was an Arhat and who was a commoner. At the critical moment five hundred Arhats exercising their magical powers rose in the air and went to Kasmir where they scattered themselves up hills and down dales. Having received the news the king sent to them a messenger to bring them back to his capital, but they declined his invitation, The king then made a gift to the church of the whole kingdom of Kasmir and built there five hundred monasteries for the residence of the saints; these monasteries received the names of the various forms taken by the saints when escaping from Pāṭaliputra, for example: Garden of Pigeon *(Kapotārāma)* etc., and the Vibhasa adds "It is reported that these monasteries are still flourishing," The king of Pāṭaliputra then conferred his favours upon Mahadeva and his disciples who lived near him. Mahādeva passed away after being held in high estimation by 'the people but, when they wanted to burn his dead body in the cremation ground, the fire could not be ignited and it was necessary to use as fuel the excrements of dogs; his body was then burnt, but suddenly a violent wind arose and dispersed the ashes of the heretic.

Now according to Vasumitra, the enunciator of the Five Propositions, remained anonymous. The Vibhāṣā, a century later, finds him a name and attributes to him quite a history. It treats him definitely as an adversary, laying against him the charge of all the unatonable crimes and invents for him an unhappy end. It should be noted that the Mahāvibhāṣā only (T. 1545) takes notice of Mahādeva and that it is not similar to that found in the Vibhāṣā of Buddhavarman .(T, 1546).

But once introduced the legend died hard. Adopted with enthusiasm by the Sarvāstivādin, it received valid recognition from the Mahāyānist teachers. But as these latter did not lose their sympathy for the Mahāsāmghikas whom they regarded as their distant precursors, they endeavoured, otherwise to clear up the memory, at least to attenuate the wrongs committed by Mahādeva, the initiator of the Mahāsāmghika schism.

Mahayanist Authors and Supporters of the Vibhasa:

1. In the Vlth century, Paramārtha (557-569) in his criticism of Vasumitra (summed up in T. 2300), and his pupil Ki-Tsang (549-623) in his Treatise on the sects (T. 1852) reproduced the account of the Vibhāṣā after introducing therein substantial modifications[6]: Upto *116* PN there did not appear heterodox opinions within the Saṅgha. After the 116th year appeared Mahādeva, of the Kauśika family, son of merchant of Mathurā. Having committed three *ānantarya-sins,* he gave up his worldly life and went to Pāṭaliputra by confering ordination upon himself. He received entrance into the palace of Aśoka where he had secret intercourse with the queen. He entered again into the monastery. He took up the Mahāyāna sūtras and incorporated them into the Tripiṭaka. He fabricated, on his own authority, many sūtras wherein was formulated the quintuple heresy and summing them up in a stanza, he recited it after the recitation of the śīlas in the Uposatha ceremony. Many controversies having arisen in the monastery, King Asoka on his own authority, took recourse to voting to settle the dispute. The partisans of Mahādeva were then greater in number. The Arhats, who were in minority, frightened the community by exhibition of some magical powers. The queen exercised her influence and had the Arhats thrown into the Ganges in boats of broken staves. The Arhats took flight and went away to Kasmir, some transforming themselves into fishing-float

pigeons, others into birds. After arriving at the destination they took again their ordinary forms. Meanwhile the queen realising her error repented and was converted. After the death of Mahādeva, Aśoka looked for the Arhats of Kasmir and invited them to return to Pāṭaliputra. As Mahādeva had introduced the Apocrypha into the Tripiṭaka, the Arhats gathered together in Council (the third since the beginning) and recited once more the canon of the scriptures. It was at that time that the divergences of opinion among them took place ending in the formation of two separate schools; that of the Mahāsāṃghikas and that of the Sthaviras.

It will be noticed that Paramārtha quickly passes over the sins of Mahādeva, seeks to acquit Aśoka of finding fault with the queen, attributes to the heretic a scriptural activity which the Vibhāṣā did not mention at all, and poses a third Buddhist council with a new compilation of the Tripiṭaka; after which only the schism was ultimately placed.

2. In the Vllth century, the master of the Law, Hiuan-tsang, sums up once more the story of the Vibhāṣā, but with more faithfulness than that of Paramārtha. The passage is found in the Si-Yu-Ki (T. 2087, k 3, p. 886 b. n-22)[7] :

A hundred years after Parinirvāṇa, Aśoka king of Magadha extended his power over the whole world; he revered the Triratna and loved all beings. There were in his capital among the religious Buddhists, 500 Arhats and 500 commoners *(pṛthagjana)* whom the king patronised impartially.

The religious commoners included in their ranks a certain Mahadeva "a man of great knowledge and of great talent, keen investigator of the Nāmarūpa" (sic) who put in treatise his personal views and his heretical observations. The controversy having burst forth, Aśoka took the side of Mahādeva and the commoners, and tried to drown the Arhats in the Ganges. But the latter fled away to Kasmir where they established themselves up hills and down dales. The king at once became repentant for their departure and himself set out to invite them to return to his capital. On their refusal to return, the king built for them 500 samghārāmas and made a gift of Kasmir to the Church.

Hiuan-tsang, agreeing with the Vibhāṣā, affirmed that the persecuted Arhats remained in Kasmir and refused to return to Pāṭaliputra. In these conditions there could be no question of the session of the third Buddhist Council, which, according to Paramārtha, had taken place at Pāṭaliputra after the return of Arhats. However, in another passage, where describing his visit to the Kukkuṭārāma of Pāṭaliputra, Hiuan-tsang (T. 2087, k. 8, p. 912 b)[8] states that King Aśoka after his conversion to Buddhism convoked in his monastery a saṇgha of thousand members "comprising of two communities: one of the saints *(ārya),* the other of the commoners *(pṛthagjana)".* In it there is a reference to the Sthaviras and the Mahāsāṃghikas but nothing said that they held a council and proceeded with a fresh recitation of the Tripiṭaka.

Though accusing his Mahādeva of heresy, Hiuan-tsang does not make at all any mention of the Five Propositions to which people refer generally. He praises his knowledge and his talent and described him as sublte investigator of the "Nama-Rupa" otherwise known as the five Skandhas. But the question of the Nāma-Rūpa preoccupied more the Sarvāstivādins than the Mahāsāṃghikas. It may be asked whether in the opinion of the Chinese master, Mahādeva was not a Sarvāstivādin teacher; but, if so, it would be contrary to the whole tradition, according to which the heretic was the initiator of the Mahāsāṃghika schism.

It seems that the great Hiuan-tsang did not try to harmonise the informations which he collected carefully from his readings, notably from the Vibhāṣā, and the many oral traditions gathered by him locally to which he refers "in bulk." His account about the settlement in Kasmir of five hundred Arhats thrown by Aśoka into the Ganges followed immediately the story of the conversion of the Kasmir in the year 50 PN. by Madhyāntika and his five hundred Arhats (T. 2087, k. 3 p. 886 a 19-886bn). Obviously it referred to an identical event, but divided into two for some chronological reasons.

3. K'ouei-ki (632-682), disciple of Hiuan-tsang, in his criticism on the Yogācāryabhūmī of Asaṇga (T. 1829, k. 1 p. 1 b) tries to rehabilitate Mahādeva by presenting him as a victim of calumny: "High was his reputation, great his virtue; though young he had realised the Fruit; he was respected by kings and nobles and venerated by monks. And that is the reason for which were imputed to him the three ā*nantarya-sins* to which were added the Five Propositions...".It is not the only text favourable to Mahādeva. There was already an earlier commentary on the Ekottara, half-Mahāsāṃghika half-Mahāyānist, the Fen-pie-kong-to-louen, translated into Chinese between 25 and 220 A.D. which spoke of a saintly king Mahādeva endowed with four *brahmavihāras* and qualified him as *Ta-che,* or great Bodhisattva (T. 1507, k. 1, p. 32 c 8-10.)

MAHADEVA II: In order to complete the record it should be noted that besides Mahādeva I, the initiator of the Five Propositions and instigator of the schism, the sources point out the existence of a second Mahādeva, a Mahāsāṃghika teacher who lived 200 years PN, continued to teach the Five Propositions and provoked new secessions inside the Mahā-sāṃghika sect. This Mahādeva II[9] is well known to Vasumitra who it is seen did not make any mention on Mahādeva I. Here are some references:

1. *Vasumitra, tr. Kumarajiva* (T. 2032 p. I8a 17-20). "Then in two hundred years Mahadeva a heretic *(trthika)* gave up his worldly life and resided in the Caityasaila. In the Mahasamghika sect developed anew three sub-sects: Caityika, Aparasaila and Uttaraśaila."

2. *Vasumitra, tr. Paramartha* (T. 2033, p. 20 b 2-4): "When two hundred years had elapsed, there was a heretic called Mahadeva who eschewed the worldly life and joined the Mahasamghika school; he resided alone in Mount śaila and taught to the Mahasamghikas the Five Propositions. Thence there were two new secessions: school of Caityasaila and school of Uttarasaila (and according to the Tibetan version, school of Aparasaila)"

3. *Vasumitra, tr. Hiuan-tsang* (T. 2031, p. 15 b 1-4): "When two hundred years had elapsed there was a heretic who left the worldly life, gave up falsehood and reverted to the correct mode; he was called also Mahadeva. Being recluse of the Mahāsamghika sect he received full ordination; he was erudite *(bahuśruta)* and energetic *(viryavān);* he resided in the Caitya-saila. To the community of this sect, he explained again the Five Propositions which provoked discussions and sub-divisions into three sects: Caityasaila, Aparasaila and Uttara-saila.

4. *Śāriputrapariprccha,* tr, by an anonymous writer between 317 and 420 A.D. (T. 1465 p. 900 c 6-12) "In the Mahāsamghika school, two hundred years after my Nirvāna, there will appear as a result of disputes the schools ; Vyavahāra, Lokottara, Kukkulika, Bahuśrutaka, Prajnaptivāda. Two hundred years after the discussions, will be added to those Five schools, the School of Mahadeva, that of Caityika and that of Uttarasaila".

5. *Paramartha and Ki-tsang:* When two hundred years had completed, an upāsaka-king of Magadha (according to K'ouei-ki, king *Hao yun* "Loving the clouds") propagated widely the Law of Buddha, and in order to take advantage of his bounties, all the heretics took to religious life. Mahadeva who was ordained by himself took upon himself their headship, received new disciples and ordained them in his own saṅgha. The king made a selection among those monks who were "parasites" (ste*yasṃvasika)* and authorised only one party among them, the three hundred more intelligent ones, to live in Magadha. Mahādeva being no more tolerated by them left the place and established himself separately in the mountain with his partisans. Then among those mountain-dwellers themselves, arose certain differences of opinions and thus were formed the two schools called Caityaśaila and Uttaraśaila.

Should one see in this Mahadeva II localised by all the sources in the mountainous regions of Andhra an arbitrary division into two Mahadevas? or should one reject the historicity of the two Mahādevas and see only in them an expedient intended to show the progress of a heresy originating in Southern India among the Nāgas of Mahārastra, and spreading from Saṃgha to Saṃgha, ending ultimately in Mahasamghika schism, and after many advancements it finally triumphed over some churches, notably the Caityika and Śailas of Andhra? We leave to the reader the responsibility of answering these questions.

MAHADEVA IN THE PALI SOURCES : The Ceylonese school was firmly pronounced against the Five Propositions which it exposed and refuted in the Kathāvatthu II, 1-5 (p. 163-203), but did not furnish any reference to their author. The commentary restrained itself by stating precisly that the heretical propositions were taught by the Pubbaseliyas, Aparaseliyas and others.

Among the numerous Mahādevas known to the Pali tradition, Professor Malalasekera has pointed out no less than nine[10], none of whom makes a good heretic figure. Two among them were contemporaries of Aśoka: One Mahadeva minister of Aśoka who took measures for despatch to Ceylon a branch of the *Bodhivṛkṣa* (Mahavamsa XVIII, 20); a Mahādeva Thera who played a considerable role at times as a religious master and as a Buddhist missionary. In fact he conferred the ordination *(pabbajjā)* on Mahinda, son of Asoka (Dipavaṃsa, VII 25; Mahavamsa, V, 206; Samantapāsādikā p. 51); then after the council of Paṭaliputra, in 236 PN, he set out to preach the Good law to Mahisamaṇḍala where he converted 40,000 souls and conferred ordination on 40,000 young men (Dipavaṃsa VIII,5; Mahāvaṃsa, XII, 3 and 29; Samantapāsdikā, p. 63, 66). In Mahisamandala, Andhra and the region of Dhānyakaṭaka where the Pubba and Aparaseliya sects had their seat, some authors think that Mahādeva was founder of those schools which issued out of the Mahāsāṃghika stock and which adhered to the Five Propositions[11]. But if the Mahādeva in question had been a heretic, it becomes difficult to explain how the Ceylonese Chronicles make him a disciple and confidant of a very orthodox monk like Moggaliputta Tissa, a declared Vibhajy-avādin, and could count him as one of the great propagators of the True Law. Then Mahisamandala is not certainly the country of Andhra, but may be Mysore, may be and still more probably Mahiṣmat or country of the Mahi-akas, associated by the Purānas with Mahārāśṭra which had as its capital Māhiṣmatī on the Narmadā.[12]

THE SAMMATIYA TRADITION : It is mentioned for the first time in the VIth century by Bhavya or Bhāvaviveka, author of the Tarkajvālā (Mdo XIX, p. 162 b c-163a 3; cf. Mdo XC, No. 12)[13], reproduced later with some modifications in the XIVth century by Bu-ston (tr. Obermiller, II p. 96), in the XVth by Gzon-nu-dpal (Roerich, *Blue Annals,* I, p. 96), and in the XVIIth by Tāranātha (tr. Schiefner, p. 52). According to this tradition, in the year 137 after Nirvana, under the King Nanda and Mahāpadma (sic), an assembly took place at Pātaliputra in which participated the Sthaviras holding the same view as Mahākāśyapa, Mahāloma, Mahātyāga, Uttara, Revata, etc. A monk (of the name of Bhadra) taught the Five Propositions and because of them a great schism was produced in the assembly. The sthavira Nāga and Sāramati- better Nāgasena and Manoratha-adopted the five Propositions and conformed them to their teaching. Now the religious men were divided into two schools: Sthavira and Mahāsāṃghika, and the quarrel between the two groups lasted for 63 years. Then in the year 102 (correctly in 200) after Nirvāṇa, the sthavira Vātsīputra revised the doctrine correctly.

It is here no more the question of Mahādeva but of a Bhadanta whose heretical views were supported by a Nāga or Nāgasena, whose name recalls the Nagas, already pointed out by Vasumitra. The schism broke out, not under Asoka in the year 100 PN (short chronology) but formerly under Mahāpadma of the dynasty of the Nandaṣ in 137 PN (long chronology). The Saṃmatiya tradition follows in fact an identical computation or very near the Ceylonese chronology which counts 218 years between Nirvāṇa and the coronation of Asoka and which attributes the reign of Nandas from the year 140 to 162 PN (346-324 B.C).

BHAVYA: In his Tarkajvālā, Bhavya just referring to the Saṃmatiya tradition summed up above, ascribed in his own account to the Mahāsāṃghika schism a later date: "One hundred and sixty years after the Parinirvāna, while king Dharm-Āśoka reigned over Pātaliputra, a great schism arose in the Saṃgha after some controversies, and the saṃgha was split up into two ' schools, Mahasamghika and Sthavira[14]" But the proposed date: "160 in the reign of Asoka" does not respond to any known computation and does not tally either with the short chronology which places Asoka in 100 PN or with the long chronology that makes him reign from 219 to 256 PN. However the same date, 160 PN, is still mentioned by other authors and notably by Bu-ston (II, p. 96) who attributes the origin of the schism not only to the advent of the Five heretical Propositions but also to the fact that the Arhats "read the speech of Buddha in four different languages; Sanskrit, Prakrit, Apabhraṃśa and Paiśācika".

CONCLUSIONS : The scrutiny of the records has brought to light the doubts and the chronological contradiction concerning:

1. *The date of schism :* in 137 PN during the reign of the Nandas; in 100, 116 or 160 during the reign of Asoka.

2. *The instigator or instigators of the schism:* the Nagas of the Southern India helped by their neighbouring Pratyantika and the Bahuśrutas; a monk called or surnamed Bhadanta; lastly Mahādeva. The last one is presented either as a culpable criminal of the three ānantaryas, or as a man full of knowledge and of talent, unjustly slandered, or lastly as a Sarvāstivādm, "a subtle investigator of the Nāmarūpa."

3. *Causes of the schism:* the controversies provoked by the appearance of the Five Propositions, the introduction of Mahāyānist "stras in the Tripiṭaka or even the translation of the Scriptures in four different languages.

4. *The consequences of the schism:* Having taken refuge in Kasmir the Sthavirian Arhats established themselves there finally or again after a short sojourn returned to Pāṭaliputra where they convoked a new council. As to the instigator of the schism (Mahādeva) either he lived at Pātaliputra till his death or he went to the mountainous regions of Andhra where he continued to teach his thesis to the Pūrva, Apara and Uttaraśailas. But some sources regard Mahadeva the teacher of the śailas as a personage different from Mahadeva, the originator of the schism.

The contradictions lead us to reject the chronology as apocryphal. Moreover it is of very little importance. It matters little whether the heresy originated under Asoka or century earlier, whether its author is called Nāga, Mahadeva or Bhadanta, or whether the Sthavirian Arhat took refuge temporarily or permanently in Kaśmir. The fact seems certain that, between the death of Buddha and the reign of Asoka the Maurya, the Buddist community had been subject to centrifugal forces which must have brought about finally the secession. The causes of dissension were multiple. Some religious men in possession of the Fruit of Arhat claimed to monopolise the sanctity; they roused the jealousy of the commoners *(pṛthagjana,')* and the latter invented the Five Propositions for the sole purpose of humiliating the Arhat and of outraging their honour. Some monks who, whether assembled again in councils or not, had recited in common the words of Buddha, gave themselves out as the only depository of same and wanted to impose on their colleagues the canon of their compilation which they had just put together. But the latter resisted the imposition; they had themselves memorised the words of the Master or did not consider the canon as closed and found out the introduction therein of new compositions more or less conformable to the primitive teaching. At least there was no unanimity in regard to the secondary points of doctrine and discipline: in the matter of Vinaya notably the laxist tendencies were manifest in some communities (Vaiśāli, Kauśāmbi). The dispute brewed for a long time before resulting in a secession. If an old evidence is to be believed, we mean that of the Mahāprajnā-pāramitopadeśa or of its translator Kumārajīva (T. 1509, k 2, p. 70 a), the Great Community remained intact till the time of Aśoka; "When Buddha was dead, when the Law was recited for the first time, it was still like the time when Buddha lived. A hundred years after, King Aśoka called a big quinquennial assembly *(pancavarṣaparisad)* and the great masters of the Law held discussions. Because of their differences, there appeared some distinct sects *(nikāya),* each having a name, which eventually became developed."

The fact is that the division of the Saṃgha did not at all put an end to the polemics, and that the Five Propositions continued to be discussed. The Theravādin and the Sarvāstivadin combatted them in the Kathāvatthu, the Jnānaprasthāna and its Vibhāṣā respectively. The Saṃmatīya, the Vātsiputriya and the Mahiśāsaka rejected them in the same manner. As a set off, they found some defenders among the Mahāsāmghika and their sub-sects Bahusrutīya, Caitya and Śaila, and were even adopted by a school of the Sthavirian stock, that of the Haimavata.[15]

Et. Lamotte

FOOTNOTES

1. Les textes pāli sout cites d'apres les éditions de la *Pāli Text Society* de Londres; les textes chinois . d'après l'édition du *Taisho Issaikyo* de J. Takakusu et K. Watanabe (T).
2. Sur. ce . texte,. voir Ś. *Śāstī. Jñānafrasthānaśāstra retranslated into Sanskrit,* vol. I, Santiniketan, 1955.
3. P. Demiéville, *L'origine des Secies bouddhiques d'apres Paramārtha,* Mélanges Chinois et Bouddhiques, I, 1932, pp. 15-64. On trouve dans cet ouvrage la traduction du Traité de Ki-tsang et des fragments du commentaire de Paramārtha au Traité de Vasumitra.
4. Sur Vasumitra voir J. Masuda, *Origin and doctrines of early Indian Buddhist Schools,* Asia Major, II, 1925, pp. 1-78; E. Teramoto et T. Hiramatsu, *Samayabhedoparacanacakra...,* Kyoto, 1935; A.

Bareau, *Trots traites sur les sectes bouddhiques attribués a Vasumitra, Bhavya et yinītadeva,* Journal Asiatique, 1954, pp. 229-266.

5. Cf. J. Przyluski, La *legende de l'empereur 'Aśoka,* Paris, pp. 366-369.
6. P. Demiéville, *L'origins..',* pp. 33-40.
7. Cf. T. Watters, *On Yuan Chwang's Travels,* London, 1904,1, p. 26 f.
8. *Id.,* II, p. 89.
9 Sur l'existence de deux Mahādeva ou d'un Mahādeva redouble, voir déja N. Dutt, *Early Monastic Buddhism,* Calcutta, 1945, II, p. 120; P. Demiéville, *A, propos dn Concile de Yaiśālī, I'*oung Pao, XL, p. 268.
10. G. P. Malalasekera, *Dictionary of Pali Proper Names,* London, 1938, II, pp. 505-506.
11. Voir notamment E. Frauwallner., *Die buddhistischen Konzile,* Zeitschrift der Deutschen Morgenländischen Gesellschaft, CII, 1952, pp. 240-249.
12. Cf. D. C. Sircar, *Text of the Puranic List of Peoples,* IHQ., XXI, 1945, p, 307.. Voir aussi B. C. Law, *Geography of Early Buddhism,* London, 1932, p. 22; *India as described in Early Texts,* Londres, 1941, p. 74, 104.
13. M. Walleser, *Die Sekten des alten Buddhismus,* Heidelberg, 1927, p. 81-82.
14. Td., *Ibid.,* p. 78.
15. A. Bareau, *Les Sectes bouddhiquas du Petit Vehicule,* Saigon, 1955, p, 291.

8

SOME BUDDHIST THINKERS OF ANDHRA

A historical study of the Buddhist philosophical literature reveals the great contributions made by the ancient Andhra area to the growth of the various systems of Buddhist thought. In two earlier papers[1] an attempt has been made to trace the growth of Buddhism in Andhra from the time of the Buddha; and it was also shown that Nāgārjuna and Aryadeva came from the same area in Andhra. Here it is proposed to find out the place from which certain other Buddhist thinkers hailed. Sometimes these thinkers had their main field of activity in the Andhra area.

1. In a Chinese work (Shittanzo) Asvaghosa was considered to belong to South India[2]. The Nāgārjunakonda bas-reliefs present in full the story of *Saundarananda*. The first of these shows the Buddha's conversation with Nanda and Sundari; the second reveals Nanda after the shaving, with a figure holding his head-dress; the third is the visit to Indra's paradise. The dress of the Buddha and Nanda recalls the tenth canto of *Saundarananda*. Another figure shows Arhat Nanda going to preach almost reminding us of 18.58,62 of the poem. It is not possible to say whether these sculptural representations were based on the poem, or the poem itself was written to depict them. Johnston has ably argued that Aśvaghoṣa belonged to the Bahuśrutiya sect[3], and this accords with the fact that

an āyaka pillar at Nāgārjunakonda caitya mentions the existence of the Bahuśrutiyas in that locality[4].

2. *Manjuśri-mūla-tantra* assigns Aryadeva to Saihnika-pura[5], and calls him a non- Aryan. Buston, following the lead of this text, puts him in Simhala, while other Tibetan chronicles observe that his father ruled over Seṅ-ga-gliṅ. Yuan Chwang speaks of Deva P'usa of Chishih-tzu-kuo[6] which may be a transliteration or a rendering of Simhadharaputrapura. The *Bṛhatkathā* observes that Dīpakarṇi was fortunate enough to find in accordance with a dream he had, a boy borne by a lioness. This boy was a Simhadhara, otherwise known as Sāta-vāhana or the one who was carried by a lion. Āryadeva, then, belongs to the town ruled by the Sātavāhanas; and it is called Seṅ-ga-gliṅ, Sakāla or Sagāla which was later pronounced Singala[7]. This Sagāla is the same as the modern Śrī-kā-ku-lam which was, according to the traditional accounts, the original home of the Śātavāhanas. This Śrīkākulam lies due north east of Nāgārjunakoṇḍa and as such it justiries Candrakīrti's statement that Āryadeva came southwards to meet Nāgārjuna. Seṅ-ga-gliṅ, Sagāla and Śrīkākulam refer to one and the same place which now appears in the Krishna delta near Masulipatam; and it is not surprising to believe that a place on the banks of a river in the delta could be mistaken for an island.[8]

3. Maitreyanātha has been associated with Potala which has to be located near modern Bodhan in the Hyderabad territory[9]. Of his disciple Asaṅga, we are told that he belongs to Peshawar. Here we are asked to rely on the Chinese or on the Tibetan traditions. But as Prof. Demieville observes, Chinese tradition, for all the mass of documents on which it rests, hardly affords, at least for the early period, more psitive historical information that Indian tradition with the complete absence of documents."[10] This applies to the Tibetan traditional dates as well. We find that Asaṅga was known as the sage of the Ajanta; and the caves of Ajanta in his day were known as sage of the Ajanta; and the caves of Ajanta in his day were known as Acinta-purī-vihāra[11], probably named after the original name of Asaṅga which may have been Ajita.

4. Dinnāga, as per the Tibetan tradition, was born in Simha-vaktra near Kāñci, lived in a cave on Bhoraśaila in Orissa, and sojourned in Nalanda. Fortunately enough, this misleading statement does not find a place in Yuan Chwang. Yuan Chwang entered the An-to-lo (Andhra) country, saw its capital P'ing-k'i (Vengi), and found a hill 200 li further southwest of the town. On the ridge of this isolated hill, he observes, was a stone tope where Ch'en-na (Dinnāga) P'usa composed a treatise on logic. "Manjuśri summoned him to develop for the benefit of posterity the *Yogācāra-bhtūmi-śāstra* originally delivered by Maitreya"[12]. It was on this hill near Vengi in the West Godāvari district that the *Pramāṇsamuccaya* was composed. He was born in Simhapura or Nellore.

5. Of the critics of Dinnāga's system of logic the most famous Buddhist thinkers appear to be Buddhapālita, Bhavaviveka and Candrakirti. Candrakirti, the disciple of Buddhapālita, was born in Samanta; and according to the Gaṇḍavyūha, there was a Samantamukha in the Mulaka country. This Mulaka country comprises the area round about the Bhadrācalam hills on the banks of the Godāvari. Samanta, Samataṭa, Samantamukha are one and the same.

Regarding Bhavaviveka we have definite information from Yuan Chwang. The pilgrim writes, "Not far from the south side of the capital (Dhānyakaṭaka) was a mountain cliff in the Asura's palace in which the Sāstra-master P'o-p'i-fai-ka (Bhāvaviveka) waits to see Maitreya when he comes to be the Buddha. Then we have the story of this renowned dialectician, who externally displaying the Sāṅkhya garb, internally propogated the learning of Nāgārjuna"[13]. Bhavaviveka not only belongs to Dhanyakaṭaka, but was originally a follower of the Saṅkhya. That he was believed to be waiting for the second coming of Maitreya only proves that Maitreya originally belonged to the same place which was chosen by Bhavaviveka.

Rāhula-mitra, the *parama-gutu* of Saṅgharaksita, appears in one of the inscriptions found near Gollamūḍi in the Krishna district. Sthiramati, the student of Vasubandhu, is believed to have come from the Daṇḍaka which extends over a very wide area from the Marāthi speaking tract in the west to the Telugu speaking zone in the east.

6. Next we have the famous logician Dharmakirti who has been accepted by tradition to be the relative (nephew) of Kumarila. The Jina-vijaya records:

आंध्रोत्कलानां संयोगे पवित्रे जय मंगले

ग्रामे तस्मिन् महानद्यां भट्टाचार्यः कुमारकः।

आंध्र-जातिस्तित्तिरिको माता चंन्द्रगुणासत्ती

यज्ञेश्वरः पिता यस्य महावादिर्महान् घोरः॥

Kumārila was an Andhra hailing from a village called Jayamaṅgala on the banks of the Mahānadi. Dharmakirti was supposed to be born in Trimalaya or Tirumalaya. The prefix Tri or Tiru is the Dravidian cognate of Sri; and the word malai means a mountain. Thus Tirumalaya is the Dravidian translation of Sriśaila or Sri-Parvata. In his Vāda-nyāya we read the interesting statement :[14]

यस्तु नक्कशब्दं मुक्कुशब्दमेव वा नासापर्यायं

वेत्ति न नासाशब्दं सकथमपशब्दात्श.

Here Ḋharmakirti is giving the words *nakka, mukku,* and *nāsika.* These three are from three different languages, and all mean the nose. Of these the second word is *mukku,* a pure Telugu word meaning the nose. It is not an accident that made Dharmakirti use this term. It came direct from his mother tongue. Thus a few pages later he distinguishes his mother-tongue from the Dravidian language:[15]

तत् स्वभावस्य अन्यातोऽपि सिद्धेः प्राकृतापभ्रंश.द्रमिडांध्र-भाषावत्

Prākrita, Apabhramsa, Dramiḍa and Andhra are the languages he takes for examples in his discussion of the correct and incorrect words.

7. We have found reason to disbelieve the Tibetan tradition regarding the home of Dinnāga. Yuan Chwang placed him in

Vengi. Jinendrabodhi was said to be the countryman of the venerable Bodhisattva Dinnāga. Nāgārjuna II and Aryadeva II belonged to Śri Parvata. Likewise there was at the same place a Maitrinātha who, according to Tāranatha, died nine years after Nayapāla of Bengal (c 1040-1075). .

8. Padmasambhava's chief disciple, the Tibetan lady Yeshey Tshogyal, gave an account of the life and teachings of her teacher. According to this biography, Buddha himself decided to take birth from a lotus blossom in the Dhanakoṣa (= Dhānyakaṭaka) lake in the country called Urgyan. This country was also called Udyana, Odiyana Ogyan and the like[16]. This is no other than the Andhra country. This country was ruled by Indrabodhi, who adopted Padmasambhava. Indrabodhi is the same as Indrabhūti, the disciple of Anangavajra. Padmavajra, the teacher of Anangavajra, was the author of *Gubyasiddhi*. Indrabhuti was styled Oḍiyāna-siddha, Avadhūta, Mahācārya and the like. They were practically the pioneers in the Vajrayana school of Buddhism. According to the Vajrayānists, the Buddha turned the third wheel of the law of Vajrayana at Dhānyakaṭaka, sixteen years after his enlightenment[17].

Padmasambhava married Mandaravā, the sister of Śāntaraksita and Śāntaraksita belonged to the city of Sahor in the north-western corner of the Andhra country[18]. It was at Sāntaraksita's suggestion that the king of Tibet invited Padmasambhava to Tibet. Here we have definite evidence to refer Padmasambhava, Śāntaraksita and the Vajrayana teachers to the Andhra country. It was in the same area again that the Buddhist thought and religion lingered till the thirteenth and fourteenth centuries, as the inscriptions during the times of the Velanāṭi-colas testify.

P. S. Sastri

FOOTNOTES

1. See *IHQ.*, 1955 on 'Rise and growth of Buddhism in Andhra' and on 'Nāgārjuna and Āryadeva'.
2. See B.C. Law's monograph on Aśvaghosa.
3. Johnston : *Buddhacarita*, Part 2, xxxiii-xxxv.
4. इवं विहरो स व जिन नियतो अचरियनं बहुसुतियनं पतिथपितो।
5. अपरः प्रव्रजिः श्रेष्ठः सैन्हिकपुर वास्तवी।
   अनार्या आर्य संज्ञी च सिंहलद्वीपवासिनः॥
6. Watters, II. 320. Modern Nellore, was originally called Vikrama-Simha-pura.
7. Evans-Wents : *the Tibetan Book of the Great Liberation*, pp. 113, 156-7.
8. *IHQ.*, 1955 on 'Nāgārjuna and Āryadeva'.
9. *IHQ.*, 1955 on 'The Rise and growth of Buddhism in Andhra'.
10. See Johnston : *Buddhacarita*, pt. 2, xvi.
11. Evans-Wentz, 158.
12. Watters, II. 209-210.
13. Watters, II. 215.
14. *Vādanyāya*, pp. 103-104.
15. *Ibid.*, p. 107.
16. Evans-Wentz, 105.
17. See Rāhula Sankrityayana's Preface to his edition of the *Vigraha-vyāvartani*.
18. Evans-Wentz, 142-4.

9

HARṢA: A BUDDHIST

Harṣa has generally been regarded as a Buddhist. But of late this view has been questioned by some writers, notably by Dr. R. C. Majumdar who cannot believe that Harṣa ever "formally gave up his old faith",i. e., his devotion to Śiva, and regarded other religions as distinctly inferior.[1]

That Harṣa originally was a Śaiva and remained so up to the twenty-fifth year of his reign is well known to most students of history.[2] His Bānskheṛā and Madhuban Copper-plate Grants of the regnal years 22 and 25 respectively call him a *Parama-Māheśvara,* i. e., a worshipper of Maheśvara or Śiva. His seals similarly mention him as a Śaiva, while referring to his brother. Rājyavardhana as a *Parama-Saugata,* i.e., a Buddhist, and to his father, Prabhākara-vardhana, as a *Paramādityabhakta,* i.e., worshipper of the Sun. Bāṇa speaks of Harṣa's offering worship to Nīlalohita, i.e., Śiva, before he started on his *digvijaya.*[3] His Sonepat seal bears the figure of Nāndī, the vehicle of Śiva.

To conclude, however, from this evidence that he continued as a Śaiva to the end of his life does not seem reasonable, not only in view of Yuan Chawāng's testimony which shows that by 643 A. D. Śiva had gone to the third place in Harṣa's estimation, but also on account of the testimony from Harṣa's own works and his biography by the court historiographer and poet, Bāṇa. Harṣa's two plays, *Priyadarśikā* and *Ratnāvalī* show no influence of Buddhism. They, obviously, are the works of a young author who enjoyed and liked people to enjoy life. But we have just to turn to *Nāganandā,* the last and maturest of his plays, to see the great change in his religious attitude. It begins with salutation to the Buddha, deals with the life of a Bodhisattva and preaches in uncompromising terms, the noble doctrine of Ahiṁsā.[4] It. contains veiled references perhaps also to his *Mokṣa-pariṣads* and determination, in c. 643 A. D., to fight no more.[5]

We have to notice also a passage in the *Harṣacarita,* which has so far escaped the attention of practically all writers on Harṣa's religion. When maddened by grief at the death of her husband, Harṣa's sister, Rājyaśrī, desires to become a Buddhist nun. Harṣa, while dissuading her from adopting this course, not only arranges for her instruction in the philosophy of the Tathāgata "which brings all misery to an end",[6] *but promises also to don along with her the red robes of a bhikṣu, as soon as he had finished his self-appointed task of punishing his brother's murderer, Śaśāṅka,* the ruler of Gauḍa.[7] Time, no doubt, never permitted him to implement this resolution. He died rather prematurely. But there is no reason to doubt his sincerity. An orthodox Brāhmana like Bāṇa could hardly have put this statement in Harṣa's mouth, unless Harṣa had actually in his subsequent life become a very devout Buddhist and his conduct given a clear indication that someday he would renounce the world and retire to a Buddhist monastery.

Dasharatha Sharma

FOOTNOTES

1. *Classical Age,* Bhāratīyā Vidyā Bhavan Series, pp. 119-120.
2. See R. S. Tripathi's *History of Kanauj,* p. 163.
3. *Harṣacarita,* Nirṇayasāgar Edition, p. 202.
4. See Acts IV and V and the final portion of Act III.
5. See Canto I, verse 8 which speaks of the grant of *kalpadruma* to suppliants.
6. *Harṣacarita,* p. 256.
7. *"Iyam ta grahīṣyati mayaiva samaṁ samāptakṛtyena kāṣāyāṇi"*

10

SOME BUDDHIST ANTIQUITIES AND MONUMENTS OF RAJASTHAN

Archaeological excavations and explorations in different parts of Rajasthan have brought to light sufficient material pertaining to the penetration and expansion of Buddhism in this part of the country. The Buddhist antiquities and monuments of this region are of course very few in number; but they are of great importance for a student of ancient Indian History and Archaeology. It is now proposed to describe them in brief here.

I. Bhābrū Rock Edict: —

It was in the year 1840 A.D. that Captain Burt discovered the well-known Bhābrū[1] Rock Edict of Aśoka. The same was later on transferred to the Museum of the Asiatic Society of Bengal at Calcutta. This edict is of great interest because of its having been inscribed on a stone-slab[2] *(śilā-phalaka)* as distinguished from a stone-pillar *(śilā-stambha)*. The excavations of the ancient site of Bairat have now proved that this stone-slab inscription must have originally hailed from Bairat itself. Another pillar (of Aśoka), from Bairat, was brought to light by the archaeological remains on the site popularly known as the *Bījaka-kī-Phārī*[3]. One of the fragments of such a pillar, having the usual Mauryan polish, even bears the *Brāhmī* letter *na* in the script of the third century B.C. D. R. Sahni *(ibid,* p.28) is of the opinion that the Buddhist monuments at Bairat were perhaps destroyed by the White Hun leader Mihirakula towards the beginning of the sixth century A.D.

The Bairat Edict of Aśoka of course bears testimony to Aśoka's ardent faith in the Buddhist lore and his royal injunctions to the Buddhist friars and laymen to pay rapt attention to Buddhist ideology and to devote themselves to the study of the particular passages (seven in number) from the Buddhist scriptures[4]. The text of the Bairāṭa epigraph runs thus:—

(1) *Rpi (pri) yaḍasi lājā Māgadhe saṃghaṃ abhivāde (tū)-naṃ āhā apābādhataṃ ca phāsuvihālataṃ ca*

(2) *vidite ve bhaṃte āvatake hamā Budhasi dhaṃmasi saṃghasī ti gālave caṃ rpa (pra)sade ca e keci bhaṃte*

(3 *bhagawatā Budhe(na) bhāsite save se subhāsite vā e cu khu bhaṃte hamiyāye diseya hevaṃ sadhaṃme*

(4) *cila (ṭhi) tīke hosatī ti alahāmi hakaṃ taṃ vātave. imāni bhaṃte (dh)aṃma paliyāyāni Vinaya-samukase*

(5) *Aliya-vasāṇi Anāgata-bhāyani Munigāthā Moneya-sūte Upatisa rpa (pra)sine e cā Lāghulo-*

(6) *vāde musā-vādaṃ adhigicya bhạgavatā Budhena bhasite etāni bhaṁte dhaṃma-paliyāyāni ichāmi*

(7) *kiṃti bahuke bhikhu (pā)ye ca bhikhuniye cā abhikhinaṃ Su(ne)yu cā upadhalayeyu cā*

(8) *hevaṃmevā apāsakā ca upāsikā cā eteni bhaṃte imaṃ likhā(pa)yāmi abhipetaṃ me jānaṃtu ti.*

II. The Circular Brick-Temple at Bairat: —

D. R. Sahni's excavations at Bairat also brought to light the remains of a Buddhist Brick-Temple which was circular in shape[5]. In his own words *(ibid,* pp. 30-31), "this is the oldest structural temple and one of those which furnished models for the numerous rock-cut cave-temples of Western and Eastern India. The nearest approach, both in plan and design, is the *caitya* cave of about the first century B.C. in the Tulja Lena group at Junnar...... On the outside, the walls of the temple were inscribed with the Buddhist texts in the *Brāhmī* characters of the Aśokan period. Several bricks inscribed with one or two *akṣaras* (plate V, e, o and q) were found built in the rectangular enclosure-wall around the temple. A few of them read *pāsaṃ, visa, vi, kama* etc." The existing Buddhist structure (with a *stūpa* in the interior) at Bairat has got an important bearing on the early temple-architecture in India.[6]

Referring to Hwen Tsang's notice of Bairat in the seventh century A.D. (Julien's *Hwen Tsang,* II, 206), General Cunningham *(Arch. Surv. Report,* Simla, 1871, Vol. II, p. 246) remarks that according to the Chinese pilgrim, "the capital was 14 or 15 *li* or just ½ miles in circuit, which corresponds almost exactly with the ancient mound on which the present town is built. The people were brave and bold and their king, who was of the race of *Fei-she,* or a Bais Rajput, was famous for his courage and skill in war. *The place still possessed 8 Buddhist monasteries but they were much ruined and the number of monks was small.* The Brahmans of different sects, about 1000 in number, possessed 12 temples, but their followers were numerous, as the bulk of the population is described as heretical. Judging from the size of the town, as noted by Hwen Tsang, *the population could not have been less than four times the present number, or about* 30,000, *of whom the followers of Buddha may have amounted to one fourth.* I have deduced this number from the fact that the Buddhist monasteries would appear to have held about 100 monks each, and as those of Bairat are said to have been ruined, *the number of monks in Hwen Tsang's time could not have exceeded* 50 *per monastery, or* 400 *altogether.* As each Buddhist monk begged his bread, *the number of Buddhist families could not have been less than* 1200, allowing 3 families for the support of each monk, or altogether about 6000 lay Buddhists in addition to the 400 monks" (cf. also G.H. Ojha, *History of Rajputana,* Vol. I, Hindī, 1927, p. 10; S. Beal's *Buddhist Records of the Western World,* London, 1884, Vol. I, p. 179).

III. Northern Black Polish Ware from Bairat: —

The ancient site of Bairat also yielded the well known *Northern Black Polish (N. B.* P.) *Ware* which is so characteristic of the Mauryan period[7] in India. It is now extremely essential to explore the region for the distribution of the *N. B.* P.[8] ware in Rajasthan.

IV. Remains at Nagarī: —

A fragmentary stone inscription, in the *Brāhmī* script on the third or second century B.C., was excavated at Nagarī (ancient Madhyamikā, near Chittaur, Udaipur region) and is now preserved in the archaeological section of the Udaipur Museum. It refers to a feeling of compassion for all beings in the following words[9]: —

(i) *Śa(vā)bhutānaṃ dayātham*

(ii) *(kār)* (i) *tā.*

It is just possible that this inscription was drafted and engraved under the influence of Buddhism. The explorations at Nagarī also revealed the existence of *stūpas*[10] on the site. This bears testimony to the prevalence of Buddhism there (at Nagarī) inspite of its having been an important stronghold of the *Vaiṣṇava*[11] pantheon. Describing the remains at Nagarī, Dr. Bhandarkar *(Memoirs..., op. cit.,* p. 119) writes that "it is a structure built in horizontal tiers and must be a *stūpa* as indicated by the heavy sausage-shaped garlands" (cf. *Journal of U. P. Historical Society,* Lucknow, VI (2), 19331 P. 3). Henry Cousens *(Prog. Report of Arch. Survey, Western Circle,* Poona, 1905, p. 59) also noticed an ancient lion-capital of the Aśoka period (according to his own version) lying near the image of Kaṅkālī Mātā at Nagarī. Besides this, another sculptured stone from the same site was identified as an 'architrave of some Buddhist gateway' both by Carlleyle and Cousens.

V. Stūpas on the Fort of Chittaur: —

Henry Cousens *(Progress Report of Archaeological Survey of India, Western Circle,* Poona, 1904, p. 45) also refers to the existence of a scattered group of some ten *stupas* (carved in a stone) about 4 or 5 hundred yards to the north-west of Kālikā Mātā's temple at Chittaur. According to Cousens, "the larger ones stand about 3' 3," high and 1' 8" square at the base. They are all of one pattern. The upper portion is cylindrical, with a domed top...... ....Around the base of the cylindrical part is a string-course of 16 little seated Buddhas, each in a little niche. Beneath this is a constricted circular neck with lotus leaves springing from it, an upward row and a downward row. Beneath this, again, the *stūpa* is square with projecting niches, one on each face, in each of which is a seated Buddha. There are 3 distinct positions i. e,, the meditative, the witnessing and the teaching attitudes. Beneath each of these is a symbol incised. The *stūpas* are all a good deal weather worn, so that the finer detail of the carving is lost. The hair is apparently not curly but long and is done up into a considerable knot on the top of the head." These pieces have now been preserved and exhibited in an order on an open platform in front of the Śringāra Chaurī at Chittaur itself.

VI. Absence of Buddhist Remains in Western Rajasthan :—

The ancient sites of the former states of Jodhpur, Jaisalmera, Sirohl and Bikaner[12] do not appear to have yielded anything tangible which may have some bearing on the expansion of Buddhism in Western Rajputana. But no conclu-sion can be hazarded till extensive exploration and excavation work is conducted in this direction. Hwen Tsang refers to the declining condition of Buddhism at Pi-lo-mo-lo,[12a] identified with modern Bhīnmāla or ancient Srīmāla, distant about 120 miles from Jodhpur. According to his information, there was only one *saṅghārāma* (monastery) at Bhīnmāl and that too belonged to the *Hīnayāna* sect. It was inhabited by 100 monks who were followers of the *Sarvāstivāda* Sect (cf. Samuel Beal's *Buddhist Records of the Western World,* Vol. II, London, p. 270; G.H. Ojha, *Hist, of Raj., op. cit.,* I, 1927, p. 10).

It is equally interesting to note the dearth of Buddhist finds both from Nagar or Karkoṭanagar and Sāmbhar situated in the Jaipur unit of Rajasthan. As regards the ancient site of Rairh[13] (Jaipur unit), Dr. K.N. Puri *(Excavations at Rairh,* Jaipur State, p. 57) remarked that "Buddhism had no influence, whatsoever, although traces of contact with the Buddhist world have been established by the discovery of a fragment of Chunar sandstone bowl, a few pieces of highly polished Buddhist pottery and steatite caskets similar to relic-caskets found on Buddhist sites for the enshrinement of the body relics".

VII. Remains at Lalsot: –

"The town of Lalsot, 50 miles from the city of Jaipur, once possessed an ancient Buddhist *stūpa* of a considerable antiquity. Six red stone pillars, belonging to the railings of this monument, have in modern times been utilised in the construction of the *chatrīs* or cenotaphs. These pillars are 5 feet high, square at the base and at the top and octagonal in the middle portion."[14]

VIII. Kota Buddhist Inscription: –

It is interesting to analyse the opening verses of the Kota Buddhist inscription engraved on a stone, built into a recess under a flight of stairs on the right hand as one enters the Barkhārī gate of the inner wall of the town of Shergarh (Kota Division). It records the construction of a Buddhist temple and a monastery to the east of mount Kośavardhana by the feudal chief Devadatta[15]. It specifically refers to firm belief in trinity[16], greatness of Buddha, law of Sugata, the Buddhist Church etc., in the following words: –

ओं नमों रत्नत्रयाय। जयंति वादाः सुगतस्य निर्म्मला। समस्तसंदेहनिरासभासुराः।

कुतर्कक–सम्पातनिपातहेतवो युगान्तवाता इव विश्वसन्ततेः।।१।। यो रूपवानपि विभर्ति सदैव रूपमेकोप्यनेक इव भाति च यो निकामं। आरादगात्परधियः प्रति–मर्त्यवेद्यो यां निर्ज्जितारि रजितश्च जिनः स वो व्यात्ः।।२।। भिनति यो नष्टणाम्मोहं तमा वेश्मनि दीपवत्। सो व्यादः सौगतो धर्मो भक्तमुक्तिफलप्रदः।।३।। आर्यसंघस्य विमलाः शरच्छसि जिताश्रियः। जयन्ति जयिनः पादः सुरासुरशिरोर्च्चिताः।।४।।

This testifies to State-patronage accorded to Buddhism in this area as late as the end of the 8th or the beginning of the 9th century A.D. It is of course regretted that we have absolutely no information about the Buddhist antiquities of an early period from Kota region.

IX. Buddhist Caves in the Jhalawar Region: —

Dr. Impey[17] is said to have visited the Buddhist caves at Kholvī[18] (situated in district Jhālāwār of the Kota Division) first of all. Later on, General A. Cunningham visited the place and presented a vivid-account of the caves and the topes at Kholvī in his *Arch. Survey Report, op. cit.*, pp. 280-88 and plate lxxxiv. He infers *(ibid,* p. 286) that "the Kholvī excavations are most probably of a later date than the caves of Dhamnār[19] and Bāgh in Mālwā and of Kārlī, Ellora and other places in Southern India." He *(ibid,* p. 288) even assigns them a date ranging from 700 to 900 A.D. The Buddhist caves at Kholvī thus have to play a great role in the realm of Buddhist iconography and architecture of Rajasthan during the post-Gupta period. In this connection, mention may also be made of a colossal standing figure of Buddha at Kholvī. It measures about 12 feet in height and depicts the Buddha in the mode of teaching with his left hand raised to the breast (cf. *ibid,* p. 285 for details; also consult J. Fergusson, *History of Indian and Eastern Architecture,* London, 1899, Book I, pp. 162-3 for the *later* date of the Kholvī caves).

It is equally interesting to study the cave architecture as presented by the Buddhist caves at Vināyakā (or Vināyagā or Binnāyagā) situated about 8 miles from Kholvī. Srī M.M. Śāstrī (Custodian of the Kota Museum) has recently informed me that some Buddhist caves exist at Haṭhiagor (situated in the Jhālāwār region) too. It now appears that the region round about Kholvī[20] and Vināyakā was once an important stronghold of Buddhism. Śrī G.L. Vyas (Custodian of the Jhālawār Museum) has also stated that there exist about 16 Buddhist caves at Vināyakā and that some Buddhist *stūpas* can be seen in front of these caves. Besides this, some images of seated Buddha have also been carved out nearby.

A passing reference may also be made to the discovery of the Mandsor Inscription of the *Mālava* year 524. It opens with the auspicious phrase *siddhaṃ* whereas the first verse is a *maṅgalācaraṇa* expressing adoration to *Sugata* (the Buddha;

Epigraphia Indica, XXVII, no. 1, pp. 12 ff.*):— Siddhaṃ. Ye(ne)dasamudbhavạnirodhaparaṃparāyā magnaṃ jagadvidhaduhkhanirantarāyām. Tittrāsuna tripadironiradeśi dharmmastasmai namostu Sugatāya ga(tā)ya śantim* i.e., "Obeisance to *Sugata,* wishing to save the world (which is) plunged in the uninterrupted series of births and deaths closely associated with misery in various forms, enjoined a religion consisting of 3 steps (stages) and who attained peace" *(ibid,* p. 16). It refers to the construction of a "stūpa accompanied by a well [in commemoration] of the *Buddha,* who having overcome the evil influences of all elements *(dhātu)* preached the accomplishment of all actions, the stūpa, the structure of which was as white as the *kunda* flower and the moon and the pinnacle of which touched the clouds" *(yo dhātumātre hatadhātudoṣaḥ sarvvakṛyā siddhim uvāca tasya. Kundenduśubhrobbhravighṛiṣṭaṛyaṣṭiriyaṃ kṛto dbātudharaḥ saktūpaḥ).* This *stūpa* was situated within the limits of the *Lokottara Vihāra* (verse 18) and this led M. B. Gadre *(ibid.,* p. 13) to suggest that the latter "was possibly the proper name of some local Buddhist monastery, probably named after the *Lokottaravāda* sect of the *Hīnayāna* form of Buddhism."

The phrase "*Syādvādagrahanigrahāgadavidrvvidhvastava-itaṇḍikachadmā Saugatagarvvaparvvatabhidāvajrapratāpodha-naḥ......ryabhaṅgakṣamaḥ Śrī Vedāṅgamuniḥ prasiddhamahimā yasya prasādaṃ uyadhāta*" occurring in the Inscription of V.S. 1028 from Ekaliṅgajī (14 miles from Udaipur; *JBBRAS.,* Bombay, XXII, old series, verse 17, lines 15-16, pp. 166-7) of course refers to the existence of unhappy relations between the adherents of the Buddhist and the *Śaiva* pantheons. Vedāṅgamuni, of this record, was a follower of the *Lakulīśa-Pāsupata* sect and has been described, here, as a great opponent of the Jainas (believers in the *Syādvāda* philosophy) and the Buddhists (cf. *saugata; sugata* = Buddha) alike. It is regretted that this inscription fails to throw any light on the causes of this revolt against Jainism and Buddhism in this particalar case.

This is a brief account of some Buddhist remains from Rājasthāna. The material, in this direction, is of course very scanty but the existing Buddhist monuments and remains of the region are very important for the reconstruction of the religious history of the area during the early historic and the pre-mediaeval periods.

Ratna Chandra Agrawala

FOOTNOTES

1. Bhābrū is about 12 miles in a direct line to the north of Bairat, the latter being ancient *Virāṭapura* and distant about 52 miles from Jaipur City. Virāṭapura was the capital of the *Matsya* country. For details consult B. C. Law's paper in *the Age of Imperial Unity,* Bombay, pp. *2,* n, 12 etc.
2. "This stone is an irregularly shaped block of grey granite, of the kind so abundant at Bairat and measuring about 2 feet in lengh, the same in width and a foot and a half in thickness" (D. R. Sahni, *Archaeological Remains and Excavations at Bairat,* Jaipur State, p. 18 and plate II for its photograph).
3. *Ibid,* pp. 26 ff, and plate VI. a.
4. For details consult Sahni, *of. cit.,* p. 18; B, C. Law, *Journal of the Pali Text Society,* 1946, pp, 93-8; D. C. Sircar, *Select Inscriptions,* I, 1942, Calcutta, pp. 77-8; D. R. Bhandarkar, *'Aśoka,* 1955, Calcutta, pp. 335-6; Senart, *Ind. Ant.,* XX, pp. 165 ff.; E. Hultzsch, *Corp. Insc. Ind.,* I, pp. 172 ff.
5. Cf. Sahni, *op. cit.,* plates VII, VIII; *ibid,* pp. 28 ff., for details and description.
6. Cf. Percy Brown, *Indian Architecture (Buddhist & Hindu Periods),* Second Edition, Bombay, p. 15,
7. For a comprehensive list of *N. B. P.* sites in India, consult B. B, Lal's paper in *Ancient India, Bull. of the Arch. Survey of India,* New Delhi, Vols. X-XI, pp. 50 ff. and pp. 143 ff.
8. It is equally interesting to note the discovery of the *Painted Grey Ware* at Bairat *(Indian Archaeology.* 1954-5—*a Review,* New Delhi, 1955. p, 61). This is much earlier in date as compared to the N. B. P. The Grey ware occurs in the regions of Bikaner and Alwar too.
9. Cf. D. R, Bhandarkar's *Archaeological Ramains & Excavations at Nagari, MASL,* No. 4, pp. 112-120; G. H. Ojha, *History of Rajputana,* Hindi, I, 1927, p. 358.

10. Cf. Satya Prakasha, *Rajasthan and its Traditions,* 1951, Jaipur, p. 25; G. H. Ojha, *op. cit.*, pp. 359-60; *Arch. Surv. Reports* by Carlleyle, VI, pp. 196 ff. and plates.
11. As is evident from the well known Ghosuṇḍi inscription. For details consult,, *MASl,* 4, *op. cit.*, pp. 119-20; V. S. Agrawala's paper in the Śodhapatrikā, Udaipur, IV, (3), pp. 40 ff; *Ep. Indica,* XXII, pp. 203 ff......etc.
12. Dr. L. P. Tessitory, is said to have discovered traces of the foundations of, what he thought, might have been Buddhist *stūpas* at Muṇḍa and Pīra Sultāna in the Bikaner region (H. Goetz, *The Art and Architecture of Bikaner State,* 1950, Oxford, p. 58).
12a. Some of the scholars even hesitate in accepting this identification.
13. Nagar and Rairh were important seats of the Mālava republic: cf. *Arch. Surv. Report,* Simla, VI for the finds from Nagar.
14. Satya Prakash, *Rajasthan and its Traditions,* Jaipur, 1951, p. 25.
15. For the Sanskrit text of this epigraph, consult E. Hultzsch, *Ind., Antiquary.* XIV, pp. 45-6 and M. L. Sharma's, *Kotā Rāja kā Itihasa,* Hindi, vol. I. Appendix III and p. 27; cf. also *Bhandarkar's List of Brāhmī Inscriftions of N. India,* serial no. 21.
16. i.e., *Buddha, Dharma* and *Saṅgha,*
17. Consult his paper in the *Journal of the Asiatic Society of Bengal,* Calcutta, V. p. 336.
18. About 30 miles from Augar and also 30 miles from the Dhamnār caves.
19. Dhamnār caves are situated in the State of Madhya Bharat. For Dhamnār caves, consult Percy Brown, *Indian Architecture (Hindu and Survey Buddhist),* Second edition, p. 143 ; Cunningham's *ArchaelogicalSurvey of India Report,* Simla, 1871, Vol. II, pp: 270 ff. and plates.
20. One has to pass through Dug (the headquarters of a *tahsil* of the Jhalāwār Distt.) on way to the Kholvī caves.

11

BUDDHISM IN THE CLASSICAL AGE

(AS REVEALED BY ARCHAEOLOGY)

The period under review, designated by scholars as "Classical Age", covers a period of about four centuries. It begins with the Gupta rulers in the administrative horizon of India, their glorious ascent like the midday sun, their temporary eclipse by the Huṇa invaders, and their gradual setting down. Then the twilight of various petty rulers and then the advent of the Moon in the form of Harṣavardhana with many other rulers scattered all over the country like stars in a nocturnal sky. Then with the disappearance of Harṣa, there is again a dark period, which ends with the azure with the glimpses of morning light just before the rise of another Sun in the horizon, the Pālas.

For the history of the Buddhist church in the classical period, there is a considerable number of inscriptions and archaeological remains in the form of images, shrines, *stūpas,* cave-temples, *caityas,* etc. which enable us to rebuild a complete structure of the history of the religion.

Though Buddhism was not a state religion in this period,—none of the main ruling families of this period having professed the religion of Sākya-Muni,—still, following the general Indian tradition of religious toleration which favoured the growth of diverse rival religious sects side by side in the Indian soil, most of the Indian kings patronised religions other than their own. A study of the archaeological remains reveal to us the fact that as on the one hand the Buddhist kings made religious grants to non-Buddhist communities, in the same manner the non-Buddhist kings also did not refrain from stretching their bounteous hands to the Buddhists. And this spirit of sympathetic co-operation stimulated the art, archite-cture and sculpture of this period to rise to such a level of per-fection that it drew unstinted admiration of art-connoisseurs for many centuries. Though the Gupta kings held political supremacy up to the end of the 5th century A. D., the era of art which began with them lasted much longer up to the 7-8th centuries A. D. And the influence of Gupta art spread far beyond the historical and geographical boundaries of the Gupta empire.

The Buddhist monuments consist mainly of (1) Pillars, (2) *Stūpas* (3) Railings, (4) *Caityas* or prayer halls and (5) *Vihāras* or monastic abodes.[1] The images, which play a great part in the history of the development of the Buddhist church, were introduced at a later date. In the hilly tracts, the Buddhist establishments are hewn out of living rocks—splendid specimens of rock-architecture. In fact, the earliest and the major number of the cave-temples of India are Buddhist. In the Buddhist literature the mode of preparing *stūpas* was suggested by Buddha himself[2], and the worship of *stūpas* commenced immediately after his demise. In the *Mahāparinibbānasutta* it is said that after the demise of the Buddha, a dispute arose among the Mallas, Koliyas, Śākyas and others for possession of the relics of Buddha's body, which were at last divided among eight chiefs, each of whom built a *stūpa* over them in their respective countries[3]. During the life-time of the Buddha, his religion was confined to Middle India. It was during the reign of the Emperor Aśoka that the religion gained a wide popularity. Aśoka erected several *stūpas* and pillars all over India, especially at the places associated with some memorable event in the life of Buddha. The fabulous number of eighty-four thousand *stūpas* erected by Aśoka in place of seven out of the eight *stūpas* erected over the relics of Buddha may be incredible, but that their number was quite large appears to be true. And the places around these *stūpas* must have been important centres of Buddhism for a few centuries upto about the fourth century A. D. when the building of new *stūpas* became less in number but there was enlargement or alteration of the older ones. Pillars became very rare and railings encircling *stūpas* in vogue from the earliest period of the Buddhist architecture—also became much rarer, and probably the only stone railing that may be ascribed to this period is one of the two sets found at Bodh-Gaya, the older one being of the time of Aśoka and made of the same kind of polished sand-stone peculiar to all Aśokan monoliths. The more popular Buddhist architectures of this period are the *Vihāras* or a group of monastic abodes for the residence of monks, *caityas* or prayer halls enshrining *stūpas* and images of Buddha Figures of Buddha were in some cases carved on the *stūpas* placed inside the *caityas*. These *Vihāras* and *Caityas* gained in popularity and increased in number. The *Vihāras* were used to be made by the Buddhists from the earliest period of its organisation—from the life-time of its Founder who himself lived in various *Vihāras*. *Caitya* halls were introduced somewhat later, the earliest form of paying homage by the Buddhists being the erection and worship of relic *stūpas*. With the rise and development of Mahāyāna, *Caitya* halls became more and more popular and the cultural atmosphere and the patronising spirit of the rulers encouraged the Buddhists of this age to revive their intellectual activities, particularly in the art and architecture of the *Caityas* and *Vihāras*. Lastly, with the growing popularity of Mahāyāna, and the gradual introduction of various gods and goddesses into its pantheon the family of Buddhist gods became enlarged to a considerable extent. This large pantheon gave inspiration and ample scope to the display of skill by the sculptors whose productions are really a treasure for all times. The archaeologists' spades have brought to light before us the long mute story of those forgotten far off days and we remain struck with wonder and admiration when we think of the men of that remote past who could build such magnificent structures with such delicate ornamentations and graceful and lovely figures with their hands and very meagre implements. We shall now begin our survey of the state of Buddhism during the Gupta period and commence with the extreme north-western part of India.

Buddhism reached the north-western region through the proselytising efforts of Aśoka. Three inscriptions found from Swat[4] corroborate the statement of the Chinese travellers that Buddhism lingered on this region upto the 7th century A. D. The characters of these inscriptions resemble the so-called north-western Gupta characters. These inscriptions, being quotations from the Sūtras, are very important from the literary standpoint.

It was Aśoka who was responsible for the introduction of Buddhism into the Gandhāra region. Here he built: several *stūpas* which were seen by the Chinese pilgrims.' After Aśoka, the region passed into the hands of foreign rulers who could have the religion easily rooted out from the territory but they did not do so, and on the other hand the great Kushān king Kaṇiṣka helped it in its further development. Kaṇiṣka very probably repaired the older *stūpas* or built new ones in their places, and it is said that during his time Gandhāra became a popular centre of Buddhism. The rulers, who governed this place after Kaṇiṣka, did not show much interest in Buddhism, which therefore gradually faded out in the area. But that religion of Gautama did not totally disappear from these places at least upto the 7th century, is proved by the records of the Chinese travellers as well as by archaeological discoveries. The Dharma-rajika Vihāra built by Kaṇiṣka was seen by Fa-Hian in the 5th century in a flourishing condition. Hwen-tsang, who came to India in the early 7th century, reports that he saw many *stūpas* and monasteries in this region, in a somewhat decayed condition bur their glory and sancitity were not much diminished. The Buddhist establishments of Mohra-Moradu and Kalvan appear around the Dharmarājika *stūpa*. The Archaeological reports tell us that *stūpas* and other buildings continued to be erected around the Dharmarājika *stūpa* from the 4th to 7th centuries

A. D. The Bhāmala monastery in Taxila was built about the 4th or 5th century A. D. On the tiled pavement in front of the western steps of the main *stūpa* at Bhāmala is depicted the *Dharmacakra* and various other symbols, like Swastikā, lotus, rosettes, concentric circles, quarter-foils of Pipal leaves, crosses, spirals and double-axes[5]. A few decades later, the whole of this region must have been set on fire, apparently by the formidable enemy of India, the Hūṇa invaders, Toramāna and Mihirakula as is proved by the traces of incendiarism on the sites like some half-burnt birch-bark manuscripts written in upright Gupta characters of the 5th century A. D., found from Juliāñ[6].

I. In Sind, the brick-built *stūpa* of Kahu-jo-daro near Mirpurkhās contains ornamentations and patterns resembling those at Sarnāth and at Mathurā. Clay tablets containing the well-known Buddhist formula "Ye dharma—" etc. in 7th-8th century characters go to prove that Buddhism still had its hold over this place. The *stūpa* named Sudharanjo-dafo near Tando-Mohamed-Khan, of which unfortunately nothing but the square plinth is extant, is also assigned to about the 5th-6th century A. D., on the basis of the evidence furnished by its carved bricks lying scattered.

II. That there was a net-work of Buddhist institutions with a considerable number of devotees in the Kabul valley and the Punjab region of India from the remotest period of its history is further proved by the inscriptions found in the neighbouring places. An inscription on a stone-slab from Kura in the salt-range records[7] the erection of a *Vihāra* "for the congregation of monks of Bhagavat Buddha by the lord of the Vihāra, Poṭṭa Siddha Vṛddhi, son of Roṭṭa Jaya Vṛddhi whose name was honoured by the lord of Naschira, for the benefit of the relatives of the donor and the queens, princes and princesses, of Mahārāja Toramāṇa Sāha Jauvala for the acceptance of the teachers (Ācāryas) of the Mahiśāsakas." The characters resemble the older Buddhist nail-headed inscriptions of the Gupta period with some peculiarities. The Toramāṇa mentioned in this inscription is certainly not the famous Huṇa king of the same name, who was rather a staunch antagonist to all Indian religions—not to speak of Buddhism — but might be some other independent king bearing similar name and ruling over some territory in North-Western India. Traces of Buddhism in Punjab are found in an inscribed brass image of Buddha found in Fatehpur (Kangra dist.) approximately of the 6th century A.D. which records[8] the pious gift of the Buddhist friar Dharmapriya together with his brother Dharmasiṃha and with his preceptor of the same name (viz. Dharmasiṃha), and "with all sentient beings".

III. Kashmir was a great centre of Buddhism of the Sarvāstivāda school of the Hinayāna sect from a very early period. Its later history is furnished by literary as well as architectural evidences. According to the *Mahāvaṃsa,* of the thirteen missionaries sent by Aśoka to preach Buddhism in different countries, one named Majjhantika was sent to Kashmir and Gandhāra. According to some opinion including that of Hwen Tsang, Kashmir was the venue of the Buddhist council held under the auspices of Kaṇiṣka. The *Rājatarangini,* the famous chronicle of Kashmir by Kalhaṇa, tells us that Buddhism and Hinduism flourished side by side in Kashmir during the reign of the great king Lalitāditya Muktāpiḍa (699-735) when the *Vihāras* and *Caitya* of Parihāspura (mod. Paraspur) and the Vihāra of Huviṣkapura (mod. Uskara) were built. The Vihāra of Uskara seems to have been built at least some time before that, because, Hwen Tsang, who visited Kashmir a few decades earlier and lived there for two years, is said to have spent a night in the Huṣkara Vihāra, which must be the same as that at Huviṣkapura. Another monastery mentioned by the pilgrim was the Jayendra-Vihāra. The Chinese pilgrim is said to have seen about 100 monasteries in Kashmir, but Wu-K'ung who lived at the same place about a century later, reports to have seen about 300 monasteries.[8] The most remarkable early

Buddhist remains at Kashmir are unearthed at Harwan near Srinagar. It occupies a lovely situation on a slope facing the beautiful Dal lake, with a mountain range on its background. The remains reveal a large Buddhist establishment with a *stūpa* in its courtyard, a *Caitya* hall and some monastic abodes around them. The *Caitya* hall which occupies a prominent position on the highest part of the plateau is one of the rare specimens of the type in northern India, bearing remarkable affinity to those of the rock-cut *Caitya* halls in the southern parts of India. Numerous terracotta plaques found at the site are unique specimens of Indian art. As observed by Percy Brown, "the remains at Harwan indicate that the memorable impact of diverse historical cultures, which took place in this part of Asia in the early centuries of the first millennium, also had repurcussions on the arts of Kashmir[10]." And though we have hitherto found no inscription from Kashmir, the deficiency is more than made up by the monumental discovery of a number of Sanskrit manuscripts of various Buddhist texts from a *stūpa* at Gilgit, written in characters of 5-6th century A.D. These manuscripts are supposed to be the earliest manuscripts so far discovered in India, and were hitherto known to have existed only in their Tibetan translations.[11]

IV. For the region lying between the north-western countries and Mathura, we have practically no archaeological materials to depict the story of the condition of Buddhism in these regions. Hwen Tsang reports to have seen a number of Buddhist institutions and also Buddhist devotees in this region. Mathura and its neighbourhood was a great centre of Jainism as well as of Buddhism from a very early date, the form of Buddhism being mainly the Sarvāstivāda as it is associated with the name of Upagupta, the religious teacher of Aśoka, who is said to have had great success as a missonary in this region and converted numerous people. An inscription of the time of Kaṇiṣka records that the Sāmnitiyas also resided at this place. Hwen Tsang is said to have seen the followers of Mahāyāna also. The Chinese travellers saw here about twenty Buddhist monasteries and a large number of devotees. But unfortunately no remains of any monastery have so far been found out in this area, though numerous Buddhist figures, some of which are inscribed, prove that at one time the place was a flourishing centre of Buddhism. The sculptures of Mathura had a peculiar type of its own and its school of art, which developed almost immediately after that of Gandhara, is regarded as the connecting link between the Gandhara and the Gupta school of art. Some Buddhist figures of the early Gupta period hailing from Mathura clearly manifest the vestiges of the older form of art mingled with the glimpses of the advancing Gupta art.[12] The Boston Museum of America has in its collection some images of Buddha from Mathura belonging to the Gupta period.[18] Two inscriptions inscribed on the pedestals of two standing Buddha images from Mathura have been discovered. These, on paleographic grounds, are to be placed at an interval of about a century. These are regarded as the latest inscriptions so far found in this region. The earlier one, ascribed to the middle of the 5th century A.D., is inscribed on the pedestal of a broken image of standing Buddha and records the gift of the figure by some "Vihārasvāmmi Devatā", most probably a "Mother Superior" of a nunnery, "for the acquisition of supreme knowledge by her parents and all sentient beings". The later one is the gift of another nun of the name of Jayabhaṭṭā to a monastery named Yaśovihāra.[14] Not only stone but bronze images also have been discovered from Mathura and other places which add to the glory of the artists of this period.

V. The city of Śrāvastī is prominent in Buddhist literature for continued presence and activities of Buddha himself. It is identified with the modern ruined city of Saheth_-Maheth in the Gonda and Bahraich districts of U. P. where Gen. Cunningham discovered a colossal image of Buddha with the name of Śrāvastī inscribed on it. Archaeological excavations have brought to light many of the sites mentioned by the Chinese pilgrims and those agree reasonably with their description. The Jetavana-vihāra with its eastern and northern gates, as described by Fa-Hian, has been brought to light by Gen. Cunningham at Saheth, The Aṅgulimāla-stūpa, the Gandha-kūṭī, and the Kosāmba-kūṭī have been identified by the excavators. Five brickbuilt monasteries together with a shrine and a *stūpa* have been unearthed in this area and very likely these belong to our period of survey. There are some structural remains of the Gupta and subsequent periods, as also of the earlier period testifying that the site was occupied from the Kushān upto the 11-12th centuries A.D. The sculptures so far found at this site are anterior to the classical period, and it is strange enough that no sculpture of this period has hitherto been come to light. But there are many inscribed terracotta seals and sealings bearing the Buddhist creed in scripts of the 6th-7th century.

VI. Prayaga or the district around Allahabad was the centre of Buddhism from the lifetime of Buddha. Kausāmbī, modern Kosam near Allahabad, where the Ghoṣitārāma monastery mentioned in the Buddhist literature has been unearthed together with an inscription of the earlier centuries mentioning the name of the monastery, was sanctified by the presence of the lord himself. The records of the Chinese pilgrims prove that this country continued to be a centre of Buddhism in subsequent periods also, at least upto the 7th century when Hwen Tsang visited India, and Harṣavardhana was ruling in this region. Though there is no inscription either of Harṣa or any other ruler, both Hwen Tsang and Harṣa's biographer Bāṇa depict the king as a great patron of Buddhism. The quinquennial religious assembly organised under the auspices of Harṣa is said to have taken place during the visit of the Chinese pilgrim at Allahabad. Hwen Tsang speaks eloquently of the assembly and the favour shown to Buddhism by its inaugurator, Harṣa. Two inscriptions belonging to periods earlier than Harṣa found in the neighbouring areas relate the continuation of the religion from its inception. Of the two inscriptions, the first, ascribed to the reign of the Gupta ruler Kumāragupta I, found at Mankuwar in the Allahabad district records the installation by a monk called Buddhamitra of the stone-figure of Buddha, on which appears the inscription[15]. An attempt has been made to identify this Buddhamitra with his namesake, the teacher of Vasubandhu[18]. The other inscription, found in a village named Deoriya in the same district, though undated, is assigned to the 5th century on paleographic grounds, and records the gift of the image of Buddha by a Śākya monk Bodhivarman[17].

VII. Kasia in the Gorakhpur district is the modern site of ancient Kuśīnagara, the site of hallowed memory in the history of Buddhism as the place of the *Mahāparinirvāṇa* of the Buddha, and as such one of the four great places of pilgrimage for the Buddhists. Kasia has yielded a large number of archaeological materials which show that the origin of the place goes back to a remote antiquity, even as early as the Mauryan age. Of the many Mahāparinirvāṇa *Caityas* found at this place, the main one, designated Māthā-kuvar-kā-koṭ by the local people, is supposed to have been rebuilt at this period. A colossal recumbent stone image of Buddha in the pose of attaining *Mahāparinirvāṇa* has been unearthed at Kasia. It bears an inscription under its pedestal which records the gift of the same figure by an abbot (Mahāvihāra-svāmin) named Haribala.[18] Again, in the relic chamber of a large *stūpa* behind the Nirvāṇa temple at Kasia, was found a copper vessel—probably containing the relics, with an inscribed copper lid. The inscription contains the Buddhist *Nidāna Sūtra* and also the record of the gift (of the vessel) by the pious Haribala, obviously the same person as the donor of the image mentioned above. It is also stated in the inscription that the urn belonged to the Nirvāṇa-caitya, confirming the identity of Kasia with the ancient Kuśīnagara. Further evidence of the identity of Kasia with Kuśīnagara is supplied by a number of clay seals depicting Buddha in the attitude of attaining *Mahāparinirvāṇa,* with the *Dharmacakra* or the wheel of Law underneath, and the legend 'Mahāparinirvāṇa Bhikṣusaṅghasya' on it in Gupta characters, or 'Sri Mahāparinirvāṇa mahāvihāriyārya bhikshu saṅghasya' in 8th century characters. Some official sealings with legends in Gupta characters and fragmentary stone inscriptions have also been found in the area.[19]

VIII. Sarnath had the singular fortune of being the birth place of Buddhism as well as of the Buddhist Saṅgha, the two jewels of the Buddhist Trinity. The first monastic organisation formed at Sarnath continued to exist here in subsequent days. Aśoka, who is credited with building numerous Buddhist edifices, constructed the Dharmarājika *stūpa* here, and erected one of his edict pillars, the stump of which still remain in situ. Its inscription portion has been preserved in such excellent condition that it can be read quite easily even after such a long interval of time. The *stūpa* was seen by Hwen Tsang, and it remained extant even about two centuries ago, when a local chief of Benares, Jagat Singh by name, destroyed it for procuring stones. The lion capital crowning the pillar which has been adopted recently as the insignia of the Republic of India, is exhibited in the adjoining museum. In the Suṇga, Kānva, and Andhra periods, the Sarnath monastery continued to exist in an insignificant way, but it was revived again in the Kushan period, specially under Kaṇiṣka. The most notable statue of the period of Kaṇiṣka found at Sarnath is the colossal Bodhisattva figure with the umbrella dedicated by the monk Bala. The Buddhist art attained the summit of its glory at Sarnath during the Gupta period, and a considerable number of Buddhist images which have been unearthed from Sarnath during excavations as well as those of the same period found from Mathura, are regarded as the finest specimens of Indian art. The main shrine of Sarnath is supposed to have been erected during the Gupta period, but who was its patron, is not yet clear. The famous Dhāmekh *stūpa,* still extant at Sarnath, must have been rebuilt on an earlier nucleus during this period, and show a marked distinction in its formation compared with other *stūpas* of earlier date. A fair number of inscriptions found from Sarnath help us to ascertain the condition of Buddhism in this period. An inscription of the 4th century A. D., on the pedestal of a broken image of standing Buddha, records the gift of the statue by a Buddhist nun 'Dharmmade'. The inscription below a sandstone bas-relief representation of three scenes of the life of Buddha, belonging to the 5th century (now deposited in the Indian Museum, Calcutta) records that the sculpture was made by the order of a religious mendicant named Harigupta. An inscription on a figure of Buddha, assigned to the reign of Kumāragupta (II) records the gift of the image by a certain monk Abhayamitra. Another image contains the inscription 'Deya-dharmo-yam Kumāraguptasya' which suggests that the donor was perhaps the Gupta king Kumāragupta himself. Two other inscriptions of the monk Abhayamitra have been found at Sarnath on the pedestals of two similar beautiful Buddha images standing on lotus, assigned to a later period, to the reign of Budhagupta. There are also the 5th century inscription of the gift of the monk Śilasena and the 6th century gift of the great laydevotee Narnnana as well as the gift of a pillar used as a lamp-post in the main shrine by the devout worshipper Kīrti, belonging to the 5th century. A peculiar fact about the inscriptions of this period is that they seldom state the particular sect of Buddhism to which the donors or the donee belonged. And as such we are confronted with a difficulty to ascertain the form of religion prevalent in a certain locality. This difficulty is somewhat solved by two dedicatory inscriptions on a railing-stone at Sarnath, recording the paying of homage to the Sarvāstivādin teachers. Sten Konow remarks about these inscriptions: "the inscription consists of two distinct parts in different characters. The beginning belongs to the 3rd or 4th C. A. D. The final portion... ...is older by about four centuries. It appears that the first part of the earlier inscription has been erased and a different beginning substituted." From these, it becomes evident that the Sarvāstivādins were predominant in this region, and previously some rival sect had its centre in the same region. The later sects scratched the previous names and substituted that of their own[20].

IX. The city of Paṭaliputra, modern Patna, had no less

importance in the history of Buddhism than its political one. It became the capital city as early as the time of the grandson of Bimbisāra. Aśoka too had his capital at this city, and this place must have been a centre of Buddhism from that very period. Fa-Hian in the early 5th-6 C. saw a large monastery with the adherents of the Mahāyāna sect, and another with those of the Hinayāna faith. Both the monasteries contained numerous priests and were great centres of learning. But Hwen Tsang, two centuries later, found the city almost deserted, with very few Buddhist and Brahmanic ruins scattered here and there. Archaeological excavations have brought to light what is supposed to be the palace of Aśoka, and recent excavations have unearthed some Buddhist establishments which, if further excavations are carried on, might, in the long run, be identified with those referred to by Fa-Hian.

X. The illustrious institution of Nālandā did not rise into prominence till the later part of the Gupta rule. According to Tāranātha Nālandā was a flourishing centre of Buddhism as early as the time of Nāgārjuna (i. e. and C. A. D.), who is said to have passed his academic as well as teaching career in the monastery of Nālandā. But we have no archaeological or epigraphic record in support of the statement. All the Buddhist Vihāras, from their earliest history, provided educational facilities particularly of the Tripiṭaka. In the same manner, the Nālandā monastery with its educational activities might have existed in an insignificant position from an earlier period, till it gained the world-wide reputation as a University centre at the time of the late Gupta rulers. Archaeological reports also do not prove its importance before that period. Probably it was not before the time of Kumāragupta that the Nālandā monastery came into prominence, as the coin of the king found on the site claims to prove; the inscribed copper-plate ascribed to Samudragupta is supposed by scholars as spurious; and Fa-Hian does not mention a single word about the monastery of Nālandā, though he speaks of the village Nalo and the Sāriputra tope. On the other hand, Hwen Tsang, two centuries later, speaks highly of the monastic establishment of Nalandā, of its patron kings, of the successsion of teachers, the fame of whose vast knowledge and scholasticism spread all over Asia and attracted students from far off countries. Under one of them, viz., Śīlabhadra, he himself studied for a long period. The architectural remains of Nālandā disclose several strata which indicates that the buildings were built and re-built several times, and was in a flourishing condition upto the period of the Pālas. The majority of the inscriptions from Nālandā belongs to the age of the Pālas. For the period under review, we have very few inscriptions, one of which is quite interesting. This is the inscription of the time of Yaśovarmadeva, the characters of which resemble those of Ādityasena found at Āpsaḍ, and hence is placed in the 6th century A.D. It records certain gifts of Mālāda[21], son of a minister of Yaśovarmadeva, to the temple of Buddha, erected by Bālāditya at Nālandā. Though some difference of opinion have occurred about the identity and date of the Yaśovarmadeva during whose reign the gift was made[22], this inscription is of considerable value as it confirms the state-ment made by Hwen Tsang, that the Nālandā monastery was built by 'Bālāditya Rājā'.The inscription gives the description of the Nālandā monastery as follows: "Bālāditya, the great king of irresistible valour, erected a great and extraordinary temple of the illustrious son of Śuddhodana (i. e. Buddha) here at Nālandā. Nālandā had scholars well-known for their (knowledge of the) sacred texts and art, and (was full of the) heaps of the rays of *Caityas* shining and bright like white clouds. It had a row of Vihāras, the line of whose tops touched the clouds— Nālandā had temples which were brilliant on account of the net-work of the rays of the various jewels set in them and was the pleasant abode of the learned and virtuous Saṅgha" — From the record it seems probable that the donor Mālāda himself also took to the life of a monk and his sister Nirmalā mentioned in the inscription might also have been a nun. Besides this and one or two other minor inscriptions, numerous votive inscrip-tions—some of them bearing different Buddhist sūtras—and clay seals bearing the name of the organisation of the Bhikkhus of Nālandā ('sri Nālandā mahāvihāriya bhikkhusaṅghasya'), belonging to different periods, have been unearthed during excavations. Two of the carved bricks bear on them the complete *Pratītyasamutpādastiūtra* and its exposition in Gupta characters, which is supposed to be unique of its kind[23].

XI. The township of Rājagṛha, modern Rajgir, where the Buddhistic monastic institution developed during the life time of Buddha was found by both the Chinese pilgrims as almost deserted, and archaeological reports also ascribe practically nothing to this period, except the *stūpa* of Giriyek near Rajgir, which has a shape quite different from the earlier ones.

XII. Bodh-Gaya is a place of perpetual interest not for the Buddhists only, but for everyone who is in the least interested in the religion of the Buddha, because it is here that Gautama Buddha attained his supreme knowledge, and as such, is being visited by numerous Buddhists as well as non-Buddhists from the earliest times. Aśoka made a pilgrimage to this place, in commemoration of which he constructed a railing around the Bodhi tree and the seat of the Buddha underneath it, and perhaps also erected a pillar as is supposed from some carvings of Bharhut, but this assumption docs not find support from the Chinese pilgrims. Two sets of railings arc to be found at Bodh-Gaya, one belonging to the time of Aśoka with the stories of Buddha's life carved on them, and the other belonging to the Gupta period, with the typical Gupta ornamentations pictured on them. A peculiar fact is that all the inscriptions, both old and new, are incised on the older set of railings.[24] The Bodh-Gaya temple shows marks of additions and alterations, and the nucleus of the present temple is supposed to have been originated in the Gupta period. Of the inscriptions of Bodh-Gaya pertaining to our period, the earliest is the one ascribed to the reign of Mahārāja Trikamala, possibly a feudatory of the Gupta monarchs. It records that two monks, both teachers of Vinaya, caused one Siṁharatha to dedicate the image of the Bodhisattva, evidently the one on which it is incised, with the help of two other persons, one of whom is a female lay devotee and the other an expounder of the holy text.[25] Then there are the two inscriptions of the Ceylonese monk Mahānāman, dated in the 6th century A.D., one recording the erection of a 'Maṇḍapa' for Buddha within the area of Bodh-Gaya, and the other recording the gift of a figure of Buddha, by the same person. This monk Mahānāman is recorded to be an inhabitant of Laṅkādvīpa or the island of Ceylon, and is doubtfully identified with the author of the well-known Pali chronicle of Ceylon, viz. the Mahāvaṁsa[26]. But whatever his identity might be, these two inscriptions testify to the fact that people from such a distant country like Ceylon retained their connection with this place (which began with the mission sent by Aśoka), even in this period, though it is evident from other inscriptions that these are not the first pilgrims from Ceylon to Bodh-Gaya.[27]- That pilgrims from Ceylon continued their visit to this place in subsequent centuries also, is proved from a 6th or 7th century inscription in which it is stated that some scion of the ruling family of Lanka, Prakhyātakīrtī by name, caused some buildings to be made here ("at Triratna" as the expression runs).[28] Another fragmentary inscription from the same place and the same period records the pious gift of an unknown devotee for the plastering, regular repairing, maintenance of lamps in the shrine of Buddha, and in the monastery, as well as the excavation of a well or pond for the use of monks.[29] Another inscription of the 6ch century on the pedestal of a Buddha image (now in the Indian Museum, Calcutta), records the gift of the image by two Śākya monks, Dharmagupta and Daṃṣṭrāsena, natives of an unidentified place called Tisyāmratīrtha.[30]

XIII. Buddhism must have penetrated into Bengal at least in the early years of the Christian era, as referred to in the Nāgārjunikoṇḍa inscription, even if we leave out of consideration the Mahāsthān inscription written in Maurya characters, which mentions the Chabbaggiya bhikkhus, i.e. the party of six men headed by Devadatta, and as such an anti-party of the organisation of Buddha. Of the Chinese pilgrims, Fa-Hian did not visit North Bengal, but he went to the adjacent countries like Campā in the Bhāgalpur district, and Tāmralipti, where he himself stayed for two years and studied Buddhist scriptures, and found the religion flourishing with many *stūpas* and monasteries full of monks. Hwen Tsang travelled in Bengal and is said to have seen many *stūpas* and monasteries containing both Hinayānic and Mahāyānic monks. The establishments mentioned by Hwen Tsang and other Chinese pilgrims who visited subsequently, are not yet definitely located, but the numerous ruins scattered all over the length and breadth of Bengal,—the major portion of which is at present included within the area of Pakistan,—suggest that if systematic exploration is carried out, most of the places mentioned by them will ultimately be traced. The prosperous condition of Buddhism in Bengal in the Gupta period onwards is also attested by various documents. The Gunaighar copper-plate[31] of the reign of Mahārāja Vainyagupta, a scion of the Gupta family, dated in 506-7 A.D., records the grant of land by the king at the instance of his vassal Mahārāja Rudradatta in favour of the Buddhist Avaivartaka saṅgha of the Mahāyāna sect. The saṅgha founded by Ācārya Śāntideva was living in a monastery called Āśrama vihāra, which was dedicated to Ārya Avalokiteśvara and had been established by the said Rudradatta. The plate also refers to two other Buddhist monasteries in the neighbouring area, one of which is designated Rāja-vihāra or the royal monastery. Śāntideva of the inscriptions is surely not the author of *Śikṣāsamuccaya,* who is supposed to have lived a century later[32] but some other teacher of the same name. And the name of the particular *saṅgha* viz. Avaivartaka, found for the first time in this plate, is not mentioned elsewhere. By way of explanation it may be stated that in the *Saddharmapuṇḍarīkasūtra* and other Mahāyāna texts, there are a number of references to a spiritual stage Avaivartika Bodhisattvasthānam' and also to 'Avivartika','Avaivartika teja',and 'Avaivartika' etc.[33] It seems that a sect which aimed at the Avaivartika or 'incapable of sliding back' stage, grew up in this locality, which took the name of

Avaivartika or Avaivartika saṅgha. At any rate, this record is a positive evidence that Buddhism took a firm root in Bengal even in this period, under the royal patronage. The condition of Buddhism in the 7th century in Bengal, if not the whole of India, is reflected in an inscription on a copper plate found from Kailan in the Tippera District of Bengal. It is the donation of an official of a certain king named Sridharana Rāta, to the Buddhist Triratna, as well as some other donations to a number of Brahmins for performing 'the five great sacrifices'.[34] The religious toleration which is the characteristic feature of the Indians, is once more manifested in this inscription. It supplies further evidence to the fact that Buddhism was tending towards merger with Brahmanism and devotees of the Buddha did not refrain from being respectful to Buddhism and Brahmanism in the same breath. Another inscription of a somewhat later date, found in Bengal, is also of a similar effect as the Kailan plate. It is the inscription on an image of Sarvāṇī[35] (a form of Dūrgā) dedicated by Prabhāvatī, queen of a Buddhist king named Devakhaḍga. Two copper-plates with inscriptions found from Asrafpur in Bengal[36] reveal that a number of rulers whose names ended with Khaḍga, and hence might be called the 'Khaḍga family',ruled in Bengal during the earlier part of the 8th c. A.D. The plates are significant for the fact that Buddhism received toyal recognition after a long period, as the royal records depict all of them as devout Buddhists. And further, though none of this line of Buddhist kings were as illustrious as any of the previous Buddhist rulers like Aśoka, Kaṇiṣka, or the Sātavāhana rulers, these Khaḍga rulers may be regarded as the predecessor and ancestors of a long and glorious line of Buddhist kings, viz., the Pālas. Numerous Buddhist figures have been found in Bengal, but the majority of them belong to the Pāla period. The earliest find is the standing image of Buddha from Biharail in Rajshahi district.[37] The image is to be dated from its style, not later than the 5th century A.D. and is now deposited in the Varendra Research Society Museum, Rajshahi. It bears such close affinity to those of Sarnath, that one may quite well infer that it was supplied from that place. Unfortunately the image is very badly damaged, but still it is a fine piece of sculpture. Another interesting Buddhist figure of the same period is the gold-plated image of Mañjuśrī, collected from the Balaidhāp mound near Mahāsthān, Bogra. This is undoubtedly one of the finest specimens of bronze or octo-alloy images so far found in Northern and Eastern India. The figure has the Dhyānī Buddha Akṣobhya, the spiritual father of Mañjuśrī, according to the code of *Sādhanamālā,* placed on its crown. This image is also damaged, but the loveliness of the figure prove that it was also beautiful in its original state. The execution of the limbs and drapery leads us to assign it to the Gupta period. An important point to be noticed in connection with this image is that it has changed the earlier notion that gold-plated images were made for the first time by the Siamese artists in Siam only in the 8th C. A. D. In fact, this image shows that metal images were used to be gilt long before that period in India and perhaps the Siamese artists were indebted to India in this respect also.[38]

XIV. Orissa was one of the cradles of Buddhism when it tasted the religious fervour at the time of Aśoka. The religion again took its last shelter in this country before its final disappearance from Bengal and other parts of India after the Muhammadan invasion.[39] We do not hear of any activities of the Buddhists in this part of the country during the intervening period. That Buddhism existed in Orissa in the 6th-7th centuries A. D. is proved by the statement: of Hwen Tsang who is said to have seen many Buddhist monasteries and numerous devotees in Wu-Tu (Odra or Orissa country,[40] and who was selected by Harṣavardhana to be deputed with four other scholars from Nālandā to silence the Hīnayānist monks of Orissa who were becoming vehemently opposed to the Mahāyānists.[41] The group of Buddhist monasteries in the Jajpur hills, known as Udaygiri, Lalitagiri, and Ratnagiri, have produced a large number of sculptures and images datable to Gupta period. An image of the Bodhisattva Padmapāṇi belonging to the later Gupta period has been found out from a place named Śāntamādhava in Jajpur, and a life-size image of fourarmed Avalokiteśvara on the Ratnagiri have the same pose common to the sculptures of the Gupta age. Many votive *stūpas* and architectural and sculptural fragments comprising heads of some colossal Buddha images have been found from this Ratnagiri hill. Sculptures belonging to later periods found in this place prove the continuance of this place as a Buddhist centre. At Lalitagiri there are also a large number of sculptures fixed in modern temples, which have inscriptions on them in 8th century characters, mostly containing the Buddhist creed. The sculptures represent the Buddhist gods and goddesses like Avalokiteśvara, Tārā, and Maitreya. A number of images of Buddha, Avalokiteśvara, Prajñāpāramitā and other Buddhist gods have been found in Udayagiri hill also and these sculptures too contain inscriptions in scripts of 7th to 10 or 11nth centuries. On the back of one such image of Avalokiteśvara, with the DhyanīBuddha Amitābha seated in its crest, is an inscription saying that it was the gift of a monk, Śubhagupta, written in 7th or 8th century characters.[42] The extensive ruins in these three hills prove that this locality was a flourishing centre of Buddhism from the 7th century onwards, and the cult of Avalokiteśvara and Tārā was more prevalent. The Neulpur grant of the king Śubhakaradeva[43] reveals that a line of Buddhist kings was ruling in Orissa in the 8th century, and Buddhism must have been flourishing under their patronage. In the inscritpion, instead of the conventional epithet used by all Buddhist kings and devotees, viz. 'Parama Saugata', the Kara kings of Orissa adopted a new designation for themselves, viz. 'Parama Tāthāgata' which, of course, carries the same meaning. The object of the grant is to register the gift of some villages to a number of Brāhmins by the king. Here again we are confronted with another example of the liberal charater of Indian religions, as also to the fact that Buddhism and brāhmanism were coming in closer relations with each other.

XV. The religion of Buddha was introduced into Western India during the life time of its founder who is said to have deputed his disciple Mahākaccāyana, a native of Avantī, to preach his religion there. Again, during the time of Aśoka, Aparānta, or the western country received the yavana Dhammarakṣita as the missionary despatched by the emperor. This country was fortunate enough in having the Sātavāhana rulers as great patrons of Buddhism under whom the religion flourished greatly and numerous cave-temples were excavated in the hilly tracts of Western India. The origin of these cave-temple belongs to further antiquity, perhaps to the time of Aśoka, who incised one of his rock-edicts on the hill of Girnar, though the credit of constructing the majority of the cave-temples goes to the Sātavāhans. The caves of Nāsik, Kārle, Bhājā, Junnār, Kānherī etc. bear testimony to the palmy days of Buddhism. Though they lost their importance in subsequent periods, some of them at least were not altogether deserted and were occupied or frequented by the Buddhists who made gifts to them even upto the 10th-11th centuries. In the great caitya-cava at Kānherī, there is an inscription recording the gift by a Buddhist monk of the seated figure of Buddha under which it is carved. On the verandā of the same cave, there is under a standing image of Buddha an inscription which records that the image was dedicated by a mendicant Buddhaghoṣa, the disciple of a teacher named Dharmavatsa, who was well-versed in the three Piṭkakas. In the veranda of cave no. 3 is the 'meritorious gift' of a Buddha figure by a monk Dharmagupta. near the great pillar at the same place, on a small *caitya* in bas-relief, is incised the beginning of the well-known Buddhist creed and in a small chamber stands a figure of buddha as the gift of a teacher buddharakṣita. All these inscriptions belong to the 5th to 7th centuries A.D.[44] The original architecture of Kānherī is simple but there are subsequent additions of sculpture with the develop-ment of Mahāyāna.

The Buddhist caves of Lonaḍ—a few miles off Kalyan in the Bombay presidency—seems to be an intermediate station on the long pilgrim and trade route which led from Sopara via Kānherī and other Buddhist monasteries on Salsettc islands to the Nanaghat Pass and on to the higher Deccan. Due to absence of inscriptions the date of the caves cannot be ascertained definitely, but the beautiful and lively sculptures that are chiselled out in the caves bear such close affinity with those in the later caves of Ajanta, that they may be well ascribed to that period. The sculptures in these caves depict *Jātaka* stories, some of which cannot be identified. There are also scenes of the Buddha's subjugation of the furious elephant Nālagiri, court scenes, etc.[45] That Junagarh was a fairly large centre of Buddhism at least upto the 7th century A. D., is testified by the statement of Hwen Tsang who found about fifty convents with nearly 3000 monks, belonging to the Sthavira sect of the Mahāyāna, as also by the discovery of numerous Buddhist caves near modern monastery named Bawa Pyara's Math.[46]

XVI. The Maitraka rulers of Valabhī began their career as the vassal (Sāmanta) of the Imperial Guptas. They threw off the Gupta suzerainty with the decline of the Gupta power and gradually changed their epithet from 'sāmanta' to the glorious title of Mahārājā Dhirāja.[47] These Maitraka kings, though themselves not professed Buddhists, were great patrons of the religion, and a large number of inscriptions of the rulers of this dynasty record the bounteous gifts made by those kings to the Buddhist organisations of the country. Two lady members of this royal family were devout Buddhist nuns who established monasteries of their own. One of them, Duḍḍā was the niece of king Dhruvasena. She is also mentioned as a queen in some other inscriptions. The other lady of the royal family who embraced the life of a nun is Mimmā. From the inscriptions of the Maitraka rulers it becomes clear that during their rule, the region around modern Saurāṣṭra was a flourishing centre of Buddhism with no less than thirteen monasteries, names of which are : Bhaṭārka vihāra, Gôhaka vihāra, Ābhyantarika v., Kakka v., Buddhadāsa v., Vimalagupta v., Sthiramati v., Yaksha-sūtra v., Pūrṇa-Bhaṭṭa v., Ajjita v., Bappapādiya v., Vaṁsataka v., and Yodhāvaka vihāra[48]. Hwen Tsang associates the two eminent Buddhist scholars Guṇamati and Sthiramati with Valabhi, and this is corroborated by the name of the Vihāra. In the inscriptions the mention of donations for buying books for the monasteries[49] also supports the tradition that the Valabhi monasteries were great centres of education not inferior to those of Nālandā.

XV. The missionary activities of Aśoka is best illustrated in the monuments of Sāñci, the earliest strata of the *stūpa* of which is ascribed to Aśoka. The remains of an edict pillar of the same emperor found in the vicinity lends support to this assumption. Incidentally it may be mentioned that in the Ceylonse chronicle *Mahāvaṁsa,* it is stated that Mahendra, son of Aśoka, who headed the Buddhist mission to Ceylon, visited his mother 'Devī' before his journey, at a monastery at Cetiyagiri near Vidiśā, where she was living as a nun, and stayed in that monastery for a short period. This Cetiyagiri is probably identical with the hillock of Sāñci, where the remains of the 'Devī's monastery' lie still extant. It is strange to note that none of the Chinese pilgrims seem to have visited Sāñci during their tour in India. For none of them make any mention of this centre of Buddhism, which, as is evident from the extensive ruins found at the site, was in a flourishing condition at the time of their visit to India. The main *stūpa* must have been dedicated to Buddha and the rest to the more distinguished disciples of the Master, as is proved from the discovery of the relics of Sāriputra and Moggalāna from the top of the *stūpa* no. 3. The original *stūpa* erected by Aśoka, having been damaged in course of time, was encased in a newer one and thus it became larger to a great extent than its former size. This system of constructing new *stūpas* over the older ones was not uncommon in those days. In subsequent centuries, when erection of votive *stūpas* became the custom of the day, numerous *stūpas* of different dimensions, pillars, and gateways continued to be erected on the site. Some of the very few pillars which exist in India, with the exception of those erected by

Aśoka, are found at Sāñci. One of them contains a fragmentary inscription in 5th C. characters recording the gift of the pillar by a Vihārasvāmin whose name ended in 'Rudra' and who was the son of 'Gostira-Siṁhabala'.The pillar was surmounted by the figure of Vajrapāṇi, which now remains in the Museum at Sāñci. An inscription of Āmrakardava, an officer of Candragupta II of the Imperial Gupta line, records the gifts of an allotment of land called Iśvaravāsaka, as also of some amount of money, to the Buddhist community of Kākanādabhoṭa (the name which was often mentioned in ancient inscriptions to designate Sāñci) for the purpose of feeding the monks and maintaining lamps. Another inscription dated in the year 131 of the Gupta era, records the grant of a female lay-devotee Harisvāminī, wife of the lay devotee Sanasiddha, of certain amount of money to the same community and for the same purpose[50]. Some more inscriptions incised mostly on the pedestals of Buddhist figures and dating from the 4th-7th or 8th centuries, have been found at the site. of course inscriptions belonging to earlier or later periods are not also lacking, but we are not concerned with them for the present. A fragmentary inscription in 7th C. characters has been found from the monastery no. 43 at Sāñci which is devoted to the praise of Lokanātha, who is described as having lotus in his hand and bear Amitābha (on his head), and also of Vajrapāṇi......It also mentions the lord of Mahāmālava (Malwa) and a certain ruler Vappaka Deva......a monastery with cells *(layana)* is stated to have been built. ...There seems to be further reference that the (above-mentioned) monastery belonging to a person named Tuṅga and that the benefaction recorded took place at Boṭa-Śrīparvata (i. e. Sāñci)[51]. There are numerous sculptural and architectural remains on the site which bear witness to the fact that the place was a flourishing centre of Buddhism during our period of review[52].

XVIII. Mandasor (ancient Daśapura) in the Gwalior district was known to have been a centre of Brāhmanism only. But a stone slab discovered at the place indicates that Buddhism had some place there also. The inscription on the slab records the construction of a well along with a '*stūpa*', a garden and a '*prapā*' (water stall) by Datrabhaṭa, commander-in-chief of king Prabhākara. The record is dated in the Mālava saṃvat 524 (467-68 A. D.). The inscription mentions the early Gupta king Candragupta II and his younger son Govindagupta, the donor Dattabhaṭṭa being a son of Govindagupta's general Vāyurakṣ ita[53].

Though Mandasor did not produce many Buddhist remains, the prevalence of Buddhism in the Gwalior district is amply proved by a group of Buddhist caves at Bagh in the same district. These caves, though only four in number, form a very interesting group. They belong to the classical period of Indian history, and have some sculptured figures and the most charming paintings which can very well stand in comparison with those at Ajanta. One more interesting fact about these caves is that though the caves belonged to the Mahāyānists, and there are Buddha and Bodhisattva figures carved in the caves, the main object of worship in them is the plain and simple rock-cut *stūpa* and no figure of Buddha is carved on them, as is most natural for the Mahāyānists. The very soft nature of the hill on which the caves of Bagh are excavated cannot be durable and a few of them have already collapsed leaving the four surviving ones.[54]

XIX. The most illustrious examples of rock-cut caves of this period are those at Ajanta and Ellora in Deccan. The caves of Ajanta had their beginning more than a century earlier than the Christian era, most probably under the patronage of the Sātavāhana rulers, whose dominions included this region. But in the earlier stage, the monastery of Ajanta did not prosper much. And though it continued for a period of more than three centuries, only five out of the present twenty-nine caves are said to have been used at that period. After that, the monastery of Ajanta must have been deserted for a long period of four centuries, when, about the fifth century A. D., the Mahāyānists took charge of the hill resorts, and turned them to an important centre of Buddhism. Of the 24 caves belonging to the Mahāyāna sect, there are two *Caitya* halls enshrining *stūpas* with images of Buddha carved on them as a contrast to the corresponding two *Caitya* halls enshrining *stūpas* but without any kind of carving on them, out of the five earlier Hinayāna ones. The rest twenty-two caves belonging to the Mahāyāna sect are dormitories for the residence of monks with stone beds in them and the innermost central chamber of these cave-dwellings were used as shrines sheltering colossal figures of Buddha. These caves are decorated with fine sculptures representing Buddhist figures and in one of them is carved a colossal figure of recumbent Buddha with various Mahāyānic symbols underneath. But the far-reaching fame of Ajanta caves is not so much for its architecture and sculpture as it is for its fresco-paintings on the wall of the caves. These paintings are the living embodiment of grace and loveliness which have attracted admiration from the most scrupulous critics of the world. "The artists" remarks Lady Herringham, one of the premier admirers of ' Ajanta art, "had a complete command of posture. Their seated and floating poses especially are of great interest. Their knowledge of the types and positions, gestures and beauties of hands are amazing ......the drawing of foliage and flowers is very beautiful......some of the schemes of colour and composition are most remarkable and interesting, and there is a great variety." Nothing need be added to this note of appreciation about the art of Ajanta. These paintings illustrate in addition to decorative designs, scenes from the life of Buddha and the Jātakas or the past lives of the Buddha, as also scenes from secular and court lives. The paintings are so mutilated in some places that identification of them becomes very difficult and sometimes impossible. That the religion of Buddha had travelled a long way from its primitive phase, is also well attested by the fact that amopg the paintings of Ajanta there are profuse scenes of dancing and music, which, though included among popular or court scenes, were even beyond imagination to have been painted in the dormitories of Buddhist monks, as dancing and music and some other things like toileting and garlanding (which also form the subject-matter of some scenes) were strictly prohibited for the recluses. The art of Ajanta influenced later artists not only of India proper, but also of its neighbours like Ceylon, China, Japan, and Eastern Islands. The paintings of Sigiriya at Ceylon, executed about the same period, bear a close affinity with those at Ajanta, and the 'Thousand-Buddha cave' of China, of some later days have gained world-wide reputation.

The patrons under whom the monastery of Ajanta flourished in its later phase were certainly the Vākāṭaka rulers of Deccan, in whose dominions this region was included. An inscription from the cave no. 16 at Ajanta lends further support to the assumption. Though the inscription is not preserved in full, it is interesting in that it records that the cave was excavated by order of Vīradeva, a minister of the Vākaṭaka king Hariṣeṇa. Vīradeva was a devout Buddhist. In cave no. 17, an inscription records that Acitya, a minister of Rabisāmba, a feudatory to the Vākāṭaka king Hariṣena, caused to excavate the 'monolithic, gem-like hall' with a *Caitya,* a reservoir, with cool refreshing water, and a Gandhakūṭi'.Another important inscription is that in cave no. 26. According to this inscription, it was the monk Buddhabhadra who was responsible for this cave to be excavated, and provided funds for the work. His own disciple Bhadrabandhu and another monk Dharmadatta were the supervisors of the work. The information about Buddhabhadra as is given in this inscription, suggests that he was not an ordinary roving recluse, but must have been an abbot of a great institution, —might be that of the Ajanta monastery itself and possessed a considerable amount of wealth. Possession of a large amount of wealth by an abbot was no more an unnatural occurrence in this period, though in primitive Buddhism, a monk was debarred from having anything more than the four requisites prescribed by the Buddha, as his own. That the monk Buddhabhadra also held an esteemed position is indicated by the mention of his friendship with the minister of the king of Asmaka, in whose name the cave was dedicated. Another name of importance which is mentioned in this inscription, is that of Sthavira Acala, who is described as one of the former builders of the Vihāras. This Sthavira Acala seems to be no other than the 'Arahat 'O-che-lo' mentioned by Hwen Tsang, who is credited to have built a convent in honour of his mother. Besides these important ones, there are other inscriptions, both painted and incised, recording gifts of ministers, noblemen, lay-devotees as well as monks. There are also explanatory titles of the Jatakas painted on the walls of the caves.[55]

A less known Vihāra-cave, 11 miles away from Ajanta, known as the Ghaṭotkaca cave, contains the fragments of a long inscription. It begins with invocation to the Buddha, Dharma, and Saṅgha and mentions about Hastibhoja, the minister of the Vākāṭaka king Devasena, father of Hariṣena mentioned in the cave no. 16 at Ajanta. The Hastibhoja mentioned in this inscription was the father of Vīradeva, during whose ministry the Ajanta vihāra was excavated. From the fragmentary character of the inscription, it cannot be stated definitely whether Hastibhoja or his son Vīradeva was responsible for the excavation of the Ghaṭotkaca cave.[56]

XX. Situated about sixty miles away from Ajanta, the twelve Buddhist caves of Ellora are contemporary with the later phase of those at Ajanta. These caves are richer in sculpture but lack the paintings and inscriptions of Ajanta, the only inscription at Ellora being the Buddhist formula in the Caitya-cave called the Viśvakarmā cave. There are about 35 caves scattered over a vast table land, belonging to the three main Indian sects, viz. the Buddhist, the Brāhmins and the Jains, the Buddhist group of caves occupying the southernmost part of the hill. Of the 12 Buddhist caves, all are Vihāras, except the Viśvakarmā, which is a *Caitya* hall enshrining a *stūpa* carved with a colossal seated figure of Buddha attended by two attendants on both sides. A number of colossal Buddha images are to be seen at Ellora also like those of Ajanta, but the difference between the two sets of caves lies in the fact that while at

Ajanta the Buddhas are represented without or only with one or two attendants, at Ellora, he is most frequently attended by a large number of side-figures, mostly the Bodhisattvas, and the Śaktis or the female counterparts of the Bodhisattvas. Cave nos. II and 12, are designated Do-Thal and Tin-Thal respectively, though both of them are three-storied, and contain a large number of sculptures which include the seven human Buddhas, the five Dhyānī Buddhas, and their respective Bodhisattvas, in addition to Gandharvas and other decorative motifs. Some of the Brahmanic goddesses like Saraśvatī and Kālī were being gradually incorporated into the Mahāyāna pantheon in this period, but the figure of the goddess carved on one of the walls of these caves, with books in her hand and a peacock by her side, which had so far been identified as the goddess Sarasvatī, has of late been correctly identified by Dr. J. N. Banerjea, with the personified form of the *Dhāraṇī* or 'protecting spells' named *Mahā-Māyūrī*,[57] used to be recited by the Buddhists in order to cure diseases, particularly, snake-poisoning, as the peacock was regarded as the greatest enemy of the snakes. The sculptures of the caves of Ellora conform to the mythology of the Yogācāra school of Buddhism, and it is supposed that these caves were the resorts of the same sect also. The caves of Ellora were probably the last activity of the Buddhists in this region as we do not find any other works of importance in the subsequent period.[58]

XXI. A few miles distant from Ellora, are the rock-hewn Vihāras of Aurangabad, divided into three groups. The first and the second group are certainly Buddhist, while the incompleteness of the caves and as such the absence of sculptures in the third group renders it difficult to regard them definitely as Buddhist, though there is nothing as negative evidence against their being Buddhist. Among the whole set of caves there is one *caitya* hall and the rest are Vihāras. From their features it seems that the caves were in good condition from the third to the seventh century A.D. The sculptures in these caves are lovely and are imitations of those in Ajanta, particularly the 'vase and foliage' pattern. The Viharas nos. 3 and 7 of this group are the finest and the best preserved. The carvings of the images of Buddha and other gods and goddesses are on a massive proportion. These and the group of musicians and the set of devotees carved on the walls of the caves are of a very special type.[59]

XXII. Recent as well as previous finds prove that the ancient site of South Kośala, comprising modern Bilaspur and Raipur districts, was a centre of Buddhism at least from the 5th century. Sirpur, in the Raipur district, was noticed and hinted as a site of archaeological interest by Cousens as early as 1903 in his report. The site has been recently excavated and has brought to light the remains of two large Buddhist monasteries and several other small structures including vihāras. A colossal image of seated Buddha and a life-size figure of Padmapāṇi has been found from one shrine, which, according to an inscription found at the same place, is stated to have been built by a monk Ānandaprabhu during the reign of Bālārjuna in about the first quarter of the 8th C. A. D. A considerable amount of antiquities of various kinds have been found at the site. These include a fine bronze statue of Buddha plated with gold with eyes set in silver. A number of seals with Buddhist texts, an exquisitely carved crystal *stūpa* and a gilt Vajra have also been found at an adjacent site. Of the monasteries discovered at the site, one seems to be a nunnery, from the evidence of a large number of shell and glass bangles found at the site.[60] An inscription from Ratanpur in the Bilaspur dist. (now in the Nagpur museum), confirms the view that in the 7th-8th C. A. D. this place was a populous centre of Buddhism. The inscription in question is of Bhavadeva Raṇakeśarin. It opens with an invocation to Buddha, and relates that a certain illustrious king Sūryaghoṣa built a splendid temple or Vihāra for Buddha, in order to mitigate the sorrow incurred by the accidental death of his son.......The inscription further records the restoration of the said temple after some time had elapsed after the king Sūryaghoṣa, under the supervision of Bhavadeva, who was in charge of the temple. The restoration work was done by two persons under Bhavadeva, one of whom is described as the favourite of the (then ruling) king, a Brāhmin well-versed in Buddhist scriptures, and the other, a novice in the Buddhist institution.[61] Another inscription, the Mallar plate of Mahāśivagupta of South Kośala, ascribed to the 7th C. A. D., records the grant of the said king, of a village to the Buddhist congregation of the monastery at Tāradaṁsaka. The king himself is stated to be a devout Śaiva.[62]

XXIII. Extensive ruins prove that Andhra and countries on further south were flourishing centres of Buddhism from the pre-Christian era. Though in our period, Buddhism had lost here its palmy days, it nevertheless lingered on in these countries. The Buddhist site of Salihundam is on the summit and slopes of a very fine hill in the Ganjam district. There are remains of a large and some smaller *stūpas,* fragments of Buddhist figures, a broken image of Buddha, a figure of Māricī, and such other antiquities, found on the hill-top and in the neighbouring village of the same name. The Boston Museum has in its collections a standing image of Buddha found in Buddhapād in Bezwada district. The place is not far from Amarāvatī, the most illustrious centre of Buddhism in Southern India from the 2nd-3rd centuries. The image in question belonged to the 6th C. A. D. and it is said that basketfull of images and fragments were found at Buddhapād while excavating a canal[63]. That the region encircling the *stūpa* of Amarāvatī was a flourishing centre also is well proved by inscriptions as well as sculptures found there. The *stūpa* at Goḷi is ascribed to the 4th C. A. D. The great *stūpa* of Amarāvatī was frequented and kept in repairs even as late as the 12th century. The sculptures of Amarāvatī and its neighbourhood form a different school of art. The British Museum has a very good collection of the sculptures of Amarāvatī and of the places influenced by its art. One of them is a bas-relief carved with an image of Mañjuśrī which has a lotus in one of his hands, which hold a book, and a second lotus issuing out of the stem of the first. The figure is interesting because earlier images of Mañjuśrī found in N. India, have the Dhyanī Buddha Akṣobhya in their head-dresses. The date of the image is supposed to be some time between 650 and 750 A. D[64]. The Pallava king Siṁhavarman II, who belonged to the last quarter of the 6th C. A. D., presented an image of Buddha to the *stūpa* of Amarāvati. The inscription recording the presentation, is incomplete and it records that on his return from an expedition to the North, Siṁhavarman came to a place sacred to the Buddha which was called Dhanyaghaṭa or Dhānyaghaṭaka (evidently identified with Dhānyakaṭaka, the well-known name of Amarāvatī). The lost part of the inscription evidently records the gift[65]. The Kapoteśvara temple of Chezrala shows from the remains of its constructions that it was originally a Buddhist *Caitya,* converted at a later date to a Śaiva temple, with the growing popularity of the religion in South India. The remains of Chezrala may be considered as one of the only two extant brick-built *Caitya* halls which have preserved their original structural condition, the other being at Ter, the ancient Tagara, in Sholapur dist. in the Nizam's dominions. Both are ascribed to the 5th C. A. D.[66] A number of stone inscriptions of the Ānandagotra kings, a dynasty which ruled about the 6th C. A. D., expressing their Buddhist faith are seen in the Caitya of Chezrala.[67] In Jagayyapeṭa, an inscription on a marble-slab in 5th-6th C. characters, under the figure of a Buddha, mentions Candraprabha, the disciple's disciple of Nāgārjuna; the preceptor of Candraprabha was Ācārya Jayaprabha. A similar slab has also been found from Ramireḍḍipalli.[68]

XXIV Another example of rock-cut monasteries of the Gupta period lies in the Buddhist remains on the Saṅkaram hills in the Vizagapatam district. These caves are scattered on the hill and the remains consist of a number of *stūpas,* a series of rock-cut chambers and the foundations of an extensive monastic building. Some of the *stūpas* are the largest of their kind. From a survey, it seems that the site was in a flourishing condition in the Gupta period, though its origin goes back a few centuries earlier.[69] Other places in this region which have yielded remnants of Buddhism are Nāgārjunikonda, Guṇṭapalle, Ghanṭāsālā, Rāmātīrtham, etc. Copper images of Buddha found from Buddhāni show the typical characteristics of Gupta art in their costume and features. A figure from Amarāvatī and identified as Avalokiteśvara, has its counterpart in the collection of the British Museum, ascribed to the middle of the 8th C. A.D. Another figure of Vajrapāni in the British Museum, though mutilated, has fine executions like those at Ellora.[70] Casting images in metal seems to be a common practice of this period, not only in the southern part of India, but in northern part also. So bronze images of Buddha have been found not only from this area, but the bronze image of Buddha found from Sultangañje and now deposited in the Birmingham Museum, is one of the finest, specimens of its kind. Incidentally we may refer also to the 80 feet high image of Buddha said to have seen by Hwen Tsang at Nālandā, though no further trace of the image have been possible to find.

The countries to further south have not yielded many Buddhist antiquities, though the Chinese travellers found the religion in fairly popular condition. In the Western coast, an inscription is found frem Goa (ancient W. Koṅkan). The copper-plate was issued by certain Mahārāja Candravarman, and records the grant of a piece of land to a Buddhist monastery (Mahāvihāra) at Śivapura, located in Goa. This king was probably a scion of the Bhoja family ruling in that region during the 5th century, to which period the inscription is also ascribed on paleographic grounds.[71]

From the above survey, it may be concluded that though the form of the religion had undergone great changes, and was losing its hold, it was in a fairly flourishing condition during this period. The decline of Buddhism, however, is not disappearance in the proper sense of the term because it merged into Brahmanism. The religion of Buddha started as a protest against Brahmanic ritualism, but ended in being more ritualistic than ethical and philosophical. The line of demarcation between the

Buddhists and the Brahminists was becoming narrower in the later part of our period of survey as is evident from some of the inscriptions stated above. The assimilation of Buddhism by Brāhmanism was done by including Buddha in the list of ten Avatāras or incarnations of Viṣṇu or sometimes identifying him with Śiva. This process of assimilation manifested itself in an inscription in the Varāha Perumal temple, dating about the 7th C.A.D., where the Buddha is stated as one of the ten incarnations of Viṣṇu.[72]

In our period, the religion had travelled a long way from its primitive state, both in time as well as in form. But the destination was still farther, which was reached during the rule of the Pālas in Bengal, when the religion was turned into a ritualistic Tantric one. The Tantras had not yet reached its full-fledged form, but the faint traces of its advent are hinted in some of the literature of this period. The practice of mystic rites, if practised at all, was done in secret. Hwen Tsang mentions that at Kāmarūpa, there were 'secret devotees'.This statement may lead one to believe that it was a centre of Tantric Buddhists, but it cannot be stated definitely that the Buddhist Tantras found a resort here in that period. Kāmarūpa, or modern Assam was for a long time, even a few decades ago, considered to be a place of secret practices.

The sect of Buddhism prevalent at different parts of India at the period under our consideration, cannot be ascertained from the inscriptions of the period, because very few of the numerous inscriptions of this period state the particular sect to which they belonged. But the growing popularity of Mahāyāna is manifested by some inscriptions, reports of the Chinese pilgrims, and above all, by the vast number of images found all over the country. These figures include not only those of Gautama Buddha and the past human Buddhas, but a large number of Bodhisattvas, together with their respective Dhyānī Buddhas or spiritual fathers and their Śaktis or the female counterparts. In addition to these, there are the personified forms of the sacred literature of the Mahāyānists, like the Prajñā-pāramitā, Mañjuśrī, and Mahāmāyuri etc. mentioned above.

Most of the institutions which had their beginning in previous centuries, continued to function in this period and many of those others which flourished in subsequent days, had their beginning in this period. This period may be called the mid-day of Mahāyāna Buddhism, when the Mahāyāna was on the summit of its glory. Then it changed on and on, until losing its individual existence, it finally merged itself into the Hindu religion.

Sudha Sengupta

FOOTNOTES

1. Fergusson, *History of Ind. & Eastern Architecture,* Introduction.
2. *Mahāparinibbāna Sutta, Dighanikāya,* XVI. 5- 12-13.
3. *Ibid.* XVI. 6,25.
4. *Ep. Ind.*, VI, 133-4.

5-6. Marshall, *Taxila,* vol.1, (plate 119a, 119b.)

7. *Ep. Ind.*, I, p. 238.
8. *ASI. Ann., Rep.*, 1904-5, pp. 107-8.
9. *Watters,* I, pp.25ff; cf. *IA.*,1895, p. 342ff.
10. P. Brown, *Indian Architecture,* p. 186.
11. *Gilgit Manuscripts,* ed. N. Dutt.
12. *ASI,* 1922-23, p. 168-69.
13. Cf. *Boston Museum Catalogue* by Coomaraswamy.
14. *CII,* III, pp. 262ff, 273ff.
15. *CII., p.* 45ff.
16. *IA.*, 1912. also *Allan Cat. of Gupta Coins,* p. XLII.
17. *CII.* Ill, p. 271 ff.
18. *Ibid,,* p. 272,
19. *ASI. Ann. Rep.*, 1911-22.
20. Sahni. *Guide to Sarnath,*
21. *Ep. Ind.*, XX p, 294ff.
22. *IHQ., VII,* p. 664.
23. *ASL,* Memoir 66, p. 75.
24. Cf. Barua, *Gaya* and *Bodh-Gaya,* p. II.
25. *ASI, An. Rep.*, 1922-23, p. 169.

26. For details see *CII., III,* p. *274ff.*
27. *ASI, An. Rep.*, 1908-09; Bloch's *Report on Bodh-Gaya,* p. 156.
28. *ASI, An. Rep.*, 1908-09; Bloch's *Report on Bodh-Gaya,* p. 156.
29. *Ibid.*
30. *CII.*, III, p. 281.
31. *IHQ, VI*, p. 45f.
32. Winternitz, II. p. 365.
33. Cf. *Saddharmapundarika-sūtra*—Bib. Bud. X, p. 264; also the *Gilgit Mss.* of the text, ed. N. Dutt, pt. I, p. 70, verse 5; pt. II, p. 253 v. 130; pt. Ill, p. 465. v. 1126; also p, 510. (avaivartiko bhavisyatyanuttarāyām ṣamyakśamtbodhau).
34. *IHQ.*, XXIII, p. 221 ff.
33. *Ep. Ind.*, XVII, p 357.
36. *MASB.*, I, no *6,* p. 65ff.
37. *History of Bengal,* Dacca, I. p 523.
38. N. Dasgupta, *Bāṅglāy Bnuddba^harma* (in Bengali) p. 46-47.
39. H. P. Sastri, *Bauddba Dharma* (in Bengali), p. 106-7
40. Watters, II. p. 193.
41. Beal, *Life,* p. 160-61.
42. *ASI.*, Memoir, 44.
43. *Ep. Ind.*, XX, p. 1.f.
44 *ASWI.*, V. &VI.
45. *J1SOA.*, XV, p. 84 ff.
46. *ASWI,* II, p. 139.
47. For the gradual change in their epithet see Bhandarkar's List of Inscs. In *Ep. Ind.*, XX, appendix.
48. *Anc. Hist, of Saurāstra by* Vriji.
49. *IA.*, VII, p. 66,
50. *CII,* III, p. 29ff. and p. 260.
51. Marshall, *Monuments of Sāñci,* insc. no. 842.
52. For details, see Marshall, *op. cit.*
53. *AS1, Ann. Rep,,* 1922-23 p. 189.
54. *The Bagh Caves,* Marshall also cf. *Mahabodhi,* June 55, pp, 246.
55. *ASWI,* p. 124 ff. and p. 60 (vol. IV)
56. *ASWI.*, p. 124 ff, and p. 60 (vol. IV)
57. Paper read in the *Indian History Congress* at Waltair, 1953.
58. *ASWL, V,* p. 2 ff.
59. *ASWL,* III, p. 59 ft. also cf. *Ind. Art & Lett.*, IX, new Series.

60. *ASI., Ann, Rep.*, 1203-04; *Indian Archaeology, 1954-55,* pp. 24-25.
61. *JRAS.*, 1905, p. 618 ff.
62. *EI.*, XXIII, p. 115.
63. Coomaraswamy, *Cat. Boston Museum,* II, p. 60 ff,
64. *Art and Letters,* XXVIII, no. 2. Amaravati & its influences (later school);
65. Hultzsch, *SII,* (I), p. 25.
66. P. Brown, *Ind. Architec.*, I. p. 50.
67. *MER.*, 1900, p. 5.
68. Burgess, *Amaravati & Jagayyapeta Stūpas.*
69. P. Brown., *Ind. Architec.*, I, p. 45; also ref. *ASI, Ann. Rep,* 1907-08.
70. *Cat. of the British Museum.*
71. *ABOR.*, XXIII, p. 510 ff.
72. *ASI.*, Mem., 26, p. 5.

12

BUDDHISM IN THE ŚUṄGA PERIOD

The Śuṅgas or at least the founder of the Śuṅga dynasty was the performer of the *Aśvamedha* sacrifice. This is recorded both in literature and inscription. The *Mahābhāsya*[1] of Patanjali and the *Mālavikāgnimitra* of Kālidāsa incidentally inform us that Pusyamitra, the founder of the Śuṅga dynasty performed the *Aśvamedha* sacrifice, whereas from the Ayodhyā stone inscription of King Dhanadeva, we learn that general Puṣyamitra celebrated two horse-sacrifices.[2]

The cult of Gautama Buddha flourished during the rule of the Śuṅgas, although they were pro-Brahmanic. This is indisputably proved by a number of monuments and inscriptions scattered over the different parts of India. In this paper it is proposed to point out the evidences yielded by archaeological excavations and epigraphic researches:

At Bharhut in Nagod State and Sanci in Bhopal State there was in each of these places a *stūpa* at the centre surrounded by stone railings leaving an intervening space for *pradakṣiṇa* or circumambulation with approaches from four cardinal points through four gateways. The stone railing consisting of a number of pillars is joined together by a number of *Sūcis* or lenticular cross-bars and overlaid by *uṣṇiṣa* (coping stone). The circumambulation for the second time used to be performed by the pilgrims on a higher level through a terrace to be together by a approached by a staircase. The railing and the gateways were richly decorated with bas-reliefs for the purpose of arousing religious feeling in the minds of the pilgrims. Some of the decorative designs were of religious character while others were simple auspicious symbols. There are to be found on the railings some non-Buddhist popular deities with subordinate position evidently for proclaiming that the deities belonged to the world *(arūpa)* and not *lokottara* like Buddha.

The illustrations and labels (written in *Brāhmī* characters of 2nd-1st centuries B.C.) found on the Bharhut railing offer a comprehensive picture of the state of Buddhism during the rule of the Śuṅgas.

As regards Buddhist pantheon, Gautama Buddha *(Sākyamuni)* and the past Buddhas e.g. (1) Vipaśyin, (2) Viśvabhū, (3) Krakucchanda, (4) Kanakamuni and (5) Kāśyapa are mentioned by name and indicated by individual symbols. No figure of Sākyamuni or any one of the earlier Buddhas is found there. Their presence is indicated in the following way: —

(1) *Gautama Buddha* is represented by a throne surrounded by two *triratna* symbols placed under the Bodhi tree and labelled as *Bhagavato*[1] *saka tnunino bodho*. (Bharhut Ins. No. 270)

(2) *Vipaśyin* by a throne under a *Pāṭali* tree and labelled as *Bhagavato Vipasino bodhi* (Bh. Ins. No. 87).

(3) *Viśvabhū* by a throne under a Ś*āla* tree and labelled as *Bhagavato Vesabhuno bodhi Śālo* [Bh. Ins. No. 117 (b)]

(4) *Krakucchanda* by a throne under a *Śirīṣa* tree and labelled as *Bhagavato Kakusadhasa bodhi* (Bh. Ins. No. 293 (a)]

(5) *Kanakamuni* by a throne under a *Udumbara* tree and labelled as *Bhagavato Konāgamanasa bodhi* [Bh. Ins. No. 294)

(6) *Kāśyapa* by a throne under a *Nyagrodha* tree and labelled as *Bhagavato Kasapasa bodhi* (Bh. Ins. No. 295).

For winning over the common people, the stories of the

Jātakas were depicted on stone in the form of beautiful illustrations on the railings of Bharhut and Sāñci. Representations are found on the Bharhut railings from the following Jātakas:—

Jātaka	*Illustration No.*
(1) Laṭukika	253
(2) Sujāta	327
(3) Kukkuṭa	329
(4) Nigrodhamiga	337
(5) Migapotaka	343
(6) Makhādeva	356
(7) Bhisa	362
(8) Cammasātaka	379, 381
(9) Ārāmadūsaka	404
(10) Maṇikaṇṭha	383
(11) Asadisa	376
(12) Mahā-Janaka	391
(13) Kapota	406
(14) Dabbhapuppha	412
(15) Dubhiya makkaṭa	418
(16) Vessantara	422
(17) Kinnara	424
(18) Mahākapi	35
(19) Kakkaṭa	289
(20) Mūgapakkha	290
(21) Vidhura-paṇḍita	260
(22) Chaddanta	291
(23) Alambusa	225
(24) Mahā-Ummagga	202
(25) Mahā-kapi II	317
(26) Mahā-bodhi	319
(27) Ruru	129

Some illustrations connected with the life of the Buddha are also found on the Bharhut railings, but they do not contain any figural representation of the Lord. His presence is indicated by the symbols of wheel, triratna, Bodhi tree, throne, *stūpa* and footprints.

After the shaving of the head of Buddha, his lock of hair is represented to have been taken away by gods to Heaven and worshipped there (Illustration No. 182). Thereafter we find that Arhadgupta, the angel makes announcement of the inauguration of the Law of Buddha in the assembly of gods. (No. 183)

The Buddhist conception of sin and hell also is represented at Bharhut (Illustration Noș 313-316). The torments of a couple for killing people by administering poison are depicted there.

The followers of the faith of Gautama Buddha came from various strata of the society. They belonged to widely distant places of the country. The gift of lithic pillars and cross-bars etc. at a place of Buddhist pilgrimage was considered an extremely religious act. And in this work both the monastic and the lay Buddhists used to take keen interest. It is found that pillars and other objects were dedicated by nuns some of whom were named as Phalgudevī (Ins. No. 13), Somā (Ins. No. 33), Somanā (Ins. No. 34), Nāgadevī (Ins. No. 85), Nāgilā (Ins. No. 17 b) Budharakhitā (Ins. No. 131), Bhutā (Ins. No. 133), Badhikā (Ins. No. 150), Nāgā (Ins. No. 237) and Diganāgā (= Diṅnāgā) (Ins. No. 310).

Teachers of Buddhist literature, pupils and reciters also contributed their share in showing due regard to the religion of the great Master. Thus we find that Bhadaṁta Valaka (who was a *bhāṇaka* or a reciter) (Bharhut Ins. No. 30), Ārya Kṣudra, well versed in the *Suttantas* (cf *Ayacula sutaṁtika,* Ins. No. 73), Buddharakṣita proficient in the *Five Nikāyas* (Ins. No. 127), Ārya Ṛṣipālita (who was both a reciter and superintendent of the construction work) *(navakamika)* (Ins. No. 183. b), Ārya Jāta, a master of the Piṭakas *(Peṭakino)* (Ins. No. 263) also made gifts. The sculptor *(Rūpakāraka),* (Ins. No. 180) was also not left behind. Gifts were also forthcoming from the royal household as well as from the ordinary run of people. As regards the latter, the inscriptions record a good number of names both male and female who took part in making gifts to the Buddhist *stūpa* at Bharhut. On the other hand it is evident from the inscription No. 16, at Bharhut that some gifts came from a royal consort *Nāgarakhitā,* wife of a certain king whose name is now mutilated. Another inscription (No. 108) records that the first pillar was the gift of *Cāpadevī* wife of *Revatimitra,* of Vidiśā (modern Besnagar in Gwalior state). The royal figure mounted on an elephant with a relic casket in hand just near the inscription (No. 108) is probably King Revatimitra of Vidiśā mentioned in the above record. This person is followed by a horseman holding a Garuḍa standard. This makes out the case that Revatimitra, who probably hailed from the royal family of Vidiśā was the owner of the Garuḍa standard and was thus very likely devoted to *Vaiṣṇavism.* Another figure in the Bharhut railing is also found to carry a Garuḍa emblem. Moreover we are aware that in the 2nd century B.C. the Greek ambassador Heliodoros came to Vidiśā from the Greek king of Taxila. He professed *Bhāgavatism*[3] and set up a pillar with a Garuḍa emblem in honour of god Viṣṇu. From these it transpires that Vidiśā was an important seat of Vaiṣṇavism in the Śuṅga period and that King Revatimitra was a devotee of Vaiṣṇavism.

That Buddhism was appreciated by the Hindu society is proved by the gift of *Cāpadevī,* queen of Revatimitra who appears to be a follower of Vaiṣṇavism. The person mounted on an elephant holding a relic casket in his hand has been taken by some to be King Revatimitra of Vidiśā. It this identification is correct, it may be said that Revatimitra was a tolerant king and came forward of his own accord to lead the procession for depositing the relics of the Buddha in the *stūpa* at Bharhut.

It has already been noticed to some extent that the gifts at

Bharhut were coming not only from the Buddhist order but also from various ranks of people of other sects. But now we shall see that the Bharhut *stūpa* attracted devotees and pilgrims not only from the same locality or neighbouring places but also from very distant regions. Thus we find that gifts were made from Pāṭaliputra (mod. Patna) (Ins. Nos. 44, 67, 70), Vidiśā (mod. Besnagar in Gwalior state) (Ins. Nos. 108, 119, 291, 302) and Bhojakaṭa[4] (mod. Ellichpur district, Berar) (Ins. Nos. 248,310) etc. There are some other place names which cannot be properly identified now, e.g. Moragiri (Ins. Nos. 173,177, 303), Bodhicakra (Ins. No. 249), Purika (Ins. Nos, 69,132,252), the town of Karahakaṭa (Ins. Nos. 362,6), Dabhina (Ins. No. 150), Cuḍathila (Ins. Nos. 85,, 91) etc. Another place name, e.g. Nandinagara (Ins. No. 14), which occurs at Bharhut as well as at Sanchi cannot now be properly identified. So it seems that this Nandinagara had a very important part in the activities connected with Buddhism. The other important centres of Buddhism during the Śuṅga period were at Sanci, Bodhgaya, Sarnath, Lauriya Nandangarh and some other places.

At Sanci also the lithic bas-relief contains copious illustrations from the Jātakas and interesting stories connected with the life of the Buddha. Representations from the Mahākapi Jātaka and Śyāma Jātaka etc. are found there. Here also the great Master has been represented by symbols e.g. the throne and pipal tree just as in Bharhut.

The Sāñci inscriptions show that there was a good number of corporate bodies or families which made gifts to the Buddhist stūpa.[5] Sometimes the donation comes from the village as a whole (cf 1. *vejajasa gāmasa dānaṁ* 1.17 II. *Pāḍukulikāya gāmasa dānaṁ.* II. 1.) From another inscription which reads *Bodha-gothiya dhamavadhananā dānaṁ,* 1.25., it is evident that *gosṭhī* or committee of trustees for looking after religious institutions of the Buddhists was in existence in about 2nd century B.C. As regards other corporate bodies which took part in the activities of the Sāñci *stūpas,* mention may be made of *daṁtakāras* or guild of ivory workers *(cf Ep. Ind.,* II. p. 378, No. 200, c 189; *Vedisakehi daṁta-karehi rūpakaṁmaṁ kataṁ,* (i.e. workers in ivory of Vediśā have done the carving).

Gifts were coming both from the monastic order as well as from the laity. Some of the donors both male and female were well versed in the *Suttapiṭaka* and the five *Nikāyas* (cf I. 79. *Avisinaye Sūtātikiniya maḍala chikatikāye dānaṁ* = the gift of Avinisa who is well versed in *Suttapiṭaka,* an inhabitant of Maḍala Chikata) (cf also 1.60. *Devagirino pacanekayikasa bhichuno sa atevasi* = *(gift* of monk Devagiri expert in five *Nikāyas* along with pupils).

Among the donors, the trading communities such as the Seṭhs or Śreṣṭhis and their relatives take a prominent part, the weavers (sotika=. sautrika. I. 196), carpenter (according to Bühler Vaḍaki or Vardhakin means carpenter No. 311) and royal scribe *(Rājalipikara* I. 49) etc. also find suitable mention in connection with making gifts to the *stūpas* at Sāñci.

The places whose people were attracted by the great Buddhist centre at Sāñci are the following among others:—(1) Ujjayini (I. 27, 69,95; C VI. 12,49. 55-68, 70 77), Vedisa (modern Besnagar I. 38, 1,117), Mahisati (Māhismati, mod. Mandhātā on the Narbada, I. 111), Pokhara (= Puṣkara near Ajmir, I. 106, I. 83, etc)., Pratithāna Pratiṣṭhāna (mod. Paithan on the Godavarī, I. 12,70), Erakina (Eran in the Sagar district of C.P. I. c 98), Tumbavana (= Tumain, Esagarh district, Gwalior State), Arāpāna, Bhogavadhana, Madhuvana, Navāgāma, Kurara, Kuraghara and Nandinagara etc. the last of these names i.e. Nandinagara occurs apparently also in the place names mentioned in the Bharhut inscriptions. The lion's share of the expenses for the ornamentation of the Sāñci monuments was borne by the villagers.

Although the votaries of the Sāñci *stūpa* generally come from the Buddhist community, there were some persons whose names bore the stamp of other religions or who were actually non-Buddhists but made gifts to the *stūpas* out of liberal views.

For instance, the names, (1) Agisimā (= Agni Śarmā, I. 69) (2), Bahadata (= Brahmadatta, I. 30), (3) Viśvadeva (I. 95), Mitā (I. 73), Yamarakhita (II. c. 20) etc. appear to have been mainly influenced by the vocabulary of the Vedic literature and might have been connected with the Vedic worship also. Similarly the terms Nāgā (I. 50. c. 45), Nāgadatā (I. 117), Nāgila (I. 84. II. c. 1), Nāgadina (= Nāgadatta, I. 115) are the reminiscences of the existence of the snake worship; and Vinhukā (II. c. 24) (= Viṣṇukā) seems to be the evidence of *Vaiṣṇavism;* while Śivanadi (= Śivanandī. I. 46), Nadiguta (= Nandigupta. I, 58), Naṁdigiri (I. 108) show the influence of Śaivism. Some scholars find an implied reference to the cult of *Śakti* in the word Himadatā (= Himādatta, Himā being a name of Durgā, I. c. 63).

It goes without saying that at Bodh-Gaya in Bihar, illustrations from the life and activities of the Buddha are also found on the stone railings measuring 145ft. by 1o8ft. round the holy Bodhi tree (pipal tree). This spot of enlightenment is illustrated on the Bharhut railings as a holy edifice in the 2nd century B.C.

The Bodhi tree at Bodh-Gaya was surrounded by a sumptuous railing consisting of a covered gallery with open niches resting on pillars[6]. Pilgrims from distant places used to visit this sacred place even in the 1st century B.C. This is evident from an inscription written in the script of 1st century B.C. wherein it is said that Buddharakṣita, an inhabitant of *Tāmraparṇa* (Ceylon) made a gift there, (cf. *Buddharakhitasa Tabapanakasa dānaṁ*[7]).

In this period we find that the *dharma-cakra* has found a place in the temple along with the *triratna* placed on throne. The Bodhi tree also was illustrated as a symbol of worship by the pilgrims. Buddhist *caityas* and *stūpas* also were figured in the railings for the purpose of showing reverence to these symbols. Bodh-Gaya drew also the attention of royal patrons. At one place in a half medallion a goddess who may be taken as goddess of Fortune or Fertility is found standing on lotus and being bathed by two elephants. Below her, there is an inscription in the Brahmi characters of the 1st century. B.C. which says that Nāgadevī, wife of King Brahmamitra, made a gift there (cf *Raño Brahma mitrasa pājāvatiye Nāgadevaye dana.8)*

During his visit to Bodh-Gaya Cunningham found several pillars of granite bearing inscriptions of gift in the characters used by Aśoka. One such inscription reads—*Ayāye Kuragiye danaṁ*[9] i.e. gift of Āryā Kuragi. Although Cunningham took them to be the relics of the Maurya period, they were more probably the objects of the time of the Śuṅgas on account of the characteristic briefness of the inscriptions and their donative purpose.

Then we come to Sarnath, where Buddha after his great enlightenment turned the Wheel of Law (dharma-cakra) for the first time. This place continued to be one of the important centres of Buddhism during the Śuṅga period also. Apart from the structural evidences, several inscriptions written in the Brāhmī characters of that age were discovered in course of excavations. Some of them contain the names of donors with their places of residence. Donors used to come from widely distant regions as Ujjayini,[10] and Pāṭaliputra[11] (Patna). Here also the donors just as at Bharhut, and Sāñci made gifts of pillars (and probably cross-bars and copings etc.). It appears that the gift of pillars, cross-bars, copings and gateways etc. was regarded to be one of the essential features of religious acts during the Śuṅga period. An inscription discovered at Sarnath in the Brāhmī characters of the 2nd century B.C. records the gift of a base-stone by a nun *Saṁvahikā* by name [cf. *bhikhunikāye samvahikaye dāna(ṁ) ala(ṁ)banaṁ*[12]].

So far as places of religious worship are concerned, Buddhism has left for the posterity a remarkable legacy. A place of religious importance of this period was brought to light a few years ago in course of archaeological excavations. N. G. Majumdar dug out a huge brick structure nearly 8o ft. high taking a zig zag course and showing a number of re-entrant angles at *Lauriya Nandangarh* in the Champaran district of Bihar in 1936-37. This building was polygonal and star-shaped in plan, measuring 5oo ft. across the centre and facing each cardinal point with a side 104 ft. long. There are four sides each at a distance of 266 ft. from the other. The space between the two sides in each of the quadrangles is covered by 28 smaller sides showing 14 re-entrant angles and as many as 13 corners.[13]."

In plan the monument is somewhat similar to the Main temple at Paharpur (District, Rajshahi) though the latter was built about six or seven centuries after the former which is more elaborate and stupendous. The Lauriya Nandangarh monument has at least five terraces one above the other and there is passage for circumambulation on three of them. The lowermost and widest terrace has a width of 32 ft. and the one above it is 14 ft. across.

The decoration of the structure is very plain and simple. This monument has been attributed to the Śuṅga period by the experts. In this connection the observation made by N. G. Majumdar may be quoted here. He says "There is evidence to show that this structure must have been erected not later than the 2nd century B. C. As a simple brick built edifice of such stupendous dimensions it is perhaps unparalleled in the whole range of monuments of the period to which it belongs. Although nothing definite has yet been discovered to throw light on the character of the monument it may be described as a Buddhist *stūpa* in absence of any evidence to the contrary[14]"

In Bengal also some places particularly *Bangarh* (ancient Kotivarṣa) and *Tamluk* (ancient Tāmralipti or Tāmralipta) both in West Bengal felt the sweeping influence of Buddhism during the Śuṅga period. Because two terracotta sealings[15] bearing the names, *Bhutarakhita* and *Śamana Vilala* in *Śuṅga Brāhmī* have been discovered in course of excavations at the former place. The name Bhutarakhita was generally popular among the members of the Buddhist sect and occurs in one (No. 119) of the inscriptions of the Bharhut railings of the Śuṅga period.

At Tamluk, a terracotta tablet which was recently discovered, is supposed to contain a scene from the Chadanta Jātaka. From stylistic ground the tablet is ascribed to the Śuṅga period and is now exhibited in the Ashtosh Museum of Calcutta University. From these evidences it cannot be denied that Buddhism had a favourable ground in Bengal during the Śuṅga regime.

During the rule of the Indo-Greek Kings in the North Western India in the 2nd and 1st centuries B. C. Buddhism played a prominent part in that region. Because some of the Indo Greek rulers became patrons of Buddhism and one of them, *Menander,* became a convert to the faith of Gautama Buddha. Although according to tradition Aśoka is said to have taken the initiative for preserving the sacred relics of the Buddha constructing *stūpas* in different parts of India, documentary (i.e. inscriptional) evidences are available from the Śuṅga period to the effect that the disciples and devotees were then giving particular attention to the preservation of the corporeal remains of the Great Master in the *stūpas* throughout the country for the worship and benefit of the people.

From the Shinkot steatite casket inscriptions found in the Bajaur tribal territory beyond the borders of N. W. Frontier Province it is known that in the reign of king Menander, Viyakamitra[16] (= Vīryakamitra), apparently one of the feudatories (Apraca-raja) of the former placed the corporeal remains of the Lord Śā*kyamuni* endowed with life *(praṇa-sameda-sarira)* in a casket. But in the latter part of the inscription it is stated by Vijayamitra apparently a successor of Viyakamitra that in course of time probably after the death of the depositor these remains were not treated with due honour, hence he (Vijayamitra who was a successor or subordinate ruler) re-established the sacred remains and made arrangements for their regular worship.

That the depositing of the corporeal remains of the Buddha was considered to be one of the main religious activities of this period is also proved by the Swat relic vase inscription of the

Meridarkh Theodors[17] of the 1st century B.C. It is stated therein that Greek provincial Governor (Greek Meridarkhes) Theodoros placed a casket cotainig the sacred relics of the Lord Buddha's body for the benefit of large number of the relic caskets was made in order to give somethig concrete to the ordinary followers of Buddhism as an object of worship.

It has already been pointed out that Buddhism made a favourale appeal to the foreigners and foreign rulers, some of whom became staunch devotees and generous patrons of this religion.

Buddhism made a rapid progress also in South India in 2nd-1st centuries B.C. This is proved by the Bhaṭṭiprolu Casket iscription[18] of the time of Kuberka of the Kristna district of South India. It is stated therein that two caskets—one of stone and the other of crystal were dedicated by some individuals—Kura's father, Kura's mother and Kura himself and also another person named Śiva for depositing the corporeal remains of Lord buddha. The *mañjuṣā* or stone casket was actually the gift of Kura and his father Banaba. There were other sets of stone caskets and crystal caskets being the gifts of a good number of individuals and croporate bodies and also of king Kuberaka himself. It is further mentioned that the figure of king Kuberaka, the donor was also sketched there apparently to add importance to the work. According to casket No. 2 (D) King Kuberka has been stated to be the chief of the *Simha Goṣṭḥī* clan, which dedicated another set of two caskets one being made of stone and the other of crystal. Casket No. 3 (B) records that the *goṣ ṭḥī* or cllan of Arahadina (Arhaddatta) also dedicated a set of one stone casket and a crystal casket and that the work was accomplished by one who drew the figure of king Kuberka. It is to be noted that the king who was the patron as well as one of the essential figures in the act of dedication was represented by the artist both in name as well as in portrait on the caskets to commemorate the act of depositing the relic.

The practice of representing the figure of donors is also seen in the relief of the Andhra King Sātakarṇi at Nānāghāt.[19]

In the 2nd and 1st centuries B.C., there began to grow the art of excavating caves, caitya halls and vihāras (monasteries) for the Buddhists (especially for the Buddhist monks) in different parts of India. In this connection the names of Bhājā[20] (near Poona), Nāsik[21] (District Nasik), Mānmada[22] (Junnār) and Nānāghāt[23] (District Poona) appear uppermost in our mind. The cave architecture which received a strong support from the Buddhists and patrons of Buddhism made steady progress during this period. These places besides Bharhut, Sāñci and Bodhgaya were certainly of great importance from the Buddhist point o view. Pilgrims and monks from all quarters used to flock to these places. Although the Sātavāhana kings were themselves strong supporters and staunch followers of the Brahmanical religion, yet they were liberal patrons of Buddhism, and the buddhist cave architecture of Nasik and Nānāghāt etc. flourished under them. There is record to show that during the reign of king Kṛṣṇa of the Sātavāhana dynasty a cave was excavated by the officer-in-charge of the Śramanas at Nasik[24] (or by a Śramaṇa who was himself a *Mahāmātra* or officer at Nasik). The Nānāghāt caves contain lebels bearing the names of Simuka Sātavāhana Devī Nāganikā, King Sātakarṇi, Kumāra Śaktiśrī and Kumāra Sātavāhana[25].

Kunja Govinda Goswami

FOOTNOTES

1. "*iha Puṣyamitraṁ yājaymaḥ*" under Pāṇini's Sūtra, III, 2. 123.
2. *Ep. Ind.*, vol. XX, p. 57.
3. *Arch. Sur, Ind. An. Rep.*, 1912-13, pp. 82 f.
4. Bhojakaṭa-rajya is found in the Chammak inscription of Pravarasena II. Fleet, *Corp. Ins. Ind.*, Ill, pp. 236 f.
5. *Ep, Ind.*, vol. II, pp. 87 f.
6. *Arch. Sur, Ind. An. Rep.*, 1908-09. pp. 141 f.
7. N. G, Majuṃḍar, *Guide to the sculptures in Indian Museum,* (=GSIM,) Part I, p. 67.
8. N. G. Majumdar, *GSIM.*, Part I, p. 71.
9. Cunningham, *ASR.*, vol. I, p. 10.

10. *Arch. Sur, Ind. An. Rep.*, 1914-15, p. 121, II, PL. LXVIII. 9-10.
11. *Ibid.*, p. 122. V, PL. LXVIII, 14.
12. *Ibid.*, 1906-07, p, 95.
13. *Arch. Sur, Ind. An. Rep.*, 19.36-37, pp. 47 f,
14. *Ibid.*, 1936-37, pp. 47-50.
15. K. G. Goswami, *Excavations at Bangarh,* pp. 12, 36. PL. XXIV, b.
16. *Ep. Ind.*, vol. XXIV, p. 7.
17. Sten Konow, *Corp. Ins. Ind.*, vol. II, i. p. 4.
18. *Ep. Ind.*, vol. II, pp, 323 f,
19. Coomaraswamy, HIIA., p. 30.
20. *Ibid.*, fig. 29.
21. *Ibid.*, fig. 31.
22. *Ibid.*, fig. 30.
23. *Ibid.*, p. 30; *Arch, Sur. Rep. West. Ind.*, V. p. 64.
24. *Ep, Ind.*, vol. VIII, p. 93.
25. *Arch, Sur. Rep. West, Ind.*, V, p. 64.

13

PLACE OF BUDDHISM IN INDIAN THOUGHT

It is rather striking that the early Pali texts even later Buddhist Sanskrit texts do not breathe a word about the Upaniṣads and the Upaniṣadic philosophers, although there are repeated references to the teachings of the six teachers, Pūraṇa Kassapa, Ajita Kesakambalin, Pakudha Kaccāyana, Sañjaya Belaṭṭhiputta, Maṅkhali Gosāla and Nigaṇṭha Nāṭaputta. Incidentally in the Pali texts there is also mention of the Vedic *śakhās,* viz., Addhariya, Bahvrija, Chandoka, and Tittiriya and Vedic seers, Aṭṭhaka, Vāmaka, Vāmadeva, and others who are said to have taught mainly *Brahma-sahavyatā* or the attainment of Brahmaloka, supposed to be the highest form of existence. In the sixty two views envisaged in the *Brahmajālasutta,* there are criticisms of the belief in the existence of a self and of its transmigration from one existence to another. This criticism is elaborated in later Mahāyāna texts particularly in that of Nāgārjuna.[1] In the Pāli *Nikāyas* there are several discourses of a stereotyped nature discussing the problem whether the soul is identical with the body or not, and the conclusion drawn is that there cannot arise any question of the existence or non-existence of soul, as from the Buddhist point of view it has no more existence than that of the son of a barren woman or that of a flower in the sky.[2] Hence it is an indeterminable problem *(avyākata)* to be left aside *(ṭhapanīya)*. The fundamental query of almost all the *Upaniṣads* is the nature of soul and its transmigration from one existence to another. It seems that Buddha deliberately ignored the *Upaniṣads* as in them the existence of soul is taken for granted while his main thesis was the total denial of the existence of this soul *(anatta)* and through all his philosophical discourses he tried to establish that there could not exist any permanent self unalloyed by worldly impurities. Hence, it is idle to say that Buddhism issued out of the *Upaniṣads* and was a phase in the evolution of Upaniṣadic thought.[3] On the other hand, it may be stated that Buddhism was a revolt against the Upaniṣadic thought and it was this denial of soul, which undermined the belief in the efficacy of the sacrificial rituals and ceremonies. The three primary conditions which make one a true Buddhist is the elimination of the belief in the existence, of a self *(sakkāyadiṭṭhi)* and in the efficacy of rituals *(sīlabbataparāmāsa),* to which is to be added the implicit faith in the *Triratna* by discarding all doubts *(vicikicchā)* about their excellence. This revolutionary teaching of Buddha instead of frightening away some of the Brāhmanic teachers and students, opened up a new vista before their eyes and made them not only staunch supporters but the best exponents of the new teaching.

Buddha subscribed to the theories of *karman* and rebirth but in a way completely different from those of the Upaniṣadas. The Upaniṣadic view of *karman* is linked up with the permanent and unchangeable self while Buddha's view was that changing *karman* could never be associated with an unchanging substance like the self. He was a strong advocate of *karman* and its effects and he laid the utmost emphasis on it throughout his teachings (see *infra)*. He criticised those teachers who denied or minimised the efficacy of *karman* and it is with this purpose that he discussed the doctrines of the six teachers mentioned above and condemned them in no uncertain terms. The upholders of *Akiriyavāda* were destined to hell—this was his repeated assertion. He elaborated his cosmological ideas of heaven and hell mainly with a view to educate his large number of disciples who were not spiritually advanced and to infuse into them the spirit of doing good deeds and avoiding evils in order to assure a better and happier after-life. of the six teachers he made an exception of only one, viz., Nigaṇṭha Nāṭaputta, whom he regarded as a *kiriyavādin* and passed over the views of the Agnostic teacher Sañjaya Belaṭṭhiputta.

The doctrinal views of these six teachers are presented in the Pali texts thus:

(i) Puraṇa Kassapa seems to be the oldest teacher and held views wavering between antinomianism and fatalism. His doctrine is that soul remains inactive as in Sāṅkhya and it is the body which acts, hence soul remains unaffected by the results of good and bad deeds of the body. A person earns neither merit by pious acts such as gifts, sacrifices, or by abstinence from evil acts nor demerit by killing, stealing, adultery or speaking falsehood. It is rather difficult to find out exactly what was Pūraṇa's views from such cryptic statements. It may mean that the body enjoys or suffers according to its deeds but not the soul, a doctrine which cannot reasonably, be refuted by a Sāṅkhya or a Vedānta schoolman. In Buddhism however soul and body are not admitted as two separate entities, not also as identical. Pūraṇa's doctrine is grouped in the Pāli texts as an "*Akiriyavada*" i.e. non-existence of *karmaic* effects.

(ii) Makkhali Gosāla, the founder of the Ājivika sect, was at first a follower of Pārśvanatha, the traditional founder of Jainism. One day he observed a sprout growing up again after it was trampled down. This changed his outlook and he came to the conclusion that beings were subject to re-animation and not death and destruction. He added to it the doctrine that all beings were subject to a fixed series of existence from the lowliest to the highest and this series was unchangeable *(niyati sangatibhāva)* and every existence had its own unalterable characteristic as heat is of fire or coldness of ice. He denied the effects of deeds *(karma)* and energy *(vīrya)*. He upheld fatalism of the extreme type. A being when nearing the end of the several spans of its lives becomes a human being. Its existence as such is divided into six categories, viz., (i) black *(kaṇha)* as bird catchers, hunters, fishermen etc., (ii) blue *(nīla)* as ascetics observing rigorous practices, including the Buddhists (Śākya-puttiya Samaṇas), (iii) red *(lohita)* as monks of the Jaina order, (iv) yellow *(halidda)* as lay-devotees of Acelakas and Ājīvikas, (v) white *(sukka)* as Ājīvika monks like Nanda, Vaccha and Saṅkicca, and lastly (vi) very white *(paramasukka)* as Ājīika saints. Buddhaghosa[4] has made an attempt to explain in detail the various states of existence envisaged in Maṅkhali Gosala's doctrines. In the Jaina literature[5] as also in Tamil works like the *Manimekhalai* of the 4th century A. D. and *Civañāna Cittiyar* of the 14th century, the various states of existence distinguished by colour as black, dark, blue, green, red, golden and white have been dealt with in connection with the doctrines of the Ājīvikas[6]. The distinctions made by colour, though not now intelligible, must have been a prominent feature of Ājīvikism. It is not unlikely that the term *'niyati'* was introduced into Indian thought by the Ājīvikas and it cast a definite influence on the Epics particularly the *Mahābhārata*. Manu and compiler of *Hitopadeśa* tried to disabuse the minds of the people of this faith in fatalism though Bhartṛhari extolled it in his *Nītiśataka*. The Ājīvikas, it seems, attained great popularity in post-Aśokan age. There is a tradition that king Bindusāra consulted Piṅgalavatsa (Janāsana in Pali chronicles) an Ājīvika monk for ascertaining which of his two sons, Aśoka and Vītaśoka would succeed him to the throne. Aśoka's mother was very likely a follower of the Ājīvikas. After Aśoka's demise his grandson Daśaratha dedicated a few caves to the Ājīvika saints specially, showing thereby that the successors of Aśoka preferred the Ājīvikas to the Buddhists. Dr. Basham has collected reliable evidences to show that this sect became popular in South India and was in existence up to the mediaeval period.[6]

(iii) Nigaṇṭha Nāṭaputta (fetterless son of the Nāya clan) or Mahāvīra happened to be an older contemporary of Buddha. Like Buddha he came of a noble family, perhaps the chief of the clan. He led for some time a married life and then renounced the world. He revived the teachings of Pārśvanātha, and formed an order of monks who however led a much more austere life than that of a Buddhist monk. His philosophical views are as follows: There are nine substances *(navatattva)* viz., (i) soul *(jīva)* present in all that is conscious including a tree or a fruit; (ii) non-soul *(ajīva)* which serves as the basis for the functioning of soul *(jīva)* as body is of the soul; (iii) merits and demerits *(puṇya, pāpa]* which are also substances produced by actions *(karman)* of *jīva* through mind, speech and body; (v) impurities *(āsrava)* which flow into the body due to *karmaic* effects; (vi) self-control *(saṃvara)* which arrests the flow of *karmaic* effects, and also neutralises them; (vii) bondage *(bandha)* of the soul caused by *karmaic* effects transformed into ā*srava* and leading to repeated existence *(saṁsara),* (viii) elimination *(nirjarā)* of *karmaic* effects or ā*sravas* through s*aṃvara* as prescribed for the Jaina monks; and lastly (ix) liberation *(mokṣa)* attained by a monk who has perfected himself in the disciplinary practices and realised the truth as inculcated in Jaina philosophy.

In Jaina philosophy no definite statement *(syādvāda)* can be made about any object, not even about the highest truth. Every object is subject to three momentary states, viz., origin *(atpāda),* continuity *(sthiti)* and decay *(vināśa)*. The object in its state of continuity may be regarded as the substance *(dravya)* while in the other two states it is subject to change *(paryāya)*. According to *anekāntavāda* an object is permanent from the standpoint of continuity *(nitya),* but it is impermanent *(anitya)* from the other two standpoints. Every object has to be determined from different standpoints, as it has several aspects and so there can be no absolute statement regarding the nature of an object. This is known as the Jaina doctrine of *Anekānta-vāda*. In order to have a true knowledge of an object, its examination is necessary from various aspects and it is by this means alone that the perfect knowledge can be attained. For the sake of practical application, the *Anekāntavāda* has been condensed into seven members *(saptabhangī)* thus:—From seven different standpoints a being is (i) permanent; (ii) impermanent; (iii) both permanent and impermanent; (iv) indescribable; (v) permanent and indescribable; (vi) impermanent and indescribable; (vii) both permanent and impermanent as also indescribable.

This religion with its great emphasis on asceticism and rigorism imposed on monks and nuns has maintained its existence in India up to the present day. Its lay followers however are limited and still observe many hard and fast rules of self-discipline.

(iv) Sañjaya Belaṭṭhiputta did not give out any definite views about the ultimates. He is generally described as a sceptic unwilling to give any definite answer to the ultimate problems, which were, according to him, were indeterminable, a view not incompatible with Buddha's declaration that the problems: whether the soul is identical with body or not, whether an emancipated being exists after death or not, and so forth are also indeterminable *(avyākata)* and should be left aside. Sañjaya happened to be the teacher of Sāriputta and Moggallāna who joined the Buddhist order along with the other disciples of the teacher and who were much impressed by Buddha's theory of causation, which explained that the beings of the world were in a ceaseless state of flux governed by certain causes and conditions.

(v) Ajita Kesakambalin was a materialist. He denies an after-life and so according to him there is no need of earning merits by good deeds, sacrifices or service to parents. There is no spiritual advancement or perfection in knowledge likewise. There is no demerit if one commits evil deeds. A being is composed of five elements: earth, water, air, fire and space *(ākāsa)*. After death each of these returns to the corresponding mass of great elements while the senses *(indriyas)* pass into space. A person's earthly existence ends in the funeral pyre. Nothing survives after death *(bhaṣmībhūtasya debasya punarāgamanaṃ kutaḥ)*.

This doctrine of Ajita is clearly a restatement of the Lokāyata or Bārhaspatya school of thought. Dhīṣaṇa, to whom is attributed this type of doctrine in the *Padma Parāṇa,* asserts that there is no God. The variegated world exists by itself. He admits only four elements and not the fifth *ākāśa*. The combination of the four elements produces consciousness *(caitanya)* as liquor is produced by the fermentation of rice and molasses. When everything ends in death, there is no sense in performing sacrifices or in seeking heaven. It was an anti Vedic movement and established that a being should seek his own happiness by whatever means he can devise, and not perform acts which are supposed to bring fruits in the next life. It identifies soul with body, a doctrine which has been bitterly criticised by Buddha and classed as annihilationism *(ucchedavāda),* i.e., the doctrine that a being disappears for ever with the dissolution of the body.

(vi) Pakudha Kaccāyana was a pluralist and a semi-materialist. Like Ajita he holds that a being is composed of seven elements ; earth, water, air, fire, pleasure *(sukha),* pain *(dukkha)* and soul *(jīva)*. These seven elements are neither created nor moulded. They are barren and fixed as a rock or a stone-pillar and do not produce anything. They neither move nor change nor hinder one another so as to cause pain or pleasure or indifference. Hence, there is no killer nor instigator of killing, no hearer nor preacher, no learner nor teacher. If a sword passes through the body of a being, it does not destroy it but only slips through the interspaces of the elements forming the body. It is a form of atomism without any parallel. It has been criticised by Buddha as a kind of eternalism (*sassatavāda}* and grouped with Ajita's teaching of annihilationjsm *(ucchedavāda),* i.e., everything ends with death.

Besides these six renowned teachers there was another class of religious men known as the Paribbājakas or Wanderers. These moved about all over the country either singly or in groups. There were provisions for their residence called *Paribbājakārāma* in important villages and towns. This shows that the Paribbājaka fcrm of life was in vogue in ancient India in the 5th century B.C. or even earlier. The Paribbājakas could be either Brāhmanic or non-Brāhmanic. From their nature of discussions with Buddha it seems that they had no confirmed doctrinal views but not without predilections for either a Brāhmanic or a particular non-Brāhmanic system. The problems broached by them with Buddha related to soul, *karman,* efficacy of ascetic practices, elimination of mental impurities, attainment of perfect knowledge, soundness of views of Nigaṇṭ ha Nāṭaputta and so forth. A number of Paribbājakas were impressed by Buddha's teachings and became lay-devotees and a few became full-fledged monks. The Paribbajakas were generally in quest of the Truth and tried to find out what was the best teaching which of course they did not necessarily accept. They may be regarded as students of religion and philosophy with a receptive mind, and some of them ultimately joined a particular religious order or reverted to a householder's life. From the discourses specially delivered to them, as embodied in the *Nikāyas,* it appears that they formed an important part of the religious and philosophical movement of ancient India." It is also evident that in those days change of doctrinal views was the rule of the day and there was no slur on a person even if he changed his religious affiliation. Had it not been so, Buddha could not have formed his band of disciples, whom he recruited largely from the Brahmanic and Śresthī families and *paribbājakas*.

The Paribbājakas or the Saṅghas or Gaṇas of the six heretical teachers formed a very small section of the religieux of ancient India. In spite of Buddha's silence about the *Upaniṣads* it cannot but be taken for granted that the Upaniṣadic thinkers held the torch of religion, philosophy and culture in pre-Buddha days. There are at least ten Upaniṣads, viz., *Bṛhadāraṇyaka* and *Chāndogya, Aitareya* and *Taittīrīya, Īśa, Kena* and *Kaṭha, Praśna, Muṇḍaka* and *Māṇḍukya,* which are attributed to a date much earlier than Buddha's time. These are mostly compilations of dialogues and monologues of Brāhmanic seers and not systematic expositions of a particular school of thought. In some of them there are traces of *Sāṃkhya, Yoga* and *Mīmāṃsā* schools of thought but the central theme of most of them is the exposition of the monistic philosophy, well known as *Vedānta,* developed with great subtlety in the two principal Upaniṣads, *Bṛhadaraṇyaka* and *Chāndogya.* The oneness of Brahman or the Reality, and the world as a diversified superimposition on the Reality are the keynotes of this philosophy.

The Sāṅkhy a school of philosophy, the origin of which is traced in the *Katha* and *Śvetāśvatara Upaniṣads*[7] took a modified Vedāntic view. It explains that the appearance of worldly objects is due to ignorance *(avidyā)* of the separateness of the two reals, *Puruṣa* and *Prakṛti.* It however held that the appearance of phenomenal world is not wholly baseless or a delusion as the primeval cause *(prakṛti)* does undergo a change *(pariṇāmī)* and the changed object is substantially the *prakṛti,* the change being confined to characteristics *(nimitta)* only of the basic cause *(upādāna).* For this reason it is called '*satkāryavāda*' or the view that cause exists in its effect. The untenability of the Sāṅkhya view, as argued by the Buddhists, lies in the fact that it admits two reals with different characteristics, which are not logical, viz., one, *Puruṣa,* as unchangeable and the other *Prakṛti* as changeable *(pariṇāmī).* The latter being real and eternally existing *(nitya)* it is further led to the fallacy that an eternal entity undergoes change. According to the Sāṅkhya view, the evolution of the *Prakṛti* takes place thus: Out of *Prakṛti* issues *Mabān* or its cosmic aspect or *Buddhi* or psychical aspect. It is the unindividuated cosmic intellect which gives rise to *Ahamkāra* (egoism) or individuated intellect, which is also a substance, an active agent. In its *sāttvika* (pure) aspect it leads to the origin of *Manas* (mind), the function of which is determinate perception; it is the central organ of the sense-organs and their perceptions. *Ahaṃkāra* also gives rise to five subtle essences *Tanmātra,* which in their turn evolve into five gross elements: earth, water, fire, air and ether. Out of these originate the five sense-organs : eyes, ears, nose, tongue and body as also the five physical organs: voice, feet, hands, anus and generating organ. The process of evolution as shown in the *Buddhacarita*[8] is a little different. It is as follows: The primal or ultimate cause *(Prakṛti)* and its evolutes *(vikāra)* constitute a being *(sattva)* with the concomitants: birth, old age, disease and death. The primal cause manifests itself in five great elements *(pañcabhūta)* in their minutest states *(tanmātra),* egoism *(ahaṃkāra)* and unindivduated *(avyakta)* cosmic intellect *(buddhi* or *mabān).* Their evolutes are the sense-organs and their objects, the hands and feet, the voice, the organs of generation and excretion and also the mind. There is the soul *(ātman)* which is conscious of the body. This consciousness or awareness is intellection, which was possessed by saints like Kapila. It is the absence of intellection that produces the world of beings. Those who develop individuation *(vyakta)* and are unable to go beyond the notion of I-ness get entangled in worldly joys and sufferings while those who discard the notion of I-ness and maintain an unindividuated mind go beyond the world of pain and pleasures. This type of Sāṅkhya teachings, according to the testimony of Aśvaghoṣa's *Buddhacarita,* was imparted to Prince Siddbārtha by his spiritual teachers, Ārāḍa Kālāma and Rudraka Rāmaputra and might have some influence on his mind in his formulation of the law of causation *(paṭ iccasamuppāda).*

The Yoga philosophy is similar to that of Sāṅkhya. It has only added the existence of the God. It developed the meditational practices which perhaps were well known to the Upaniṣ adic seers. There is much in common between the Yoga and the Buddhist systems of meditation including the meditational terms.

The Mīmāṃsakas also admit the reality of the world. According to them the souls are eternal, permanent as also the material elements composing the universe. Their universe consists (a) of living bodies, in which the soul reaps the *karmaic* effects *(bhogāyatana),* (b) of sense-organs *(indriya-bhoga-sādbana)* and (c) of sense-objects *(bhoga-viṣaya).*

The Nyāya-Vaiśeṣikas go a step further and in place of two reals of the Sāṅkhya admit six categories of reality, viz., substance *(dravya)*, quality *(guṇa)*, motion *(karman)*, universality *(sāmānya)*, particularity *(viśeṣa)* and inherence *(samavāya)*. Their *dravya* consists of the four eternal constituents: space *(ākāsā)*, time *(kāla)*, mind *(manas)* and soul *(ātman)*. Their viewpoints can also be traced in the Upaniṣads. They are opposed to mere subjectivity of the Vedāntists.

Prince Siddhārtha, educated as he was and engaged in search of the truth, must have been acquainted with most of the non-Buddhistic doctrines stated above. He no doubt denied the existence of a permanent soul but he accepted the theory of *karman* and rebirth, which, of course, he had to interpret in a way suited to his non-soul doctrine.

The doctrine of impermanence *(anityatā)* of the phenomenal world must have appealed to him most and led him to give up his princely life and luxuries. He recognised at the same time that the only means to get out of the clutches of *anityatā* was spiritual exercises as a recluse. The principle of retirement from worldly joys and pleasures is denoted as pessimism though strictly speaking the underlying force for retirement is not so much disgust with the world as the attainment of *nityatā* (eternality)—an ineffable state surpassing the highest conceivable form of worldly existence, which is unalterably associated with birth, old age, disease and death, the four factors, which according to the Buddhist traditions filled the mind of Prince Siddhārtha with consternation not so much for himself as for the humanity in general. The impetus to the Prince's retirement came from human misery and so the Prince directed his mind to evolve a path that might put an end to that misery and not so much for the unfolding of the eternal Truth, on which was concentrated the attention of the Upaniṣadic seers. But there can be no enunciation of the path unless the Truth is known and so the Prince went through a long course of spiritual exercises and succeeded ultimately in visualizing the Truth—the truth of oneness which of course was different from the oneness of *Jīvātman* and *Parāmatman*. It is not known if the Upaniṣadic teachers had formulated any code of duties or chalked out a course for the guidance of their followers; perhaps it was kept secret and handed down esoterically from teacher to disciple. Buddha made no secret of the path of achieving the goal and so he laid bare his scheme of life before one and all who approached him with the sincere desire of exerting to overcome the worldly sufferings. His ethical teachings and his monastic discipline marked a complete departure from the old ways of attaining perfection in knowledge.

Dukkha (Duḥkha): Misery of phenomenal existence had already got hold of the minds of the Upaniṣadic thinkers. In the *Chāndogya* (vii.1.3) it is stated that a wise man, the knower of self, goes beyond the sea of misery *(tarati sokarn ātmavit)* while in a late text like the *Vedāntasāra* (31) appears the statement that a person oppressed by death and rebirth, and worldly fire should approach for the true knowledge a learned teacher conversant with Brahman, the Truth. The Sāṅkhya schoolmen spoke of the misery of human existence and analysed it under three heads, viz., internal *(ādhyātmika)* due to physical disorder and mental agitation, external *(ādhibhautika)* due to injuries caused by men and beasts or by any outside agency, and supernormal *(ādhidaivika)* due to supernatural factors, or the great elements *(mahābhuūtas)*. Thus it is evident that the pessimistic view of life was already in the air and Buddha only picked it up and made it a starting point of his teachings. Buddha told his monks to realise that the tears shed by a being in his innumerable existences if accumulated would exceed the water of a sea *(Saṃyutta Nikāya,* II, pp.178f). In Pali texts,[9] human misery has been sub-divided in a different manner thus: mental and/or physical pain *(dukkha-dukkhatā),* pleasure turning into pain *(vipariṇāma-dukkhatā)* and pain which arises and disappears due to change *(saṅkhāra-dukkhatā)*. Of the four truths *(cattāri ariyasaccāni)* the first truth to be realised by the wise is "*dukkha*" pain or suffering concomitant to phenomenal existence. Its popular exposition is the non-fulfilment of one's desire causing resentment or disappointment, separation from the dear ones or association with the undesired causing mental pain. This *dukkha* is suffered by the commoners and not by the elect *(ariya),* and so, strictly speaking, such *dukkha* is not *ariyasacca. Dukkha* in the eyes of an advanced monk *(ariya)* is the possession of one's body of five constituents *(upādāna-khandbas),* of wealth and property, because of the fact that one's earthly possessions are evanescent and subject to decay *(vayadhammā),* to impermanence *(aniccatā).* Unless and until this nature of *dukkha* is fully comprehended by a monk, the next three truths, viz., desire as the source of *dukkha,* end of desire as the termination of *dukkha* and eighthfold path as leading to the end of *dukkha* remain incomprehensible to him. Realisation of *dukkha* therefore forms the first step in the Buddhist code of spiritual practices and its interpretation is more comprehensive than that of the earlier systems. In almost every school of Indian thought the woes and worries of a living being due to unfulfilled desires are spoken of and there are also suggestions about the means of avoiding the same[10]. The Buddhists however have worked out the problem of *dukkha* in as thorough a manner as possible.

Aniccatā (Anityatā): There can be no two opinions about the fact that the pessimistic view of life *(dukkha)* is based on impermanence or rather evanescence *(aniccatā)* of phenomenal objects. Buddha repeatedly reminded his disciples of this fact by saying '*aniccā vata saṅkhārā uppādavayadhammino*' (impermanent are the composites which are subject to origin and decay). Except *Nibbāna* and *Ākāsa* there is nothing unconstituted in this world. Even the infinitesmal atoms of earth, water, air and fire (i.e. *rūpa)* contain all the four elements and the four qualities: colour *(vaṇṇa),* smell *(gandha),* taste *(rasa)* and nutritive essence *(ojā)* which cannot be separated, and as such each of the material elements as distinct objects exists in thought only so are the other *khandhas,* viz., feeling *(vedanā),* perception *(saññā),* impressions *(saṅkhārā)* and knowledge derived through the senses *(viññāṇa).* A being therefore is a conceptual entity and has no real existence. The Buddhist point of view differs substantially from that of the Nyāya-Vaiśeṣikas, according to whom, there are six irreducible categories of reality. The Jaina school of thought goes a step further and asserts that matter *(pudgala)* is constituted of atoms *(paramāṇu)* which are real and eternal while its action *(karma)* is also material *(paudgalika)*. The 5arvāstivadins (or the Vaibhāṣikas or the Ābhidhammikas) advocated, according to some scholars, 'radical pluralism erected on the denial of substance (soul) and the acceptance of discreet momentary entities' and 'change as the replacement of one entity by another, it is the cessation' of one and emergence of another. The combination (of constituents) is not real over and above the constituents. The components are real *(vastusat)*, the combination is appearance *(prajñapti-sat)*.' The true import of the words '*sarvam asti*' of the Sarvāstivādins is something different from what has been said above. It is a fact that the Sarvāstivādins offer a list of seventy two *dharmas* under the heads: (i) Matter *(Rūpa)*—11; (ii) Mind *(Citta)*—*1*; Mental states *(Caitasikas)* —46; and Non-mentals *(Citta-viprayuktas)*—14. By "all exists" *(sarvam asti)* the Sarvāstivādins mean existence of concepts of past, present and future *(trikālasai)* and not the eternal existence of phenomenal objects or of their minutest elements, which also are impermanent but not as false as a mirage or objects seen in a dream. It is through the realisation of their impermanence and making one's mind completely free from the notion of existence of phenomenal objects that an adept can attain emancipation. Hence, the Sarvāstivādins do not really mean that all objects are real and exist eternally. *Khaṇikatta* (Kṣ aṇikatva): The Buddhists qualify impermanence *(anityatā)* with momentariness *(kṣaṇika)*, i. e., the phenomenal objects are subject to change every moment, and within one moment take place origin *(utpatti)*, duration (*sthiti)* and decay *(vināśa)*. As against this contention of the Buddhists, it is argued that momentariness cannot be directly perceived and further it leads to the admission of the absence of any cause *(ahetukatva)* for the origin of the second moment, because the first momentary existence disappears then and there and cannot be effective in producing the second momentary state.[11] The counter-argument of the Buddhists is that momentariness cannot, it is true, be established by direct perception but it should be noted that momentariness is the characteristic nature *(svabhāva)* of effectiveness *(arthakriyākāritva)*. By momentary cessation of an object is meant the absence of immediately preceding state *(svādhikaraṇa-samaya-prāgabhāva)*. If momentariness as explained above be not admitted, then an object would remain the same for more than one moment, and the object that produces an effect in the present would also produce the same effect in the past and future and would be subject to the fallacy that there could not be an accomplished effect *(kṛta-kāritā)* of an object, in other words, the purpose of an object would not be served.[13]

Hence the Buddhists rightly contend that an object is momentary and produces its effect then and there and not in the past or future. It may be argued that an object retains its potentiality which will be effective in future but this argument is also fallacious because of the fact that two opposite characteristics, viz., presentness and pastness, or presentness and futurity cannot exist together. Therefore it should be admitted that the momentariness of an object can only establish the fulfilment of a purpose and this is not possible if an object remains unchanged for more than one moment. The subtlety of the Buddhist interpretation of *kṣaṇika* is rather unique and may be regarded as a contribution to Indian thought. In short, it explains fully the dynamism of worldly objects or ceaseless change that takes place in worldly objects, in nature.

Paṭiccasamuppāda (Pratītyasamutpāda): The question that arises next is whether this ceaseless change is accidental or predestined or is effected by certain causes *(hetu)* and conditions *(pratyaya)*. The Buddhists reject the first two views and accept the last and offer their formula of the law of causation, *Paṭiccasamuppāda,* popularly known as *Dharmacakra* or the ceaseless cycles of existences of a being. The word "*samutpāda*" created a confusion in the minds of some who took the word in its literal sense and attempted to interpret the formula as Buddha's conception of the origin of the world of beings. Buddhaghosa the great Pali commentator of the 4th century A.D., pointed out in his *Visaddhimagga* that the word *samutpāda* (origin) was used to counteract the false notion of nihilism *(asat-dṛṣṭi)* while the other word *pratītya* (dependent) as an antidote to the notion of real existence of worldly object *(satdṛṣṭi)*. Buddha repeatedly asserted that his interpretation of the Truth kept clear of the two extreme views of existence *(sat /asti)* and non-existence *(asat / nāsti)* of worldly objects, of eternalism *(śāśvata)* and annihilationism *(uccheda)*, of their limitedness *(antavān)* and unlimitedness *(anantavān)*. This is described as the middle path *(majjhimā paṣipadā)*[13] developed later by Nāgārjuna as *Mādhyamika* or Śū*nyatā* philosophy,. and by Asaṅga as Yogācara or *Vijñaptimātratā*.

In the Abhidhamma texts like the *Paṭṭhāna* appears an exhaustive, study of the causes *(hetu)* and conditions *(paccaya)*. The formula of causation has been explained both externally in connection with material objects and internally in relation to living beings. The origin of an earthen pot depends on several causes viz., clay, water, fire, potter, wheel and so forth, while that of a sprout on seed, water, gardener, etc. The origin of a being is due to non-realisation of the Truth *(avidyā)*, thirst *(tṛṣṇā)*, deeds *(karma)* which give a shape to its constituents, organs of sense, and mind. The *Paṭṭhāna* states that there are in all twentyfour kinds of causes, more than one of which are applicable to the origin of an object or a being. Some of these causes, again, mean invariable sequences. In fact, the complete cessation of the previous momentary state cannot produce the succeeding one, and again, there is nothing to pass from the former to the latter. In that case, the law of causation really means only the law of invariable sequence which is observed in nature. The *Laṅkāvatāra sūtra* (p. 103) denies causal origin and speaks of sequence of objects, but it also discusses six kinds[14] of causes which are quite different from those of the

Paṭṭhāna. Nāgārjuna in his *Mādhyamakakārikā* refers to four[15] out of the twentyfour causes mentioned in the *Paṭṭhāna*.

The Mādhyamikas and the Yogācāras like the Vedāntists do not admit the existence of the phenomenal world and so they relegate the law of causation to conventional truths *(saṃvṛtisatya)* and utilise it to establish the relative appearance of objects, e.g., long and short, red and black are mere conventional terms used relatively and have no existence whatsoever. Nāgārjuna remarks that as objects that have origination do not exist and so its existence cannot be established as uncaused, or as caused by itself, or by non-self, or by both self and non-self.[16] The *Laṅkāvatara* states that the ignorant only conceive of objects as originating out of causes and conditions, and for not knowing the true law takes repeated births in the three worlds.[17] In the *Brahmastūtra* there is the statement that there can be no origination of an ever existing substance[18]. Thus, there is complete unanimity between the Mahāyānists and the Vedāntists about the ever existent Real as causeless and conditionless.

The question then arises, why the Mahāyānists take the law of causation into their consideration. They state that this law has two-fold purpose, first to point out the relative appearance of phenomenals objects and secondly to establish by inference that the Real has nothing to do with cause and condition *(apratītyasamutpanna)*. This law is needed to initiate the unliberated into the Truth of non-existence of the phenomenal world and thereby into the uncaused Truth Both the Hīnayāna and Mahāyāna texts state that one, who comprehend the law of causation, realises the Truth and visualises the Buddha[19]. The law of causation leads to the realisation of the fact that the Reality remains undisturbed by origin and decay and is beyond any description[20] and so the law is called fondly by Candrakīrti as the mother of Buddhas of ten powers[21].

Slightly different is the line of reasoning adopted by the Hīnayānists for showing that the law of causation leads to the realisation of the Truth. They have developed a chain of illustrative terms such as ignorance *(avidyā)* of past life causing certain impressions *(saṃskāra),* which in turn produce consciousness that takes rebirth *(pratisandhi-vijñāna).* It is followed by the present life consisting of the five constituents *(nāma-rūpa),* six sense-organs and their objects *(ṣaḍāyatana),* contact *(sparśa),* feeling *(vedanā),* thirst *(tṛṣṇā),* strong attachment *(upādāna)* and lastly, clinging for rebirth *(bhava).* After this, takes place another existence *(jāti)* which ends ultimately in old age and death[22].

Lest this formula of twelve terms creates the impression that it represents the Buddhist view of the tree of life similar to that of Sāṅkhya, Buddhaghosa pointed out in his *Visuddhimagga*· (p. 525) that according to the Sāṅkhya school, the first term *Prakṛti* is uncaused and is the primeval source of the tree of life whereas *Avidyā* is not necessarily the first term in the Buddhist law of causation and also it is not uncaused and hence it cannot be the primeval source. The chain of terms may commence at any link, say, thirst or even birth. *Avidyā* has for its cause thirst or wrong views, etc. The terms illustrate only some invariable sequences.

Avidyā (Ajñāna): Like the Buddhists, Śaṅkara also states that ignorance *(avidyā)* cannot be the primeval cause but he argues against the Buddhist contention that *avidyā* cannot be the cause of mental impressions *(saṃskāra)* because, logically, negation or absence of something cannot be a productive cause. In reply the Buddhists state that *avidyā is* not a mere negation but is something positive—it is the misguided knowledge due to wrong views *(mithyā-darśana).*[23] It is impure and acts as a hindrance to knowledge. It is produced by attachment, hatred and delusion *(rāga, dveṣa, moha)* and belief in a self *(satkāyadṛṣṭi)* leading to erroneous apprehensions *(viparyāsa)* e.g., evil as good, unhappiness as happiness, impurity as purity, non-soul as soul and so forth. It is due to incorrect mental application *(ayoniso manasikāro).* It means a clouded and deluded mind[24], Śaṅkara in his comment on *Brahmasūtra* (I. 1) points out that *avidyā* means the apprehension of certain qualities superimposed on the attributeless Reality, the Pure Soul. The opponents argue that "uperimposition can take place only upon an object directly perceived and not on an imperceptible pure self, Śaṅkara in reply points out that sky *(ākāśa)* has no objective existence still the unenlightened men speak of the sky as blue or compare it with cauldron upturned and so forth. He argues further that though the pure self is attributeless still it serves as the basis of the notion of I-ness, hence it is not as nonexistent as the sky. The knowledge derived through supermposition on an object and its consequent misapprehension, e.g., nacre as silver, rope as snake, is known as Nescience *(Avidyā)* in Vedānta. In his comments on *Brahmasūtra* (II. 1. 14) Śaṅkara offers another exposition of *Avidyā*. He writes that name and form *(nāma-rūpa)* are manifestations of ignorance *(avidyā)* and as such they are indescribable as existing or non-existing and are included in Īśvara or the God, the creator and are known as Cosmic Nescience *(Māyā)*, Energy *(Śakti)*. Īśvara is different from *nāma-rūpa* but is its upholder or is circumscribed by *nāmarūpa*, i.e., *avidyā* is similar to space in an earthen jar. He is therefore the moulder of a conscious being. From the standpoint of *Avidyā*, Īśvara is supreme, omnipotent and omniscient, and from the highest standpoint He is identical with Brahman, the ultimate Truth. In His subtlest form He is Īśvara, the omniscient and in His grossest form the manifested world in its infinite diversity.

The later Vedāntists have given more positive conception of nescience *(Ajñāna= Avidyā)*, saying that it is composed of three qualities ; purity *(sattvas)*, activity *(rajas)* and impurity *(tamas)*, which in turn produce the five subtle elements and so forth as found in the Sāṅkhya system. The *Ajñāna* of the Vedāntists is said to be neither existing nor non-existing because though it does not exist in reality, it has an apparent existence which is indescribable but causes delusion. The *Laṅkāvatāra* (p. 106) uses the term *Bhrānti* in place of Vedantic '*Ajñāna*' and expatiates on it saying that the glow of a circling fire *(alātacakra)* is seen by the wise[25]. It is devoid of both existence and non-existence but at the same time it is in a sense eternal *(bhrāntiḥ śāśvatā)*. It continues to exist so long as one's knowledge functions but it ceases when one puts at rest all his thought constructions[26]. In other words, the *Laṅkāvatāra* supports the Vedāntic conception of *Ajñāna*.

Kamma (Karman): The Buddhists fully recognise the influence of *Karman* and its effects on a being's repeated existences. Of the twelve terms or links in the chain of causation, the second and the tenth i.e. mental impressions *(saṃskāra)* and desire for re-existence *(bhava)* are regarded as resultants of acts of one's past life and present life respectively.[27] The fact that a being is born with name and form, i.e., mental and material constituents, implies that in its previous existence it had mental obsessions due to lack of true knowledge *(avidyā)* and collected the so-called merits and demerits and developed certain mental dispositions *(saṃskāras)* which produced the consciousness for rebirth *(pratisandhi-vijñāna)*, which in its turn brought about its re-existence and gave it a name and form. After re-existence the being in due course becomes subject to the roots of evils, viz., attachment, hatred and delusion[28] and reaches the end of its life with a desire *(bhava)* for another existence. And so it is said in the *Mahāvastu*[29] that the first and the eighth links, nescience and thirst, are the roots of *Karma* leading to rebirth. In Buddhist texts it is repeatedly stated that a being is subject to his deeds, inherits the good or bad effects, and has its origin out of his own past deeds.[30] It is on account of an individual's deeds that one becomes a cultivator, an artist or a king[31]. Deeds are divided into three categories thus: those which produce fruit (i) in this life *(diṭṭhadhammavedaīya)*; (ii) in the next life *(uppajjavedanīya)*; (iii) in a future life *(aparāpaniyavedarīya)*. Some of the *Avadānas* and *Jātakas*, particularly the *Vimānavatthu* and *Petavatthu* and *Mahākarmavibhaṅg*[32] illustrate through stories the effects of good and evil deeds.

It is by the elimination of deeds *(kamma)* that a person attains full emancipation.[33] Self-exertion is the only means of

Nirvāṇa, said Buddha and by self-exertion he meant the performance of certain deeds, spiritual or otherwise. Hence the greatest emphasis was laid on one's acts and exertion and non-dependence on a superior power or on any ritual and ceremony. *Kamma* is inexorable and can only be counteracted by proper exertions as Aṅgulimāla got rid of his sins of indiscriminate killing by his spiritual exercises *(sadhanā)*. Again, Buddha himself could not escape the effects of his past deeds as is illustrated by the event of his being wounded by a stone chip of a missile thrown by Devadatta. Śaṅkara also admits that man is the architect of his destiny and that his *karma,* past and present, must produce fruits which are to be exhausted by enjoyment or suffering. According to the Vedāntists[34] however, *karma* connotes not only meritorious and demeritorious deeds but also fulfilment of duties prescribed for a particular caste *(Varṇa)* and stage of life *(āśrama),* as well as performance of sacrifices and expiatory ceremonies *(prāyaścitta)*. Liberation is to be attained, according to Rāmānuja, not only by true knowledge *(jñāna)* but also by *karma,* by which, he meant, rituals prescribed in the śās*tras*. It is also enjoined in the Vedāntic texts that *karma* should be free from any desire for reward *(niṣkāma)* and such *karma* can destroy the accumulated effects of one's past life. *Karma* is divided into three categories : (i) deed already commenced *(prārabdha),* (ii) deed already accumulated *(sañcita),* and (iii) deed that is being accumulated *(sañdyamāna)*. Of these three, the first must take its own course while the second can be destroyed, and the third prevented by acquisition of true knowledge.

There is a general agreement between the Vedāntic and the Buddhist view of *karman* and its elimination, except that the former relies partially on rituals and ceremonies for neutralizing *karmaic* effects—a view wholly unacceptable to the Buddhists.

Soul and Rebirth: As the Buddhists do not admit the existence of a permanent self, they replace the word "transmigration" by "rebirth".

The conception of ātman in the *Upaniṣads* has given rise to two views: (i) that the self is similar to a spark issuing out of a mass of fire; and (ii) that the self is similar to space within an earthen jar. Śaṅkara gives preference to the second view and describes it as eternal, unchanging, undecaying, immaculate.[35] It is not gross, not eyes, not life-force, not mind, not doer, it is just pure intelligence.[36] It pervades the whole body though it is infinitesmally small. At death it passes out of the eyes, or skull or some other portion of the body.

The living self limited by the adjuncts of the body of an individual, his sense-organs, mind, intelligence and notion of I-ness becomes an empirical self, perceiving pleasant and unpleasant feelings. It is unaware of its true nature and is in the grip of nescience; its power and knowledge become limited and it becomes an agent, an enjoyer of acts, by which it accumulates merits and demerits.

The Buddhists contend that in the ultimate analysis of the constituents of a being there is no trace of a permanent soul, which according to the Vedāntists, is unconstituted *(asaṃskṛta)*. They argue that the unconstituted, immaculate and permanent substance has nothing to do with the constituted *(saṃskṛta)*, and logically also, two objects, having opposite characteristics, can never exist together as light and darkness. Hence they uphold the doctrine of the non-existence of a real self. They point out that the five constituents forming a being (i.e. *upādāna-skandhas)* as distinguished from the mass of elements *(skandharāśi)* give rise to the wrong notion of I-ness or *satkāyadṛṣṭi*. They do not also accept the position taken by the Sammitīya Buddhists that the five constituents on combination produce a sixth constituent called *Pudgala* which lasts as long as the *upādāna-skandhas* continue. They deny the existence of empirical self of the Vedantists or of *Pudgala* of the Sammitīyas. Such denial leads to the question as to how the Buddhists explain the transference of *karmaic* effects of an individual from one existence to another.

The Vedāntists hold the view that the empirical self serves as the transmitter of *karmaic* effects. It continues after the death of a living being and transmigrates like a caterpillar from one existence to another. It does not give up the old body till it obtains a foothold in another body.[37] In his comments on *Brahmasūtra* (III. 1.1) Śaṅkara states that the living being at the time of his death dreams of his future existence and grows an attachment for it, and so the empirical self extends its creative effort; it is a continuation or extension *(dīrghikaraṇa)* and not exactly similar to the movement of a caterpillar. The empirical self carries with it the subtle body *(sūkṣma-śarīra=liṅga-deha)* composed of three vestures or sheaths *(koṣa)*[38] This subtle body carries with it all the merits and demerits accumulated in past existences as also nescience *(avidyā)* along with the impressions left by past experiences *(pūrvaprajñā janmāntarīya saṃskārāḥ),* leaving behind all material elements, gross or subtle. This subtle body remains along with the empirical self till the attainment of liberation.

Regarding the transference of *karmaic* effects, the Buddhist view is wholly different from that of the Vedānta. The Buddhists take their stand on their doctrine of momentariness, and explain that the mental and material constituents *(nāmarūpa)* of a being undergo change, in other words, birth and death, cessation and re-appearance, decay and origination, occur at every moment, which has not even an infinitesmal duration. These are as dynamic as nature and are never static even for a moment. Hence the *karmaic* effects are transmitted every moment. At the time of death the *nāmarūpa* obtains the subtlest form modified by the impressions of past life and develops a will for re-existence *(pratisandhi-vijñāna)* which in turn gives rise in the next existence to the nascent mental state *(bhavaṅga-citta)* similar to the Yogācāra conception of *ālayavijñāna* or consciousness-receptacle. This *bhavaṅgacitta* comes out of the womb or the egg-shell and develops the nascent sense-organs. Hence, according to the Buddhists, there is rebirth and not transmigration and the reborn *nāmarūpa* carries with them all the *karmaic* effects of past life.

They explain the continuity of a constituted being and its *karmaic* effects as a ceaseless flux like fire passing over dry grass in a field. In the day to day life of an individual, this ceaseless change is perceptible. An individual never remains identically the same from day to day i.e. from moment to moment. In this unending flux death and rebirth are mere sequences. The flux ceases only when the individual realises the Truth and arrests the flow of *karmaic* effects or mental dispositions *(saṃskāra)*.

The Mahāyānists do not admit the existence of the phenomenal world of beings and objects, which according to the Yogācāra school, is the mental creation of a being out of desires conserved in a latent form from time immemorial *(anādikālavāsanā)*. It is a conceptual world *(prapañca)* of its own — a world which has no more existence than objects seen in a dream[39]. Hence the Yogācārins do not speculate about *nāmarūpa* or their momentariness. The Mādhyamikas go a step further and do not even admit that the phenomenal world is an extension of.mind. They simply state that the origin, continuity and. decay of the phenomenal world has no more existence than delusion, dream or city of Gandharvas[40], or the two Moons seen by jaundiced eyes.

The Buddhists regard that the Vedāntic conception of *Jīvātman* stands in the way of the removal of the notion of I-ness *(ahaṅkāra)* which is the only means for attaining liberation.

The Reality or the Highest Truth : The conception of *Brahman* or the Absolute varies slightly in the different Upaniṣads. Śaṅkara has tried to reconcile them to propound his own *Advayavāda* or Monism. On the basis of statements mainly of the *Chāndogya Upaniṣad,* he says that Brahman is ever existent and is identical with the universe. It is both infinitely large and infimtesmally small. It is one, real, eternal, non-dual and attributeless. In the *Bṛhadāraṇyaka-upaniṣad* (II. 3. 1.)[41] there are references to the two aspects of Brahman, as *Parabrahma* and *Aparabrahma*. The former represents the Brahman which is pure, subtle, immortal, undefined, attributeless (*nirupadhi),* transcendent, beyond description with the limited vocabularies of the world. The latter represents Brahman as superimposed by Nescience *(Ajñāna)* when it appears as gross, limited, mortal, determinate, and possessed of certain attributes *(sopadhi)*. These two aspects are expressed in the words "*tattvam asi*" (Thou art that)[42] and compared to a snake and its coils, the snake being the Real self and the coil the individuated self. A simpler simile is unlimited space limited within a jar, the former being *Parabrahma* and the latter *Aparabrahma*. In the *Bṛhadāraṇyaka, Chāndogya* and *Taittirīya Upaniṣads,* Brahman is described as the supreme bliss *(paramānanda)* and pure intelligence *(vijñana)*. In the *Māṇḍukyakārikā* Brahman is said to be indeterminate, inexpressible, eternally refulgent and trans-empirical, while in the *Brahmasūtra* (III. 2.22) it is stated that Brahman can only be referred to by negations of known concepts *(neti neti)*. The conceptions about Brahman in the various texts may be summed up thus:

(i) *Brahman* is non-dual, inexpressible, trans-empirical and can be spoken of by negative concepts only; (ii) *Brahman* is immanent in the universe, and (iii) *Brahman* exists, it is pure intelligence and supreme bliss *(sat-cit-ānanda)* and (iv) Brahman may become limited, gross and endowed with attributes from the conventional but not from the highest standpoint.

The Monistic philosophy of Vedānta finds a better exposition in the Buddhist, specially Mahāyānic texts, in which the Truth is repeatedly referred to as non-dual and non-divisible *(advayam advaidhīkāram)*. In the Pāli texts Nirvāṇa is described by negatives only as not born, not diseased, not dying, not happiness, not unhappiness and so forth. It is only in popular phraseology we come across its positive account as tranquil, i. e., undisturbed by origin and decay *(śāntam),* happy *(sukham)* and deathless *(amṛtapadam)*. The Mahāyānists are emphatic in their statements that the Reality is attributeless *(sūnyatā),* oneness and sameness *(tathatā),* the end of phenomenal existences *(bhūtakoṭī),* the sum-total of all existences *(dharmadhātu)*. It is ever existent, urionginated and undecaying, and as such it is unchangeable and infinite and can in no circumstances become limited. Thus, it is apparent that the Buddhists were more accurate than the Vedāntists in their exposition of the Monistic philosophy.

The first fundamental difference between Vedānta and Buddhism regarding the highest Truth is the former's attempt to offer a positive description of the Reality as existent *(sat)*, pure consciousness (*cit*) and supreme bliss *(ānanda)*. Excepting the attribute '*sat*' and that also used very discreetly, the other attributes are not acceptable to the Buddhists, who contend that any positive description of the transcendental implies its opposites viz., non-existence, non-consciousness and non-bliss and that any characterization of the Reality is false representation *(prapañca)*. The only approach to the highest Reality, they state, is possible by negation alone. The Mādhyamikas confine themselves therefore to the description of *nirvāṇa* in pure negative terms thus : Nirvāṇa is that which is neither to be eschewed nor to be obtained; which is neither eternal nor subject to extinction; which is beyond origin and decay.[43] But they do not say that Nirvāṇa or Buddha or Tathāgata is non-existent. They agree with the Vedāntists in holding that the Absolute is not non-existent. They hold that those who attempt to characterize the inexpressible undecaying one get bewildered by characterization and do not visualise the Tathagata.[44]

The second fundamental difference between Vedānta and Buddhism lies in the Vedantic conception of the Absolute becoming limited temporarily although superficially. The Buddhists are unrelenting in their arguments that the Real must remain the Real for ever and suffer no change even superficially and temporarily because it can no longer be called Absolute. They have used the terms unreal or conventional *(samvṛti)* and real or absolute *(paramārtha)* but they regard the former as non-existent as objects seen in a dream. They hold that there is no *via media* between the two, hence, they do not accept the conception of *Aparabrahma*. Even the temporary and superficial association of two with opposite characteristics, viz., purity and impurity, unlimitedness and limitedness, they state, is as illogical as the co-existence of blackness and whiteness, of hotness and coldness.

It is noteworthy that the Vedāntic conception of the identity of Brahman with the universe[45] is fully endorsed by the Mādhyamikas who state that there is not the slightest difference between *Nirvāṇa* and the phenomenal world *(Saṃsāra)*[46].

The Yogācārins hold a view midway between the Mādhyamikas and the Vedāntists in that they qualify the Absolute as not only existent *(sat)* but also as pure mind or consciousness *(vijñānamātra)*. They have also introduced the conception of *Tathāgatagarbha* which bears comparison with the Vedāntic conception of *Jivātman*. In the *Laṅkāvatāra* (p. 77) it is stated that the Teacher spoke of the *Tathāgatagarbha,* which is pure and refulgent by inherent nature, dwells in every living being, encased in sense-organs and other constituents forming a being. It is like an invaluable jewel wrapped in a dirty cloth. It is ever existent, unchanging, tranquil and eternal. In the text, care however has been taken to point out that their conception of *Tathāgatagarbha* is not identical with the heretical doctrine of the soul-theorists, as they do not admit the existence of the Highest Soul *(Paramātman)*.

N. Dutt

FOOTNOTES

1. See *Early Monastic Buddhism,* vol. I.
2. Cf. *Abhidharmakośa,* IX, 4-5 :

   असत्त्वाद्भगवान् जीवं तत्त्वान्यत्वेन नावदत्।
   नास्तीत्यपि च नावोचन् माभूत प्राज्ञप्तिकोप्यसन्।।
   यत्र हि स्कन्धसन्ताने शुभाशुभफलास्तिता।
   जीवाख्या तत्र सा न स्याज्जीव नास्तित्वदेशनात्।।
   प्रज्ञप्तिमात्रं स्कन्धेजु जीव इत्यपि नावदत्।
   अभव्यः शून्यतां बोद्ध तदानीं तादृशो जनः।।
3. T. R. V. Murti writes in his *Central Philosophy of Buddhism, p.*

20 "The Upaniṣads and Buddhism belong to the same spiritual genus, they differ as species, and the differentia are the acceptance or rejection of the *ātman* (permanent substance). Cf. V. Bhattacharya, *Basic Conception of Buddhism,* pp. 70-75.

4. *Sumaṅgalavilāsinī,* pp. 161-4.
5. *Bhagavatisūtra,* XV, 550; *Uttarādhyayana,* xxiv.
6. Bashatn, *History & Doctrines of the Ājīvikas,* pp. 243ff.
7. *Kaṭha.* I, 3. 10-11; *Śvetāśvatara,* V, 7.8.12; IV, 5.1.3.
8. *Buddhacarita,* Ch. XII.
9. *Visuddhimagga,* p. 499; *Mādhyamikavṛtti,* p. 475 n.
10. Cf, Gauḍapāda: Ā*gamaśāstra,* III. 43: दु:खं सर्वमनुस्मृत्य कामभोगान् निवर्तयेत्।
11. Cf. *Brahmasūtra,* II. 2, 20: उत्तरोत्पादे च पूर्व निरोधात्।
12. Cf. Bertrand Russell, *Mysticism and Logic,* p. 185: Cause cannot have a duration...the cause after existing placidly for some time should suddenly explode into effect...is illogical, Again, cause cannot be static, no such cause is to be found in nature.
13. There is the other popular exposition that Buddha prescribed a middle path of spiritual culture, which discarded a life of ease as also a life of extreme asceticism. The life of a monk, as chalked out by his Teacher, was one approved by him as a general rule, exception however being made in the case of those who were bent upon asceticism and took up the *Dhūtaṅga* practices.
14. *Laṅkāvatāra,* p. 83 : भविष्यत्हेतु ; सम्बन्धहेतु ; लक्षणहेतु ; कारणहेतु ; व्यञ्जनहेतु; उपेक्षाहेतु।
15. *Madhyamakakārikā,* I, 2.
16. *Madhyamakārikā,* I, 7; XXI. 13; XXIII. 20:
न स्वतो नापि परतो न द्वाभ्यां नाप्यहेतुत:
उत्पन्ना जातु विद्यन्ते भावा: कचन केचन
cf. *Gauḍapāda*, IV. 22 : खतो वा परतो वापि न कञ्चिद्वस्तु जायते।
सदसत् सदसद् वापि न किञ्चिद्वस्तु जायते।।
17. *Lahkāvatāra,* p. 105-6.
18. *Brahmasūtra,* II. 3.9 : असम्भवस्तु सतोऽनुपपत्ते:।
19. य: प्रतीत्यसमुत्पादं पष्ठयति स धर्मं पष्ठयति। यो धर्मं पष्ठयति स बुद्धं पष्ठयति। See *Aspects of Mahāyāna Buddhism,* p. 51.
20. *Madbyamakakārikā,* VII, 16 : प्रतीत्य यद्यद्भवति तत्तत् शान्तं स्वभावत:।
21 *ibid.* सकलदष्ठाबलजननीं प्रतीत्यसमुत्पादमातरम्।
22. Cf. *Laṅkāvatāra,* p. 103.

23. *Abhidharmakośa,* III, 29.
24. See *Mādhyamikavṛtti,* p. 452 quoting *Pratītyasamutpādasūtra.*
25. भ्रान्तिरार्याशमपि ख्यायतेऽविपर्यासतः । Cf. *Laṅkāvatāra,* p. 298.
26. *Laṅkāvatāra,* p. 295:
सर्वप्रपञ्चोपष्ठामात् भ्रान्तो नाभिप्रवर्तते।
प्रज्ञा यावद् विकल्पन्ते भ्रान्तिस्तावत् प्रवर्तते।।
27. *Kośa,* III, 24.
28. *Nettippakaraṇa,* 13; *Aṅguttara,* V, p. 2.62 : कम्मनिदानानि-लोभदोसमोह।
29. III, p. 65.
30. *Suttanipāta,* 654: कम्मण वत्तति लोको कम्मणा वत्तति पजा। *Majjhima,* III, p. 203 ; *Aṅguttara,* III, pp. 72, 186 ; V, pp. 81, 288 : कमस्मका सत्ता कम्मदायादा कम्मयोनी कम्मबन्धु ख्र यं कम्मं करोन्ति कल्याणं वा पापकं वा तसस दायादा भवन्ति।
31. *Suttanipāta,* 653: कस्सको कम्मणा हेति सिप्पिको होति कम्मणा-राजापि होति कम्मणा।
32. Edited by S. Lévi, Paris, 1942.
33. *Saṃyutta,* I, p. 134 : सब्बकम्मक्खयं पत्तो विमुत्तो उपधिसंखये। Cf. *Aṅguttara,* V.p. 262.
34. *Brabmasūtra,* III. 1. 8.
35. नित्यशुद्धबुद्धमुक्तसत्यस्वभावं प्रत्यकचैतन्यमेवात्मतत्त्वमिति।
36. प्रत्यगस्थूलों अचक्षुरप्राणः अमना अकर्ता चैतन्यं चिन्मात्रं सत्। नित्यचैतन्योऽयमात्मा।
37. *Bṛhadāraṇyaka,* IV, 4. 3.
38. (i) *Vijñānamaya* = consciousness as an active agent,
(ii) *Manomaya*=*will* as instrumental,
(iii) *Prāṇamaya* = vital breath or physical organism as energy.
39. *Laṅkāvatāra,* p. 274 :
मायास्वप्ननिभाभावगन्धर्वनगरोपमाः।
मरीच्युदकचन्द्राभाः सविकल्पां विभावयेत्।।
cf. *Gauḍapāda,* 31 :
स्वप्नमाये यथा दृष्टे गन्धर्वनगरं यथा।
तथा विश्वं इदं सृष्टं वेदान्तेजु विचक्षणैः।।
40. *Madhyamakakārikā,* VII, 34
यथा माया तथा स्वप्नो गन्धर्वनगरं यथा।
तथोत्पादस्तथा स्थानं तथा भङ्ग उदाहृतम्।।
41. द्वे वाव ब्रह्मणो-रूपे मूर्त चैवामूर्तं च, मर्त्यं चामष्टतं च, स्थितं चच्च, सच्च तच्च।
42. *Chāndogya,* VI. 8. 7,

43. *Madhyamakakārikā,* XXV. 3 :
अप्रहीणमसंप्राप्तमनुच्छिन्नमशाश्वतम्।
अनिरूद्धमनुत्पन्नमेतन्निर्वाणमुच्यते।।
cf. *Gauḍapada.* 32 :
न निरोधो न चात्पत्तिर्ण बद्धो न च बाधकः।
न मुमुक्षुर्णवैमुक्तक इत्येषा परमार्थता।।
44. *Madhyamakakārikā,* XXII. 15:
प्रपञ्चयन्ति ये बुद्धं प्रपञ्चातीतमव्ययम्।
ते प्रपञ्चाहताः सर्वे न पष्ठयन्ति तथागतम्।।
45. *Chāndogya,* III. 14. 1 : सर्वं खल्विदं ब्रह्म।
46. *Madhyamakakārikā,* XXV. 19.
न संसारस्य निर्वाणात्किं चिदस्ति विशेषणम्।
न निर्वाणस्य संसारात्किं चिदस्ति विशेषणम्।।

14
DUḤKHA-SATYA

The first Noble Truth of Buddhism, *Dukkhaṃ ariyas-accaṃ,* is generally translated by almost all scholars as "The Noble Truth of Suffering", and it is interpreted to mean that life according to Buddhism is nothing but suffering and pain. This translation and interpretation are highly unsatisfactory and misleading. It is because of this narrow translation and interpretation that many people are misguided to regard Buddhism as pessimistic. First of all, Buddhism is neither pessimistic nor optimistic. It takes a realistic view of life and of the world. It looks at things objectively. It does not falsely lull you to live in a fool's paradise, nor does it frighten and agonize you with all kinds of ideas of imaginary fears and sins. It tells you exactly and objectively *(yathābhūtaṃ)* what you are and what the world is, and shows you the right way to perfect freedom, peace, tranquility and happiness.

It is true that the Pali word *dukkha* or Sanskrit *duḥkha* in ordinary usage means "suffering", "pain" or "misery" as opposed to the word *sukha,* meaning "happiness", "comfort" or "ease". But the term *dukkha* as the first Noble Truth has a philosophical meaning and connotes an enormously wider sense. It is admitted that the term *dukkha* in the first Noble Truth contains the ordinary meaning of "suffering" or "pain", but in addition to that it includes also deeper ideas such as "imperfection", "impermanence", "emptiness", "unsubsta-ntiality", "conflict". It is difficult therefore to find one word to embrace the whole conception of the term *dukkha* as the first Noble Truth, and so it is better to leave it untranslated than to give an incomplete and wrong idea by conveniently rendering it as "suffering" or "pain".

Buddhism does not deny happiness in Life. On the contrary it admits different forms of happiness, both material and spiritual, for laymen as well as for monks. But all that is included in the dukkha. Even the very pure states of *dhyāna* attained by the practice of higher meditation, which are free even from a shadow of suffering or pain in the accepted sense of those words and which may be described as unmixed happiness, and also the state of *dhyāna* which is free from sensations both pleasant *(sukha)* and unpleasant *(dukkha)* and which is only pure equanimity and awareness—even these extremely high, pure spiritual states are included in the *dukkha.* Not because they are suffering or pain, but because they too are *saṅkhārā,* conditioned, subject to change, impermanent and unsubstantial.

The conception of the dukkha as the first Noble Truth may be viewed from three aspects: (1) dukkha as ordinary suffering *(dukkha-dukkha),* (2) dukkha as change *(vipariṇāma-dukkha)* and (3) dukkha as condioned state *(saṅkhāra-dukkha).*[1]

All kinds of suffering in life like birth, old age, sickness, death, union with unpleasant conditions, separation from beloved ones and agreeable conditions, not getting what one desires, grief, lamentation, distress—all such forms of physical and mental suffering, which are universally accepted as suffering and pain, are included in the dukkha as ordinary suffering *(dukkha-dukkha).*

A happy feeling, a happy condition in our life is not permanent, not everlasting. It changes sooner or later. When it changes it produces an unhappy feeling, an unhappy condition. This vicissitude is included in the dukkha as change *(vipariṇāma-dukkha).*

These two forms of dukkha, namely *dukkha-dukkha* and

vipariṇāma-dukkha, may be included in the first Noble Truth according to the conventional *(saṃvṛti)* sense.

But the third form of dukkha, i.e. dukkha as a conditioned state *(saṅkhāra-dukkha),* is dukkha in the ultimate sense *(paramārtha),* and calls for a little analytical explanation of what we consider as "being", as "individual" or as "I". According to Buddhist philosophy what we call a "being", "individual" or "I" is only a combination of everchanging physical and mental energies which may be divided into five aggregates *(pañcakkhandhā).* The Buddha says: "In short, these five aggregates of attachment are dukkha" *(saṅkhittena pañcupādānakkhandhā dukkhā).* Here it should be clearly understood that the dukkha and the five aggregates are not two different things; the five aggregates themseleves are the *dukkha.* We will understand this point better when we get an idea about the five aggregates.

Now what are these five aggregates which constitute the so-called being?

The first is the aggregate of matter *(rūpakkhandha).* In this term "the aggregate of matter" are included the four great elements *(cattāri mahābhtūtāni,* namely, the elements of solidity, fluidity, energy and motion, and their derivatives *(upādāya-rūpa).* In the "derivatives of four great elements" are included our five material sense organs, i.e. the faculties of eye, ear, nose, tongue and body and their corresponding objects in the external world, i.e. visible form, sound, odour, taste and tangible things and also some ideas or thoughts which are objects of mind. Thus the whole sphere of matter, both internal and external, is included in the aggregate of matter.

The second is the aggregate of sensations *(vedanā-kkhandha).* In this group are included all our sensations, pleasant or unpleasant or neither pleasant nor unpleasant, experienced through the contact of our sense organs with the external world. That is to say, the sensations experienced through the contact of the eye with visible forms, ear with sounds, nose with odour, tongue with taste, body with tangible objects and mind (which is the sixth faculty in Buddhist philosophy) with mind-objects or thoughts or ideas. All our physical and mental sensations are included in this group.

The third is the aggregate of perceptions (*saññākkhandha*). Like the sensations, perceptions also are produced through the contact of our sense faculties with the external world.

The fourth is the aggregate of mental formations *(saṅkhārakkhandha)*. In this group are included all volitional mental activities, both good and bad, which produce karmic effects, such as attention *(manasikāra),* will *(chanda),* determi-nation *(adhimokkha),* confidence *(saddhā),* concentration *(samādhi),* intelligence or wisdom *(paññā),* energy *(viriya),* desire *(rāga,),* repugnance or hate *(paṭigha),* conceit *(māna),* idea of self *(sakkāya-diṭṭhi)* etc. There are 52 such mental activities which constitute the aggregate of mental formations.

The fifth is the aggregate of consciousness *(viññāṇakkhandha)*. Consciousness is a reaction or a response which has one of the six sense faculties (eye, ear, nose, tongue, body and mind) as its basis and an external phenomenon as its object. E.g. the visual consciousness has the eye as its basis and a visible form as its object. So is the consciousness connected with other faculties.

Very briefly these are the five aggregates. What we call "being" or "individual" or "I" is only a name or a label given to the combination of these five groups. They are all impermanent. They are in a state of flux of momentary arising and disappearing. One thing disappears conditioning the appearance of the next in a series of cause and effect. There is no substantiality in them. There is nothing behind them that can be called a permanent, unchanging self *(ātman),* individuality or any thing that can be called "I", apart from these five aggregates. Everyone will agree that neither matter, nor sensation, nor preception, nor any one of those mental activities, nor consciousness can really be called "I". But when these five physical and mental aggregates, which are inter-dependent, are working together in combination as a physio-psychological machine we get the idea of "I". But this is only an imaginary idea which is nothing but one of those 52 mental formations of the fourth aggregate, which we have just men-tioned. These five aggregates together, which we popularly call a being, are the *dukkha* itself *(saṅkhāra-dukkha)*. There is no other "being" or "I" standing behind these five aggregates who experiences the *dukkha*. There is no unmoving mover behind the movement. It is only movement. In other words, there is no thinker behind the thought. Thought itself is the thinker. If you remove the thought there is no thinker. Here one cannot fail to notice how this Buddhist view is diametrically opposed to the conception of Cartesian cogito.

This is the Noble Truth of Dukkha. This does not at all make the life of a Buddhist melancholy or sorrowful, as some people wrongly imagined. On the contrary, a true Buddhist is the happiest in the world. He has no fears or anxieties. He is always calm and serene, and cannot be upset or dismayed by changes or calamities, because he sees and takes things as they are. The Buddha was never melancholy or gloomy. He was described by his contemporaries as "eversmiling" *(mihita-pubbangama)*. In Buddhist paintings and sculptures the Buddha is always represented with a face happy, contented and serene. Never a trace of suffering or agony is to be seen. There are two ancient Budhhist texts called the *Thera-gāthā* and the *Therīgāthā* which are full of happy and joyful utterances by the Buddha's disciples, both male and female, who found peace and happiness in his teaching. The king of Kosala once told the Buddha that unlike many a disciple of other religious systems who looked haggard, coarse, pale, emaciated and unpre-possessing, the disciples of the Buddha were "joyful and elated *(haṭṭhapahaṭṭha)*, jubilant and exultant *(udaggudagga)*, enjo-ying the religious life *(abhiratarūpa)*, with senses pleased *(pīṇitindriya)*, free from anxiety *(appossukka)*, serene *(pann-aloma)*, peaceful *(paradavutta)* and living with a gazelle's mind *(migabhūtena cetasā)*" i.e. light hearted. The king added that he believed that this healthy disposition was due to the fact that "these venerable ones had certainly realized the great and full significance of the Blessed one's teaching."[2] Buddhism is quite opposed to melancholic, sorrowful and gloomy attitude of mind which is considered a hindrance to the realization of Truth. On the other hand, it is interesting to remember that joy *(pīti)* is one of the seven essential qualities to be cultivated for the realization of Nibbāna *(Bojjhanga)*.

W. Rahula

FOOTNOTES

1. *Visuddhimagga* (PTS), p. 499; *Abhidharma-samuccaya,* pp. 36. 38 (ed. Pradhan, Santiniketan, 1950).
2. *Majjhima-nikāya* II (PT.S). p. 121

15

NIRODHA-SATYA

In the Abhidharma all objects (dharma) are classified under two heads, saṁskṛta (constituted) and asaṁskṛta (unconstituted). Objects as are caused or constituted are called 'saṁskṛta' and those which are not caused or constituted, that is to say, which are eternal, are called 'asaṁskṛta'. Asaṁskṛta objects are of three types,— 'ākāśa'; 'pratisaṁkhyā-nirodha' and 'apratisaṁkhyā-nirodha'. In the present paper we confine ourselves to the study of 'nirodha'. In this connection it should be borne in mind that according to the Sautrāntika view, asaṁskṛta objects are denied physical and intellectual existence. The Sautrāntika thinks that as all objects are fluxional in character, their physical or intellectual existence is a contradiction in term. It is for this reason that the Sautrāntika has not recognised 'nirodha' as physically or intellectually existing (dravyasat) though its existence (as prajñaptisat) is acknowledged in the Śāstras. TheVātsīputrāyas state that 'nirvāṇa' alone is asaṁskṛta, and therefore they do not also admit its dravyasattā. The Yogācāra school does not recognise the dravyasattā of 'nirodha' apart from consciousness. The Mādhyamikas also cannot posit 'nirodha' as physically existing. It seems therefore that it is only in the opinion of the Vaibhāṣika that 'nirodha' possesses dravyasattā, and it will be our endeavour in this article to discuss 'nirodha' as described by the Vaibhāṣika.[1]

Nirodha is classified under three heads, viz., 'Pratisaṁkhyanirodha', 'Apratisaṁkhyā-nirodha' and 'Anityatānirodha'. It is worthy of notice that in the original Abhidharmakośa we come across two types of nirodha,—Pratisaṁkhyānirodha and Apratisaṁkhyā-nirodha. But the Anityatānirodha also has been specifically mentioned in the Sphuṭarthā.

It is to be seen that the two terms, 'nirodha' and 'nirodha-satya' have not been used as synonyms. Because the term 'nirodha' has been used to refer to three types of 'nirodha', while the term 'nirodhai 'Satya' denotes only pratisaṁkhyānirodha and apratisaṁkhyā-nirodha. It is for this reason that when the Abbidharmakośa describes 'nirodhasatya' as one of the four 'Ārya-satyas', it means pratisaṁkhyānirodha and apratisaṁkhyānirodha only and does not take notice of anityatānirodha.

The term 'nirodha' is generally used to denote negation. The expression 'nirodha of a jar' means the negation or the destruction of a jar. Similarly the sentence 'the current of the stream has been niruddha (stopped)' conveys that the stream which had been flowing on from before has ceased, that is to say, the current is no more and has been destroyed. But in the present article, where we propose to review the nirodha-satya from the Vaibhāṣika point of view, it cannot be maintained that the term conveys the sense of negation, inasmuch as according to the Vaibhāṣika, negation is a figment of imagination like the rabbit's horn. Nirodha has been described in Buddha-vacana as an Ārya-satya. Further the Vaibhāṣika includes pratisaakhyānirodha and apratisaṁkhyānirodha in the list of asaṁskṛta objects. And, as such they are recognised as eternal entities. Hence, pratisaṁkhyānirodha and apratisaṁkhyānirodha are not, in the opinion of the Vaibhāṣika, of the nature of negation.

Let us now analyse the derivative meaning of the term 'nirodha'. The suffix to imply 'bhāva' has not been attached, but it conveys the meaning of the agent (kartṛ). As such the derivative meaning of the word 'nirodha' is, that which retards or shuts out. It is for this reason Yaśomitra has described 'visaṁyoga' or pratisaṁkhyānirodha as 'a closed door, which shuts out the different kleśas'. So the Vaibhāṣika conceives of the pratisaṁkhyānirodha and apratisarhkhyanirodha as different kinds of 'invincible walls' which are eternal entities. The person striving for Nirvāṇa does not create pratisarhkhyanirodha and apratisaṁkhyānirodha, but he collects those ever-existing entities for his own purpose i.e., for the attainment of Nirvāṇa.

Pratisaṁkhyānirodha

The Vaibhāṣika texts have mentioned only two varieties of nirodha-satya, viz., pratisaṁkhyānirodha and apratisaṁkhyānirodha. The term pratisaṁkhyānirodha may be explained as nirodha, which an individual secures by means of pratisaṁkhyā. It is with the help of the Ānantarya-mārga' (the 16th kṣaṇa of the Nirvedhabhāgiya) the individual drives out the kleśas, and with the help of the 'Vimukti-mārga' (the first fifteen kṣaṇas of the Nirvedhabhāgiya) the door of the visaṁyoga or pratisaṁkhyānirodha is shut against these different kleśas. It is therefore to be understood that the 'nirodha' which the individual attains through the pursuit of vimuktimārga is called pratisaṁkhyānirodha.

But it should be pointed out that the aforesaid meaning of pratisaṁkhyānirodha cannot be endorsed in view of the fact that the Vaibhāṣika texts have laid it down that certain apratisaṁkhyānirodhas too may be secured with the help of pratisaṁkhyā or vimuktimārga. It is therefore quite in the fitness of things that Vasubandhu has sought to describe or define it in a different way. In his opinion pratisaṁkhyānirodha is an object which retards contact. The prefix 'vi' in the term visamyoga suggests 'opposition',and as such the term (visaṁyoga) means 'that which opposes or retards contact'.

It should be mentioned here that though pratisaṁkhyānirodha means 'what retards contact',still it does not set forth the full connotation of the term. From a critical study of Yaśomitra's Sphūṭārthā it appears that pratisaṁkhyā-nirodha means those objects which invariably oppose the attainment of contact with 'sāsrava' objects. The individual who is fortunate enough to realise pratisaṁkhyānirodha will no more come in contact with sāsrava objects. As the nirodha is obtained through pratisaṁkhyā it is called pratisaṁkhyānirodha. The 'asravas',such as kleśas and others cannot reside in the asaṁskṛta objects as ether and the like, and as such asaṁskṛta objects are not sāsravas. Even some saṁskṛta objects, such as mārga-satya and others cannot be the locus of the āsravas. So mārgasatya and such others are not sāsrava. It is to be seen that the nirodha of those sāmskṛta objects, whether sāsrava or anāsrava, which may have been born but never come to life (anutpatti-dharmā), is not called pratisaṁkhyānirodha in the Abhidharma text. So the object that invariably retards the attainment of contact with the sāsrava objects that are past, born and are in the embryo form, is called the pratisaṁkhyānirodha.

It is to be carefully noticed that 'saṁyoga' and 'prāpti' are not synonymous, according to the Vaibhāṣika text. Both 'sattvākhya' and 'asattvākhya' objects may have saṁyoga, but according to the Vaibhāṣikas, prāpti has been admitted in the case of "attvākhya objects only. Those that relate to objects endowed with life, are called sattvākhya. The Vaibhāṣika admits 'prāpti' in the case of pratisaṁkhyānirodha, though the latter is not a sattvākhya object. To be precise, what waxes with the waxing of the body and wanes with the waning of the body is called sattvākhya. But pratisaṁkhyānirodha is an eternal entity and cannot be looked upon as a sattvākhya object, still its prāpti has been admitted by the Vaibhāṣikas.

It has been stated above that pratisaṁkhyānirodha is an object which invariably retards the attainment of contact with sāsrava objects. Now, a question may be raised here, if it were said that pratisanhkhyanirodha is the object invariably retarding the contact with sāsrava objects, and not the attainment of contact with them as stated in the description, the description of the pratisaṁkhyānirodha could have been quite accurate and precise. In answer to this, it may be pointed out that the pratisaṁkhyānirodha cannot retard the contact with the sāsrava objects in general, but it can only oppose the attainment of contact with the sāsrava objects. The raison d'etre is this that when the individual with the help of the 'ānantarya-mārga' drives out the kleśas, and the pratisaṁkhyānirodha shuts the door against them, the contact of kleśas with the individual ceases; but that does not mean that the kleśas cannot have any contact whatsoever with any other things outside the individual. It comes to this therefore, that if pratisaṁkhyānirodha was described only as the object retarding the contact with sāsrava objects, and not as the object retarding the attainment of contact with the sāsrava objects, the description would not have been correct and adequate.

Pratisaṁkhyānirodha has no 'sabhāgahetu', because 'sabhā-gahetu' is possible only for the saṁskṛta objects. According to the Vaibhāṣikas, the pratisaṁkhyānirodha has been included in the list of asaṁskṛta objects. So it is an eternal entity. Pratisaṁkhyānirodha can neither be described as past nor as 'anutpattidharma',but it lives in the present. It is for this reason that the pratisaṁkhyānirodha cannot be retarded by anything else. It should be stated here that pratisaṁkhyānirodha does not also become the sabhāgahetu of any other object. Apratisaṁkhyānirodha and anityatanirodha are called nirodhas, but there is no similarity between them and the pratisaṁkhyā-nirodha. So pratisaṁkhyānirodha is decribed as 'a-sabhā-ga',i.e., having no similarity with others, and it is an eternal entity. Pratisaṁkhyā-nirodha is not negation and as such it has no negatum (pratiyogi object).

Vasubandhu opines that pratisaṁkhyānirodhas are innumerable; and, those are not uniform either. As otherwise, on the attainment of pratisaṁkhyānirodha as a result of the knowledge of one of the Āryasatyas, such as, 'dharma-jñāna with duḥkha as its content',the pursuit of other kinds of Āryasatyas, such as, 'dharma-jñāna relating to samudaya' etc., would become useless. And, in view of the fact that pratisaṁkhyānirodha obstructs the way, the Ānantaryamārga can no longer drive out the kleśas. But if we admit the plurality of pratisaṁkhyānirodha such anomalies would be obviated. For, the particular pratisaṁkhyānirodha, which is obtained by 'dharmajñāna relating to duḥkha',does not obstruct the way through which kleśas are driven by 'dharmajñāna-kṣānti' relating to samudaya-satya and so on.

Apratisaṁkhyā-nirodha

Prima facie apratisaṁkhyānirodha is that which is 'not pratisaṁkhyānirodha'.But this interpretation is not accurate, as anityatānirodha is also 'not pratisaṁkhyānirodha'. Vasubandhu defines apratisaṁkhyānirodha as that form of nirodha which permanently obstructs the creation of objects (vastu), thereby distinguishing it from anityatānirodha. The latter does not obstruct the creation of objects, but it obstructs the existence of the created objects (utpanna-vastu). It is for this reason the Buddhist philosophers believe in the transitoriness or fluxional character of all created objects.

Apratisaṁkhyānirodha cannot also be explained as the nirodha which is 'not attainable by means of pratisaṁkhyā or vimukti-mārga',as in that case also it becomes applicable to anityatānirodha. Moreover such an explanation often proves to be inadequate. As for example, according to the Vaibhāṣikas, a 'srotāpanna' person, (one who is in the stream leading to Nirvāṇa) has no more to suffer from 'apāya-gati' (i. e., he is not to be reborn in the preta or tiryak-yoni). The apratisaṁkhyānirodha form of barrier against his future 'apāyagati' has thus been obtained by means of pratisaṁkhyā. This nirodha cannot be pratisaṁkhyānirodha as it obstructs apāya-gati, which is anutpattidharmā, whereas the function of pratisaṁkhyānirodha is to retard the sāsrava objects, past, born or yet to be born (utpatttdharmā).

It has also been suggested that apratisaṁkhyānirodha is obtainable by a form of 'pratyayavaikalya' (absence of the totality of creative elements), which is 'a-pratisaṁkhyā' (not pratisaṁkhyā). In this definition pratyayavaikalya has been equated with apratisaṁkhyā, and thus it indicates the process of attainment of apratisaṁkhyānirodha. But, according to the Vaibhāṣ ikas, absence or abhāva being illusory (alīka), absence of the totality of creative elements (pratyayavaikalya) can hardly be accepted as the means of attainment of apratisaṁkhyā-nirodha.

Vasubandhu's definition of apratisaṁkhyānirodha (nirodha which permanently obstructs the origin of dharma or objects) helps us to distinguish it from anityatānirodha and also from pratisaṁkhyānirodha. The former obstructs the existence of constituted objects and not their origin, while the latter prevents the attainment of contact with sāsrava objects and not their existence or origin.

According to the Vaibhāṣika a person who is 'sattvāvāsastha' is described as 'Asarṁjñikasattva'. An asaṁjñikasattva person during his 'sattvāvāsa' naturally acquires certain condition or state of spiritual upliftment when he is not baffled by future sāsrava objects. During this state of asaṁjñikatā, therefore, the very creation of sāsrava objects is obstructed for a specific period. This makes it almost similar to apratisa-ṁkhyānirodha, and may be mistaken for the latter. On analysis, however, it will be found that there is a subtle difference between the two. Apratisaṁkhyānirodha permanently obstructs the creation or origin of all objects, whereas the asaṁjñikatvā prevents the origin of sāsrava objects only during the state of asaṁjñikatā, while out of the state of asaṁjñikatā a person may once again be baffled by the sāsrava objects.

The Vaibhāṣikas mention another form of nirodha, viz., Asaṁjñikanirodha-samāpatti or Nirodha-samāpatti. This may be acquired by a person, susceptible to all desires, by means of meditation. On its attainment sāsrava objects do not originate in a person, expert in meditation, during the period of his meditation. So during the state of Nirodha-samāpatti also the origin of sāsrava objects is obstructed temporarily for him. But the expression, 'permanent obstruction' of the origin of objects in respect of apratisaṁkhyānirodha, will enable us to distinguish it from the above-mentioned nirodha-samāpatti, which effects a temporary obstruction only.

Apratisaṁkhyānirodha effectively and permanently retards the origin of Anāsrava objects as well. A 'srotāpanna' person, free from the two kleśas born of low sight and low thoughts, becomes 'Anāgānu' (i.e., one who will be born once more only to attain Nirvāṇa). Such persons are generally averse to the acquisition of more and more higher states of existence, and those anāgāmīs who attain nirvāṇa during their 'antarābhava' (the period intervening between the death in one existence and rebirth in another) do not require these higher planes. By means of their knowledge or pratisaṁkhyā they obtain a form of apratisaṁkhyānirodha which obstructs the origin of future anāsrava higher planes for them. Though it is attained by means of pratisaṁkhyā still it retards the origin of anāsrava constituted objects.

In summing up it may be observed, therefore, that the existence of all constituted objects, sāsrava and anāsrava, is obstructed by anityatānirodha; the attainment of contact with sāsrava objects, past, born or yet to be born is obstructed by pratisaṁkhyānirodha; and, the very creation or origin of anutpattidharmā objects, sāsrava or anāsrava, is permanently obstructed by apratisaṁkhyānirodha. The first strikes at the existence, the second at the attainment, and, the third at the very origin.

The constituted objects are related to anityatānirodha by their own creative elements, as they are created in collaboration with that nirodha. The pratisaṁkhyānirodha is attainable only by pratisaṁkhyā or vimuktimārga and by no other process. Apratisaṁkhyānirodha may, however, be obtained by nature as well as by pratisaṁkhyā. Some even believe that it may be attained by pratyayavaikalya, which is not accepted by the Vaibhāṣikas.

Ananta Kumar Nyaya-Tarkatirtha

FOOTNOTES

1. The present article has been written on the basis of the Abhidharmakośa of Vasubandhu and its Commentary, Sphūṭarthā of Yaśomitra. For a more comprehensive account of 'Nirodha-Satya' the reader may consult the book entitled 'Vaibhāṣika Darśana' (in Bengali) written by the writer.

16

PRATĪTYASAMUTPĀDA

Pratītyasamutpāda is one of the modes of casual relation in Buddhism—the other being Paṭṭhānanaya. It is 'a mode marked by the simple condition of the happening of a phenomenon on the occurrence of its sole invariable antecedent phenomenon.'[1] It states that things of the world are neither due to one cause (ekahetuka) nor are they causeless (ahetuka). It proves that things are due to manifold causes (nānāhetuka).

Buddhaghoṣa states that pratītyasamutpāda is one of the four difficult subjects[2] (catvāri duṣkarasthānāni) to be expounded. It is to be understood under four different aspects of profundity (catvāri gambhīrasthānāni), *viz.*, meaning (artha), doctrine (dharma), teaching (deśanā) and penetration (prativeda). It should further be known according to the four different methods as to the meaning (catvāra arthanayā) and these are the method of unity (ekatvanaya), of diversity (nānātvanaya), of non-occupation (abyāpāranaya) and of the nature of being such (evaṃdharmatānaya). This formula is characterised as the order of becoming (dharmasthitatā), happening of things (dharmaniyamat), suchness (tathatā), uncontrariness (avitathatā) and this-conditioned nature (idapratyayatā).

Pratītya (prati+√i+ya) means after reaching (prāpya), or depending on (apekṣya), and samutpāda means origination. Combining the two we get dependent origination. It establishes that things have only a dependent origination.

We are told that the Buddha, while sitting under the Bodhi tree, determined to acquire enlightenment, realised at the third watch of the night the root cause of all sufferings and sorrows, which is comprised in the second noble truth (samudayasatya), the concatenation of causes and effects, *viz.*, pratītyasamutpāda (dependent origination) with its 12 nidānas or links. They are: (1) avidyā (ignorance), (3) saṁskāra (impression), (3) vijñāna (conciousness), (4) nāmarūpa (mind and matter), (5) ṣaḍāyatana (six organs of sense), (6) sparśa (contact), (7) vedanā (feeling), (8) tṛṣṇā (desire), (9) upādāna (attachment), (1o) bhava (existence), (11)jāti (birth) and (12) jarāmaraṇa (old age and death). This is the wheel of life revolving day after day from birth to death and death to birth.

Here is given a brief exposition of the terms constituting the formula. Avidyā (ignorance) is the non-comprehension of the four Noble Truths (āryasatya), the past (pūrvānta), the future (aparānta), both the past and the future (purvāntāparānta) and pratītyasamutpāda (dependent origination).[3] It is identified with delusion (moha). Saṃskāra (impression) denotes actions which are (i) meritorious (puṇyābhisaṃskāra), (ii) sinful (apuṇyābhisaṃskāra) and (iii) static (āneñjābhisaṃskāra). Puṇyābhisaṃskāra appertains to eight kāmāvacarakuśala and five rūpāvacarakusalacetanās (volitions), apunyābhisaṃskāra to twelve akuṣalacetanās (volitions) and āneñjābhisaṃskāra to four arūpakuśalacetanās (volitions) ony. They are thus wholesome and unwholesome worldly volitions (cetanās). These three together with the three kinds of deeds belonging to the body (kāyika), speech (vācasika) and mind (mānasika) are the six saṃskāras (impressions) which are conditioned by ignorance (avidyā). Vijñāna (consciousness) means here pratlsandhlvijñana (rebirth consciousness) and pravṛttivijñāna (a continuous flow of mental states). Pratisandhivijñāna is of nineteen kinds while pravṛttivijñāna is of thirty-two laukika vipākas (resultants). Nāmarūpa (mind and matter) denote pratisandhināma and pravṛttināma, and pratisandhirūpa and pravṛttirūpa. Pratisandhināma means thirty-five cetanās (volitions) associated with ninteen pratisandhis while pravṛttināma denotes thirty-five cetanās (volitions) associated with thirty-two laukika cittas. By pratisandhirūpa is meant the nineteen kinds of pratisandhi and karmajarūpa (form arising out of deeds), and by pravṛttirūpa is taken the pravṛtticittajarūpa (form arising out of mind in this life), Ṣaḍāyatana denotes cakṣāyatana (eye-base), śrotrāyātana (ear-base), ghrāṇāyatana (nose-base), jihvāyatana (tongue-base), kāyāyatana (body-base) and manāyatana (mind-base). Cakṣāyatana is cakṣuprasāda (sensitivity of eye) and so on while manāyatana is thirty-two laukika vipākas (resultants). Sparśa (contact) is of six kinds corresponding to the six kinds of āyatanas (bases). Cakṣusparśa (eye-contact) is contact associated with eye-consciousness (cakṣuvijñāna), śrotrasparśa (ear-contact) is contact associated with ear-consciousness (śrotravij-ñāna), and so forth, but manosparśa (mind-contact) is but con-tact associated with twenty-two laukika vipākas (resultants). Vedanā (feeling) is also of six kinds corresponding to six sense-organs. Cakṣuvedanā (feeling born of eye) is feeling associated with eye-consciousness (cakṣuvijñāna) and so on while manovedanā is but feeling associated with thirty-two laukika vipākas (resultants). Tṛṣṇa (craving) is of six kinds, *viz.*, rūpatṛṣṇā (cra-ving for form), śabdatṛṣṇā (craving for sound), gandhatṛṣṇā (craving for smell), rasatṛṣṇā (craving fot taste), spṛṣtavyatṛṣṇā (craving for touch) and dharmatṛṣṇā (craving for objects). Rūpatṛṣṇā is craving for the visible objects. Similarly śabdatṛṣṇā is craving for the sounds and so forth. Upādāna (attachment) is of four kinds: kāma, dṛṣṭi, śīlavrata and ātmavāda. Kāmupa-dāna is mental concomitants rooted in greed (lobha-cetasika). Dṛṣṭ upādāna is the wrong view that there is no resultant of the gift. Śīlavratupādāna is the belief that ceremonial observances lead to purification. Ātmavād-upādāna is the belief in the existence of one's individuality. Bhava (existence) is of two kinds: karmabhava and utpattibhava. Karmabhava is twenty-nine kuśala and akuśala cetanās (wholesome and unwholesome volitions) and twenty ways of good conduct and of evil conduct associated with these cetanās (volitions). It represents the active side of life. Utpattibhava is the resultant of thirty-two laukika vipākas and thirty-five ceta-sikas and the material phenomena produced by karma. Jāti (birth) is the appearance, of the five skandhas (aggregates) of a being who is reborn. Jarā (decay) is the decay of those skandhas. Marana (death) is the passing away of those skandhas.

Pratītyasamutpāda refers to three periods—the past, present and the future. Avidyā (ignorance) and saṃskāra (impression) belong to the past, vijñāna, nāmarūpa, ṣaḍayatana, sparśa, vedanā, tṛṣṇā, upaādāna and bhava to the present, jāti and jarāmaraṇa to the future. It has twelve factors (aṇga) as mentioned above. It has also twenty modes (ākāra). Thus in the past there are five causes and in the present there are five resultants. Similarly there are five causes in the present and five resultants also in the future. There are four groups (saṅkṣepa) in this formula: one casual group in the past, one resultant group in the present, one casual group in the present and one resultant group in the future. It has three connections (sandhi): one between saṃskāra and vijñāna, one between vedanā and tṛṣṇā and one between bhava and jāti. There are three rounds (vṛtta) in it. They are kleṣavṛtta, karmavṛtta and vipākavṛtta. It has further two roots —avidyā and tṛṣṇā. Lastly, it is taught in four different ways: (i) from the beginning to the end, (ii) from the middle to the end, (iii) from the end to the beginning and (iv) from the middle to the beginning.

Pratītyasamutpāda (dependent origination) is one of the most fundamental doctrines of Buddhism, as Buddha himself has declared: 'He who realises pratītyasamutpāda sees dharma (truth) and he who sees dharma (truth) sees pratītyasamutpāda'.It is a very important philosophical doctrine in Mahāyāna philosophy. Nāgārjuna, the founder of the Mādhyamika system, has established his whole philosophy on pratītyasamutpāda. According to this doctrine it is the nature of all things (bhāva) to depend on a number of causes and conditions for their origination, and what are so produced cannot be said to have independent origination and are without any reality and nothing can, therefore, be declared of such unreal things. In the invocatory verses at the beginning of his *Mādhyamikakārikā* Nāgārjuna has described pratītyasamutpāda by eight negatives. He says that there is neither origination nor cessation, neither permanence nor impermanence, neither unity nor diversity, neither coming in nor going out in the principle of pratītyasamutpāda. Here the negatives describe the unrelatedness of everything produced through this principle and pratītyasamutpāda is rightly declared as the cessation of phenomena (prapañcopaśama) and all quiescence (śiva). Elsewhere (ch. 24) he has further stated that looked at from the relative standpoint (samvṛtisatya) pratītyasamutpāda means, origination of the world-order depending on a concurrence of causes, but from the absolute standpoint (paramārthasatya), it means non-origination at all times and is equated with Nirvāṇa. This is the basic principle of Nāgārjuna's philosophy.

Anukul Chandra Banerjee

FOOTNOTES

1. Tabbhāvabhāvibhāvākāramattopalakkhito paṭiccasamuppādanayo.
2. The other three are noble truths (satya), being (sattva) and pratisandhi (rebirth).
3. This is the meaning in the Abhidhammapiṭaka while in the Suttapiṭ aka it *means non-comprehension of the* four Noble Truths.

17

BUDDHIST PSYCHOLOGY

In Buddhism there is a very well-defined psychological study, vying at times with many a modern concept. The complex and intricate internal life of human beings has been sought to be analysed and explained in the Pali *Tipiṭaka*. In *Abhidhamma* texts it is stated that the human mind is based on certain notions, preconceived as well as originating, so that no one state of mind can be a full explanation of any human type. There are, so to say, different designations of human types on the psy-chological analysis and the consequential metaphysical status of the human individual. In the *Puggalapannatti*, a Pali cano-nical text under the *Abhidhamma*, it has been clearly stated at the outset that there are six such designations on the psycho-metaphysical side of analysis[1]. Now, apparently all these six types of designations of the know*i*ng individual may not be found to be of a strict scientific division inasmuch as there are over-lappings, *e.g.*, between the *āyatana-paññatti* and the *dhātu-paññatti;* yet there are good grounds in each for special kind of stress, as on the *objective* side in the former and on the *mental* side in the latter.

In this psycho-metaphysical analysis of the human individual, the very first *sine qua non* is the doctrine of 'the designation of groups' (*Khandha-paññatti*). In general Buddhist theory of *pañca-skandha* or five-fold aggregate consisting of the inner and the outer worlds in all acts of cognition, this enunciation of the *Khandha-paññatti* as the first 'designation' assumes a significant role in Buddhist psychology of the Idealistic type. The *rūpa* (material form), *vedanā* (sensation), *saññā* (perception)[2], *sankhāra* (confection)[3], and *viññāna* (consciousness) have been put under this group, giving a broad classification of the different requisites in an act of cognition. It is well known and admitted almost as a universal rule that the mind is the seat of all cognitional processes. In Buddhist theories of the mind and its processes of *knowing,* it has been generally accepted, in both Hīnayāna and Mahāyāna schools with certain doctrinal modifications, that the mind is the seat of consciousness. This basic recognition of the mind in the psycho-physical and consequential philosophico-metaphysical doctrines of origin and control of mental states and systematisation of knowledge in realising the Ultimate Truth, has been the backbone of Buddhist tradition. Starting from the material form which is out and there, Buddhist writers have given a predominant role to our inner world of the mental processes, culminating through various notions, in the actual psychological re-actions. It is here that the Buddhist theory is not purely psychological, but psycho-physical and ultimately psycho-ethical. It has been a vexed question whether psychology should be studied from an ethical attitude, but it has been nonetheless generally accepted that ethical studies have a great anticipation of psychological analyses. Mrs. Rhys Davids in her *Buddhist Psychology* (a translation of the *Dhammasaṁgaṇi* under the *Abhidhamma)* has discussed, in the learned Introduction, this question and this attitude in the Buddhist tradition at great length. Psychology is, according to the tradition which is the subject of our discussion, pre-eminently suited to an analysis of the human mind in the hope of its exposure to an ethical adjudgment.

If we examine, on a general study, the five-fold *Khanda-paññatti* enumerated and described above, we shall find that the sensory organs have their respective fields and roles in the enumeration of different kinds of 'sensation' *(Vedanā)*. It is, therefore, evident that this first 'designation' *(Paññatti)* is mainly a description of the internal states and conditions re-acting, under specific circumstances, on particular external stimuli coming from the objective world. In this regard, Buddhist writers have given us a scientific basis as the starting-point in psychology. The next 'designations' as enumerated in the text, *Puggala-paññatti,* are the gradual exposition of this fundamental hypothesis. The numbers and groupings may appear to be not strictly scientific to modern minds, but that there are different groupings depending on, and elucidating, peculiar points of view in a psychological situation, is undeniably true. The *āyatanapaññatti* is a twelve-fold group and the *dhātu-paññatti* an eighteen-fold group, elucidating the second and the third 'designations' respectively.[3]

These ā*yatna-* and *dhātu-paññatti* aggregates are enumerated to show that in the Buddhist theory, the psychological processes are sensory, motor and even reflex, depending on the seats or organs and reactions. The *āyatanas* are these seats as well as the specific qualities adhering to the external world that the former are capable to grasp. It is interesting here that even the *manas* or *citta* that is the specific internal conscious state is also included here along with *dhamma* which quality it is capable to grasp. This *dhamma* is the three-fold group without form *(arūpa khandhattayo)* of *vedanā, saññā* and *saṅkhara.*[4] In the *dhātu-paññatti* aggregate are listed the same twelve-fold group *plus* six types of *viññaṇa* belonging to six organs including the mind *(citta)* The *dhatu-paññatti* aggregate is, therefore, enumerated after the *āyatana-paññatti,* for the fact that when specific seats or organs are capable to grasp specific objects in their specific qualities, then the actual grasping through a deeper region, so to say, takes place. This is the *dhātu-paññatti* aggregate which is not merely an aggregate of seats but also of actual *re-acting agents.* Perhaps on that account has the *viññaṇa* (consciousness), that has been specifically included in the first 'designation' of *Khandha,* been once more added to this aggregate to show that sensory processes depend on consciousness for actual psychological results to be achieved. It is, however, an hypothesis worked out from the Idealistic position of Buddhism.

Let us turn a little from the main path to study, in brief, certain other implications which are corollaries. The *citta,*-which we have translated as 'mind' in Western terminology for want of a better equivalent, though imperfectly—is, in the Buddhist tradition, generally of four types. These types of mind, as enumerated and explained, are judged not merely from the psychological point of view, but also, and more so, from the ethico-metaphysical point of view. These are: (1) *Kamāvacara*—it is the 'mind of desire' having good *(kuśala),* bad *(akuśala),* indifferent *(kriyā)* and ripe *(yipāka)* kinds, depending on the nature of our mental propensities; (2) *Rūpāvacara*—it is the 'mind of sublation' having good *(kuśala),* indifferent *(kriya)* and ripe *(vipāka)* kinds, possessed by super-human beings residing in higher regions; (3) *Arūpavacara*—it is the 'mind of trance,' also of three kinds as *Rūpāvacara,* but possessed by still higher Beings residing in *nirākāra* (formless) regions, yet having some *karmic* propensities to manifest; (4) *Lokottara*—it is the 'mind of realisation,' having as its object the bliss of *Nirvāṇa,* and having two kinds depending on the Path and the Result. It is the highest Perfection and the ultimate Goal. Buddha-hood is included in this category, and in nothing else. It is, therefore, evident that all these classes are not purely psychological. Ethical, metaphysical and spiritual evaluations are implicated in the four different kinds of *citta* as briefly enumerated and explained above. But, however lower or higher the *citta* may be, it is admitted generally in the Buddhist tradition that the three-fold formless group *(arūpa khandhattayo)* of *vedanā, sañña* and *saṅkhāra* is the resultant of such 'graded minds'. This three-fold group has its origin in mind which again is of lower or higher propensities.

Consciousness, again, in Buddhist tradition is everchanging. But every consciousness has two elements—one Constant and the other Variable. Now, this constant element is the Form of Consciousness which is reached in an Order of Thought by mind in well-defined Paths *(Vithi).* The subjective element can rise above the changing processes in its state of 'stream of being' which is free from process of thought *(Vithi-mutta),* but the objective process-consciousness *(Vitht -citta)* which is the Matter and the Variable element is ever the functional aspect of the knowing individual. All these varieties of consciousness, however, have three moments of genesis, existence and destruction. The mind, therefore, has an infinite series of thought-processes in the construction of a system of thought though the Form it reaches. The variability of consciousness is the mind's inner process but the constancy of consciousness is its system of Form in the synthetic judgments it forms. The subject, however, in its real nature is 'a stream of being' where thought-processes are capable of being transcended, and the *Vīthi-mutta* subject may stay as the metaphysical entity.[5] It is interesting to compare this analysis of the Buddhist theories of mind and its processes,the objective data and the thought-construction on them—with the Kantian epistemology and metaphysics. In germinal forms the *Abhidhamma* tradition in Buddhism seems to reflect the much later and much more developed Kantian system. The metaphysical subject, again, is tinged with the transcendental hypothesis here, though not in the Kantian sense, with the pronounced stress on the ideality of the conscious subject.

It remains for us to study the implications of *indriya-paññatti* or designation of sense-organs' in the psychological theory of Buddhism. We have discussed above the nature of the *āyatana-* and the *dhātu-paññatti* aggregates and shown their separate implications. In this designation of *indriya,* there has been a stress on the functional aspect. In fact, this aggregate is properly to be designated as 'a designation of functions or faculties'. "Indriya", says B.C. Law in his *Designation of Human Types* (p.1 f.n.) "literally means a controlling principle or force." *Indriya-paññatti* is an aggregate of twenty-two such 'principles' comprising the regions from sense-desire to the supramundane. It is, therefore, not merely the actual seats or senses that are included in this aggregate but the 'controlling principles or forces' that are working on for the control of the human body lest it should cease to function.

Buddhist psychology has a vital bearing on the Buddhist theories of morality and spirituality. It is said in the few *gāthās* in the *cittavaggo* of the *Dhammapada* that the *citta* or mind is the most perturbed and therefore the most dangerous possession of the human individual. It is always enticed away to vices, to things of ephemeral consequences, to distant paths of darkness, to *akuśalas* of the lowest form of *kāmāvacara*-state far removed from the higher and higher kinds of mental development; but it is through meditation of graded varieties (of five kinds), through good and virtuous practice and through inner control over the mind's dissipations that one can achieve peace and tranquility, and attain to the state of an *Arhat*.

Bratindra Kumar Sengupta

FOOTNOTES

1 *Cha paññattiyo :—khanda-paññatti, āyatana-paññati, dhātu-paññatti, sacca-paññati, indriya-paññatti, puggala-paññatti (loc. cit.*, Pt. I., P.T.S., ed. R. Mortis).

2 These two terms 'perception' and 'confection' as equivalaents to *saññā* and *saṅkhāra* have been used by B. C. Law in *Designation of Human Types,* P.T.S. it should be noted that *saññā* here does not mean 'name' as applied in the general *pañca-skandha* theory of outer designation, as opposed to the inner process which is described in this context.

3 *rāgañca dosañca pahāya moham sammappajāno suvimuttacitto anupadiyāno idha vā huraṃ vāsa bhāgava sāmaññassa hoti (Dhammapada,* 1/20).

In this verse there is the ethical approach to the analysis of the mind acting on the objective world through *upādāna.*

4 *manopubbaṁgamādhammāmanoseṭṭhā manomayā: Dhammapada (*1/1-2*)*

5 Cf. *Compendium of Philosophy* 5hwe Zan Aung & Mrs. Rhys Davids, pp. 25 ff.

18

BRAHMAN OF ŚAṄKARA AND ŚŪNYATĀ OF MĀDHYAMIKAS

The central point of Śaṅkara's Vedānta is that consciousness absolute is the fundamental reality and Brahman is that consciousness.[1] It is devoid of all attributes (निर्गुण) and devoid of any distinct mark (निर्विशेष). It is one indivisible unit without a second (अद्वैत) having in itself no difference (स्वगतभेद) either arising out of an individuality as a member of a certain class (स्वाजातीयभेद) or a difference arising out of an individuality belonging to another class (विजातीयभेद)[2]. Each individual is essentially the same as Brahman but it appears as other than Brahman because of adjuncts (उपाधि) that arise out of nescience (अविद्या)[3].

The world consisting of individuals is there and it has the self-same Brahman as the cause (कारण) both material (उपादान) and efficacious (निमित्त)[4]. The world emanates from it and subsists in it. Now the question is how can this non-relational (निरवयविन्) Brahman be linked up with this relational (अवयविन्) world? Śaṅkara, however, says this is possible ; The world, as it is, does not exist at all nor did it ever exist nor will it exist in future. The truly existing being is alone Brahman and all else is naught[5]. All else is *māyā* or *adhyāsa,* the principle of individuation or the principle of unifying opposites[6]—unification of the self and not-self, of the ego and not-ego, of the subject and object, of the cause and effect and of Brahman and the world.[7] Opposites can never be reconciled[8]. But unless they are reconciled no experience is possible. In our every day experience we are accustomed to reconcile such opposites.[9] We make an object identified with that which it is not. We take a rope to be a snake. There cannot be an identification, between the rope and a snake in any way. Yet they are identified. This is the case also with truth and falsehood. Very often we identify truth with falsehood. In fact, there cannot be any reason[10] for such an identification but such is the case in all human affairs. Such a nature regulates all activities,—a law that makes the world as it is.[11] A man believes as that he is identical with his body and he never explicitly denies that he is his body and never feels detached from his body.[12] The notion of this false identification (अध्यास) of the self with the body would never occur to a person who has an experience of himself as the supreme consciousness. It is only one who had realised such a distinction between self and not-self and that he would wonder at this identity.

The identity of self with not-self has the form of the self existing as embodied and not as a conscious body. An individual self means a self feeling itself as embodied.[13] The illusoriness of the embodiment is the illusoriness of the body itself as also the self's identity with it. The idea of an object as distinct from the subject is derived from the notion of this embodiment. This notion again is born in the consciousness of the self and is regarded as false in consideration of its individuality. To be conscious of one's self as an individual as in the case 'I know me' is to be conscious of *me* as illusory and of the subject, that is, I, as truth. The *me* is the prototype of the whole realm of objectivity, a sort of *you* (युष्मत्). To feel it to be illusory is to be aware of the possibility of all objects to be illusory. We can never conceive the illusoriness of the world unless we start with the illusoriness of *me*. The illusoriness of *me* leads to the feeling that the self can never be identified with not-self. This feeling forms the very background on which Śaṅkara establishes his theory of objective illusion (अध्यास). This objective illusion again calls for its counterpart the subjective illusion, the *avidyā* or *māyā*, the principle of individuation. It is an illusion primary, through which the self believes in willing and feeling that it is an individual[14]. This principle exists in Brahman prior to the beginning of actual consciousness of one's self as an individual or prior to the starting of this world as an object of experience (भोग). Through it an individual self becomes conditioned and begins to conceive individually about himself and also of his subjective experience. Due to such experience every individual thinks that there are as many individuals as there are beings.[15] This principle of individuation is entirely dependent because nothing can be conceived without being related to pure consciousness which is Brahman.[16] Absolute Brahman is independent. It has nothing to do with condition (निरूपाधिक) and has no concern with the world.[17]

This world has no ultimate reality (पारमार्थिकसत्ता) and will be perceived as such as long as the ultimate reality is not realised. Even the mental states are not real. But so long this world continues to be perceived and Brahman is not realised both the internal and the external objects are to be regarded as facts. All these objects have got some value.[18] The, world also has got a value so long its knowledge as a world persists but when the knowledge of Brahman arises (ब्रह्मासाक्षात्कार) the world with its value ceases automatically.[19]

Brahman is eternal, and has neither positive nor negative attributes. It is above all determinations. Words fail to express it. In it there is a total extinction of empirical life along with the relative distinctions of subject and object. The concept of bliss in the *Turīya* state may appear as positive[20], and although there is absence of all determinate knowledge the self persists as subject to witness this absence itself. In the ecstatic consciousness it breaks through the last vestige of subject-object consciousness and attains an absolute state; it can then truly be said that all melt into one ātman,—who knows what? The outstanding mark of this state is the sublation of all determinate knowledge where the soul regains its original purity and self-sufficiency in which there was a temporary lapse owing to its association with the limiting adjuncts of the waking and dreaming life. It is not a goal to be reached or something to be effected but is the self itself. The absolute is not an object to be attained. Freed from all limitations the self attains it *oneness* with Brahman which is undifferentiated consciousness and bliss.[21]

The cardinal point in the metaphysical speculation of the Mādhyamikas is Śū*nyatā,* that is, non-existence of everything worldly. The world, has no independent existence of its own.[22] It is a mere apparition of Śū*nyatā*[23]. The objects of the world have no existence at all. They are perceived as existing but in essence they are not so. To exist in reality is not the same as to be perceived as existing. *Esse* may be *percipi* but *percipi* is not *esse*[24]. Appearance though exists *per se* subsequently dies out and is discovered later on as never existing. Yet it has got its empirical value—an empirical reality.[25] This empirical reality is derived from the absolute where there is not even a shadow of distinction between within and without. No doubt, absolute thus reached is ineffable and indescribable and may appear as if it were identical with nothing. But this negative has its counterpart in the positive.[26] It is another way of positing a true reality. In truth it is "the very opposite of a mere nothing. For it is fulfilment, attainment, peace, the goal of life, the object of desire, the end of knowledge ...... It is our finite realm that is the falsity, the mere nothing, the absolute is all truth."[27] Naturally for the Mādhyamikas such a reality escapes all conceptual determinations, Intellect is at a miss to conceive how appearance is linked up with reality. To conceive of any relation is to allow a status to both and to a third element. The removal of differences takes away from reality its concreteness and opens it to the character of pseudo reality. Mādhyamikas, therefore, were forced to postulate an indeterminate reality which presupposes instead a determinate universe. But to be determinate and at the same time to transcend constitute a contradiction. To avoid this difficūlty the Mādhyamikas had to chalk out the principle of *avidyā*. It is not clear how and why the absolute becomes determined itself. The only plausible answer to this question is offered in the principle of *avidyā* which does justice to the determinate and indeterminate aspects of existence and at the same time avoids the error of either ma-king the indeterminate determinate or installing determinate as reality.

This *avidyā has* its *locus* not in *Śūnyatā*. This is not possible,[28] though possible from the point of view of Śaṅkara.[29] *Śūnyatā* which literally means voidness or emptiness has suffered a great deal of misunderstanding by those who are not well acquainted with the Buddhist phraseology. Mādhyamikas imagined *Śūnyatā,* as the highest truth (परमार्थसत्य) denying the existence of everything conditional as well as unconditional, relative as well as independent. It is a perfect state of consciousness than which nothing can be more excellent (अनुत्तरसम्यक्-सम्बोधि).[30] What the *Śūnyatā* doctrine positively insists on is the annihilation of the imagination that weaves the dualistic conception of the world.[31] If this could be called nihilism Śaṅkara's intellectual attempt to reach a monistic view of the universe could also be called nihilistic, for it declares as well the untenability of a separate existence of thought and matter-I and not-I.[32] It is called Śū*nya* because it transcends all forms of separation and individuation.[33] Even to attribute the notion of Śū*nyatā* to it is wrong. Language is deficient to express that state exactly. But it is to be expressed. So such terms are used. It is to be designated in a term with which we are familiar. We are accustomed to call such a state as *Śūnya*. By abnegating all phenomenal existences[34] we can reach to that state which is the highest. Mādhymikas cannot define that state arrived at by such abnegation. They, therefore, had to designate it as Śū*nya*. Ignorant minds are deeply saturated with wrong affirmations and false judgments. They are accustomed to understand everything in terms of existence and non-existence but it is neither that which is existent nor that which is non-existent nor that which is or is not at once existent or non-exis-tent. It is again, neither unity nor that which is plurality nor that which is or is not at once a unity and plurality. In it there is no origination (उत्पाद), no destruction (उच्छेद), no annihilation (निषेध), no persistence (शाश्वत), no unity (एकार्थ). In short, it transcends all modes of relativity [35]

Teachings of Buddha are based on two kinds of truth. One is conventional or empirical (संवृति) and the other is transcendental and real (परमार्थ).[36] It is called *Saṃvṛti* because it envelops the real knowledge and also that it helps to uncover which as a matter of fact is enveloped. [37] It is the same as ignorance (अविद्या)[38] on account of its completely enveloping the reality. It is characteristic with *avidyā* that it superimposes a form on a non-existent and thus creates an obstacle in having a correct view of the reality. It again implies a thing which depends on another for its existence, that is, what is subject to cause (हेतु) and condition (प्रत्यय).[39] A really self-existent thing requires no cause and condition and does not undergo any kind of tranformation such as origin and decay. So whatever is caused and conditioned is *Saṃvṛa*. *Avidyā* also refers to signs and words current in the world. The signs and words form the basis of perception which is accepted by people in general as true. The form (रूप) etc. should not be supposed to be really existing. Their existences arc substantiated by proofs which are valid from worldly standpoint[40] If all that is perceived by the senses be true, then a fool's knowledge which is acquired by his senses will also be true. The body of a woman though naturally impure is regarded as pure by a man whose mind is swayed by attachment.

The *samvṛti* or *avidya* is of two kinds; one *tathyasamvṛti* which refers to a thing which originates from some cause (किंचित् प्रतीत्यजात) and is perceived in the same way by all individuals with unimpaired organs of sensing such as colour as red or blue. The other one is *mithyasaṃvṛti* which refers to a thing or statement which is accepted as true by a few individuals and not by all. It is about a thing perceived by persons with sense organs defective.[41]

Now the question is, if *saṃvrta* is not a real truth what is the necessity of preaching it in the form of topics like *skandha, dhātu, āyatana, śilavrataparāmarśa*. These topics are said to be conventionally true but not true in a strict sense (अतत्व). This is no doubt true but the fact is that the highest truth cannot be imparted without having recourse to conventional truth.[42] The final aim of life is *nirvana*. It cannot be attained also without the realisation of what the truth is. It cannot be brought home directly to a mind which normally does not rise above the conventional distinction of subject and object, knower and the known. It must have to be imparted through conventional truths and unless it is so imparted one cannot be expected to remain aloof from worldly limitations. It is for this reason that Mādhyamikas cannot dispense with the topics of *saṃvṛta* objects and had to formulate for popular understanding the topic of *dhātu, āyatana* etc. Again, *Paramārthasatya* cannot be explained to another by signs or predications. Yet it is to by explained. The only alternative, therefore, is to explain it by negation such as *neti neti*. In Sankara Vedanta also we find similar arguments by negation of all *'aṃvrta* matters that are worldly.[43] A *paramārthasatya* is beyond the cognisance of *buddhi* (अगोचर), beyond the purview of knowledge (अविषय), beyond the possibility of detailed description (सर्वप्रपंचविनिर्मुक्त), beyond all possible form of imagination (कल्पनासमतिक्रान्त).[44] The only way to explain this ultimate truth to the worldly people is through commonplace terms and illustrations. A person with diseased eyes sees a net of hair. He is corrected by another whose eyes are healthy. He sees the real nature of things by negating that there is a net of hair.[45] Similarly a person whose right vision is obstructed by ignorance conceives the existence of *dharma, dhātu* etc as existent which are, in fact, non-existent in their phenomenal forms. Buddha who is like a person having healthy eyes knows this truly[46] and cannot help but saying that there are in reality no *skandhas*, no *dhātus* etc.

One of the essential characteristics of *Śunyatā* is that no instruction can be imparted about it (अपरप्रत्यय).[47] One is to realise this within himself (प्रत्यात्मवेद्य).[48] He cannot understand it by listening to the instruction of the perfect (आर्य).[49] Besides *Śūnyatā* everything is unreal. But the worldly people whose vision is already obscured cannot understand how the objects which they perceive directly by sense organs can be unreal. They fail to realise those abstruse arguments without the help of illustrations with which they are familiar. Accordingly they are taught with the help of illustration of a snake and rope.[50] Due to defects in vision one mistakes a rope for a snake. Due to this mistake there arises some reactions in his mind such as fear in consequence of which he runs away. This false attribution is *samāropa*.[51] That there is a snake in the form of the rope is nothing but a fabrication, is a construction (कल्पना) of the mind. The rope which is the locus (अधिष्ठान) to which the mentally created (जन्य) or imagined (परिकल्पित) snake is attributed (अध्यस्त) through imagination (अध्यास कल्पना) is true whereas the imagined (परिकल्पित) snake which is attributed is false. That this imagined attribution is false has been termed as *apavāda*.[52] The world we see about is supposed to be existent (भाव). In reality it is not so. It is false. The only reality is other than this (अभाव) which is supposed to be existent. We attribute (समारोप) existence to this world but this attribution is false (अपवाद). That is only true which is other than this existent and that is Śū*nyatā* but not an annihilation[53] (उच्छेद).

In this way through the polemics of *samāropa* and *apavāda* Mādhyamikas try to impart their teachings for the realisation of the ultimate truth.[54] The Yogācāras adopt the same method.[55] Śankarites also have done so.[56]

So the Mādhyamikas were led to think that there is nothing real in this world. Everything is devoid of its innate or independent nature. It is wrong to suppose that there is anything in its own or innate from (स्वरूप). Things we see around are no doubt there but they appear before us only in their imposed forms (समारोपित).[57] Their own form is *Śūnyatā* which is devoid of any *svabhāva* (निः स्वभाव).[58] This is called also *tathatā* or the state of such nature (तथाभाव).[59] This is not liable to any change (अविकृत) and is of permanent existence (सदैव स्थायिन्) .[60] It does not come into existence through any agency. It does not depend on anything for its creation (अनुत्पाद). In *Śūnyatā* there appears nothing nor does anything disappear.

Taking the objects of this world in this light the philosophers of the Mādhyamika school declare that anything external or internal that appears to us existing, is in fact unreal and looks like an imaginary town.[61] There is nothing either internal or external. The notion of I and Mine technically known as *satkāyadṛṣṭi*[62] disappears completely in the ultimate state where there is neither subject nor object. The disappearance of such notion is followed by the disappearance of *saṃsāra*[63] where its root is stuck deep into. The sole aim of Śūnyavāda is to nullify or to root out the notion of I and Mine. One who realises *Śūnyatā* has neither likes nor dislikes. He feels attached neither to gain nor pleasure nor does he feel aversion to loss or pain.[64] As there is no *ātman* the notion of it will not arise and when the notion of *ātman* ceases to arise the notion of mine (आत्मीय) will necessarily disappear. [65]

But, when anyone speaks of *nirvāṇa* he imagines the existence of a man and his *nirvāṇa*. Due to imperfect vision he thinks that a man can attain this ultimate state after practising the disciplinary rules. But all these are fancies (परिकल्पना).[66] It has no concern with the various development of *citta* (चित्तोत्पाद) stage (भूमि) of spiritual progress, fruits (फल) of spiritual discipline. On ultimate analysis there is neither a monk nor a *nirvāṇa* to be attained.[67] One should remove all misconceptions about the world and should realise the non-duality of all worldly things (अद्वयमेतदद्वैधीकारम्).[68]

Brahman of Śaṅkara has been characterised as *sat, cit,* and ā*nanda* but these are not determinations being each of them unspeakable, absolute beyond the determinate construction of *sat* and *cit* and *ānanda* formulated by our consciousness.[69] An individual has not only to correct his self, from the subjective illusion of individuality, not only to wait for objective illusion of individuality to be corrected[70] but also to contemplate all these corrections as false.[71] He has to contemplate *moksa* not as something to be realised or effected or remanifested,[72] not even as an eternal predicament of the self but as the absolute self itself (ब्रह्मस्वरूप).[73] An individual illusorily thinks that he is not free. So he wants to be free. But he is eternally free. For the dawning of the consciousness that he is always free there is the necessity of *sadhanā* or discipline. *Sādhanā* prepares the ground for attaining knowledge in which the enquiry into spiritual truth can start.[74] When a progressive transparency of mind is effected through *sādhanā* truth begins to shine where the knowledge of self is found to be not distinct from but as one with knowledge, the eternal Brahman.[75]

According to Mādhyamikas *nirvāṇa* is an inexpressible absolute.[76] It is the same as *Śūnyatā* of which the universe is a mere reflection.[77] According to Śaṅkara *mokṣā* is the same as Brahman.[78] It is ineffable[79] and the universe is a mere reflection of it.[80] What the Mādhyamikas and Śaṅkara aimed at was to establish a unity corresponding to the Upanisadic absolute.[81] The characteristic nature of Śaṅkara's absolute is pure intelligence (चित्) and bliss (आनन्द). The characteristic nature of Mādhyamika's absolute is quietude (शान्त) and tranquillity (शिव).[82] Both can be equated so far as their impersonal (तटस्थ) aspects are concerned.

Ajit Ranjan Bhattacharya

FOOTNOTES

1. ख्रसर्वस्याकाष्ठादेर्जगतस्तत्त्वमधिष्ठानतयाख्रच पारमार्थिकं सच्चिदानन्दलक्षणं यद्रू-पमस्ति तत् ब्रह्मष्ठाब्देनेर्यते Ramakrishna's *Pañcadaśi*, 5. 8, also 3.28.

2. वष्टक्षस्य स्वगतो भेद: पत्रपुज़्पफलादिभि:।
वष्टक्षान्तरात् सजातीयो विजातीय: ष्ठिलादित:।।
तथा सद्वस्तुनो भेदत्रयं प्राप्तं निर्वायते।
ऐक्यावधारणद्वैतप्रतिज़ेध स्त्रिभि: क्रमात्।।
Pañcadaśi 2. 15-16. also see, Commentary of Ramakrishna thereunder.
3. सदन्तरं सजातीयं न वैलक्षणयवर्ज्जनात्। नामरूपोपाधिभेदं विना नैव सतो भिदा।। *Op. cit.,* 2.19.
4. जगतो यदुपादानं मायामादाय तामसीम्। निमित्तं ष्ठुद्धसत्त्वां तामुच्यते ब्रह्म तद् गिरा।। *Op. cit.,* 1.44. 'ष्ठाक्तिद्वयवदज्ञानोपहितं चैतन्यं स्वप्रधानतया निमितं स्वोपाधि प्रधानतया उपादानञ्च भवति यथा लुता तन्तुकार्यं प्रति स्वप्रधानतया निमित्तं स्वष्ठारीरप्रधानतयो पादानञ्च भवति (*Vedāntaśara* Vedāntavāgiśa's edition has been used in this paper), pp. 38-39.
5. मायाविद्ये विहायैवमुपाधी परजीवयो:। अखण्डं सच्चिदानदं परब्रह्मैव लक्ष्यते।। *Op. cit.,* 1.48.
6. अध्यासो भेदाग्रहेण व्याप्त: तद्विरूद्धश्चेहास्ति भेदग्रह: *Bhāmatī,* Adyar, p. 7.
7. तथा जीवेन कूटस्थं सोऽन्यान्याध्यास उच्यते।
अयं जीवो न कूटस्थं विविनक्ति कदाचन।
अनादिरविवेकोऽयं मूलाविद्येति गम्यताम्।।
8. न हि जातु कश्चित् समुदाचरद्वष्टत्तिनो प्रकाष्ठातमसी परस्परात्मतया प्रतिपत्तुमर्हति *Bhāeati,* Adyar, p. 6.
9. दष्टष्यते हिं धर्मिणो विवेकग्रहणोऽपि तद्धर्माणामध्यास: यथा कुसुमाद्भेदेन गष्टह्यमानेऽपि स्फटिकमणावतिस्वच्छतया जपाकुसमप्रतिबिम्बोद्ग्राहिणि इत्यारूझयाविभ्रम: *op. cit.* p. 6.
10. न च संवष्टतिपरमार्थसतो: पारमार्थिकं मिथुनमस्ति *op. cit.,* p. 14.
11. स्वभाविक: अनादिरयं व्यवहार: *op. cit.,* p. 15.
12. अन्योन्यधर्मांश्चाध्यस्य अन्योन्यस्मिन् धर्मिणि देहादिधर्मान् जन्ममरणजराव्याध्यादीनात्मनि धर्मिणि अध्यस्तदेहादिभावे समारोप्य तथा चैतन्यादीनात्मधर्मान् देहादावध्यस्त्मभावे समारोप्य 'ममेद' जरामरण पुत्रपष्ठुस्वाम्यादि इति व्यवहार *op. cit.,* p. 13.
13. इदमस्मत्प्रत्यगोचरयोरिंति वक्तव्ये युज़्मद्ग्रहणमत्यन्तभेदोपलक्षणार्थम्। यथाहंकार प्रतियोगी त्वंकारो नैवमिदं कार: 'एते वयम्, इमे वयम, आस्महे इति बहुल्प्रयोगदर्ष्ठनात् *op. cit.,* p. 13.
14. अन्योन्यस्मिन् धर्मिणयात्मष्ठारीरदौ अन्योन्यात्मकतामध्यस्य–अहमिदं ष्ठारीरादिति *op. cit.,* p. 13.

15. अयं च जीवसाक्षी प्रत्यात्मं नाना। एकत्वे चैत्रागते मैत्रस्याप्यनुसन्धानप्रसङ्गः *Vedāntaparibhāṣā,* (Nyāyapañcānana's edition, is used in this paper) pp. 65-66.
16. तदुपहितं चैतन्यमीश्वरसाक्षी। तच्चानादि। तदुपाधिमायाया अनादित्वात्। मायावच्छिन्नं चैतन्यं परमेश्वरः। मायाया विशेषणत्वे ईश्वरत्वम्। उपाधित्वे साक्षित्वमीश्वरत्व-साक्षित्वयार्भेदः। न तु धर्मिणोरीश्वरसाक्षिणोर्भेदः *op cit.*, pp. 29-70.
17. प्रमातृभेदो नाम न तावदैक्यम्। किंतु प्रमातृसत्तातिरिक्तसत्ताकत्वाभावः। तथाहि घटादेः स्वावच्छिन्नचैतन्याध्यस्ततया विषयचैतन्यसत्तैव घटादिसत्ता अधिष्ठानसत्तातिरिक्ताया आरोपितसत्ताया अनङ्गीकारात् *op. cit.*, pp. 45-46.
18. ननु संसारदशायां बाधः । यत्र हि द्वैतमिव भवति तदितर इतरम्पश्यतीति श्रुतेः। तथा चाबाधितपदेन संसारदशायामबाधितत्वं विवक्षितम् *op. cit.*, p. 15.
19. ब्रह्मसाक्षात्कारानन्तरं हि घटादीनां बाधः यत्र तस्य सर्वमात्मैवाभूत्तत् केन कम्पश्येदिति श्रुतेः *op. cit.*, p. 14.
20. आनन्दमयाधिकरण of *Brahmasūtra,* I.I. 12*ff.* and *Śaṅkarabhāṣya* thereunder आनन्दात्मकब्रह्मप्राप्तिश्च मोक्षः। शोकनिवृत्तिश्च *Vedāantaparibhāṣa,* p. 328.
21. उपाधिभूते मायाविद्ये पूर्वोक्ते विहायाखण्डं भेदरहितं सच्चिदानन्दं परब्रह्मैव महावाक्येन लक्ष्यते Ramakrishna's commentary, *Pañcadaśi* I. 45. See also विशुद्धे ब्रह्मणि वेदान्तानां तात्पर्यमवसितम् *Vedāntaparibhāṣā,* p. 60.
22. *Bodhicaryāvtārapañjikā,* Bibliotheca Indica, 9.55, p. 447.
23. तथागतो हि प्रतिबिम्बभूतः कुशलस्य धर्मस्यानास्रवस्य *Madhyamadavṛtti,* Bibliotheca Buddhica, pp. 449-50.
24. न तु प्रतीयमानस्य परमार्थसत्ता *Bhāmati,* Adyar, p. 15.
25. परीक्षका अपि हि व्यवहारसमये न लोकसामान्यमतिवर्तन्ते *op. cit.* p. II. लौकिकं दद्वदेवेदं प्रमाणं त्वात्मानिश्चयात् *SaṅkaraBhāṣya* (Samanvaya), (Nirnaya Sāgara edition used in this paper) p. 155 also see *Bhāmati,* thereunder, Adyar, p. 244.
26. That non-existent is not thinkable and hence because negative of everything is thindable you must never have negative which is non-existent—Bradley, *Principles of Logic,* 1883, p. 148.
27. Royse, *The World and the Individual,* vol. I, pp. 170-171.
28. यदि खलु तदध्यारोपाद् भवद्भिरस्त्युच्यते कीदृशं तत्। या सा धर्मणा धर्मता नाम सैव तत्स्वरूपम् *Madhyamadavṛtti,* pp. 264-65 also see pp. 492-93 also परमार्थतः सर्वधर्मानुत्पादसमतया परमार्थतः *op. cit.*, pp. 375-75.

29. मायी सष्टजति विश्वं सन्निरूद्धसूत्रमायया *Pañcadaśi,* 6.197. also 6.212. ष्टाक्तिद्वयदज्ञानोपहितष्ट चैतन्यं स्वप्रधानतया निमित् स्वोपाधिप्रधानतया उपादानश्च भवति *Vedāntasāra,* p. 38.
30. कुष्ठलमनुत्तरायै सम्यक् संबोधाय परिणामयति'' *Pañcaviṃśatisāhasrikāprajñ-pāramitā,* p. 265 ''तेऽपि सर्वेख्रप्रज्ञापारमितायां ष्टिाक्षित्वा अनुत्तरां सम्यक् संबोधिमभिसंबुद्धाः *op. cit.*, p. 267.
31. तत्त्वं यत् सतत् द्वयेन रहितं भ्रान्तेश्च संनिश्चय। ष्टाक्यं नैव च सर्वथाभिलपितुं यञ्चा-प्रपञ्चात्मकम्। ज्ञेयं अथ विष्ठुद्धयम्मलं यञ्च प्रकृत्यामलम्। यस्याकाष्ठसुवर्ण-वारिसदृष्ठी केष्ठाद्विष्ठुद्धिधर्मता *Mahāyānasūtrākaṅkāra,* II.13.p. 58.
32. स्वकाये दष्टज़्टि आत्मात्मीयदष्टष्टि : *Vṛtti Mūlamadhyamakakārikā,* 23.5 also आत्मानुपलम्भाञ्च सत्कायदष्टष्टिप्रहाणं तत्प्रहाणाञ्च सर्वकेष्ठाव्यावष्टतिं समनुपष्ठयन् *Mahabhyamakavṛtti,* p. 340.
33. महायानेऽप्रमेयानामसंख्येयानामपरिमाणनां सत्त्वानामवकाष्ठः *Pañcavimśatisri-kāprajñapāramitā, p. 236 cf.* also धर्मधातु as अचिन्तयधातु *op cit.*, 'यश्च धर्मधातुर्या च तथता या च भूतकोटिः यश्चाचिन्त्यधातुर्यश्च निर्वाणंसर्व एते धर्मा न संयुक्ता न विसंयुक्ता अरूपिणोऽनिदर्ष्ठना अप्रितघा एकलक्षणा यदुतालक्षणाः p. 244 also see pp. 239-40.
34. अभावस्वभावः सर्वधर्मा इति *op. cit.*, p. 252 also निःस्वभावतयासिद्धा उत्तरोत्तरनिश्रयात्। अनुत्पन्नानिरूद्धादियष्ठान्तप्रकृतिनिर्वष्टताः *Mahāyānasūtrā-laṅkāra,* Reconstructed from Chinese version. See French Translation, Tome II. p. 122, also see the commentary thereunder.
35. अनेकार्थमनानार्थमनुच्छेदमष्ठाश्वतम्।
एतत्तल्लोकनाथानां बुद्धानां ष्टासनामृतम्
Mūlamadhyamakakārikā 18.11. also कात्यायनाववादे च अस्ति नास्तीति चोभयम्। प्रतिज़िद्धं भगवता भावाभावाभिभविना *Mūlamadbyamakakārikā* 15.7. also *Madhyamakavṛtti,* p. 269. ''अस्तीति ष्टाश्वतग्राहो नास्तीति उच्छेतदर्ष्ठनम् *op. cit.*, Kārika, 15.10 also Catustava (Acintya stava) 21.
36. द्वे सत्ये समुपाश्रित्य बुद्धानां धर्मदेष्ठाना।
लोकसंवष्टतिसत्यश्च परमार्थतः।।
Mūlamadhyamakakārikā, 24.8. also दुबे सञ्चानि अकःखासि संबुद्धोदतां वरो। सम्मुतिं परमत्थं च ततीयं नुपलव्भति quoted in *Kathāvatthu,* (Aṭṭha Kathā) PTS. p. 30; also *Sumaṅgalavilāsini,* PTS. p. 251.
37. संव्रियते आव्रियते यथाभूतपरिज्ञानं स्वभाववषवरणादावष्टतप्रकाष्ठानाञ्च नयेति संवष्टतिः *Bodhicaryāvatārapañjikā,* p. 352, also see p. 361. *cf.* also

तुच्छानिर्वचनीया च वास्तवी चेत्यसौ त्रिधा। ज्ञेया माया त्रिभिर्बोधे: श्रोतयौक्तिकलौकिके: *Pañcadaśi,* 6.130. *et. seq.*

38. अविद्या मोहो विपर्यास इति पर्याय: *Bodhicaryāvatārapañjikā,* p. 352.

39. प्रतीत्यसमुत्पत्रं वस्तुरूपं संवष्टतिरूच्यते *loc cit.*

40. प्रत्यक्षपि रूपादि प्रसिद्धया न परमार्थत: *op. cit.*, pp. 374-75 also Verite conferme a l'assentiment universel mais erroni' *Journal Asiatique,* 1903, Tome II, p. 302.

41. *Bodhicaryāvatāra, p.* 353.

42. व्यवहारमनाश्रित्य परमार्थो न देष्टयते *Mūlamadhyamakakāridā* 24.10. also उपायुक्त व्यवहारसत्यमुपेयभूतं परमार्थसत्यम् *Bodhicaryāvatārapañjikā,* p. 372 also सत्य इमे दुवि लोकविदूनां दिष्ट स्वयं ग्रश्रुणित्व परेज्ञां। संवृति या च तथा परमार्थ सत्यु न सिद्धति किं च तृतीयु quoted *op. cit.*, pp. 361-62.

43. न ष्ठून्यवादी लोकधर्मै: संह्वियते निराश्रितत्वात् *Aryadharma Saṁgitīstūra,* quoted in *Śikṣāmuccaya,* p. 264. नित्यानित्य वस्तुविवक्षत्वात् बह्मैव नित्यं वस्तु ततोऽन्यदखिलमनित्यमिति विवेचनम् *Vedāntasāra* Section 7.

44. *Bodhicaryāvatārapañjikā,* pp.366-67.

45. also न मष्टतो दष्ठामस्तीति श्रुत्वाप्तवचनं तदा पराक्षत्वेन दष्ठामं वेत्ति स्वर्गादिलोकवत् *Pañcadaśi*,7.26 *et seq.*

46. सयं ञ्रभिञ्ञा सच्छिकत्ता *Digbanikāya*, PTS,III. p. 76.

47. सर्वोलम्भोपष्ठाम: प्रपञ्चोपष्ठाम: ष्ठिव: । न क्वचित् कस्यचित् कश्चित् धर्मो बुद्धेन देष्ठित:।।

Mūlạmadbyamakakārikā, 20, 25. also नोदाहृतं त्वया किश्चित् एकमप्यक्षरं विभो।

कष्टतस्नश्च वैनेयजनो धर्मवर्ज़ेण तर्पित:।। *Nirupamastotra*, Tucci edition, *JRAS.*, 1932 pp. 309 ff. also स हि परमार्थोऽपरप्रत्यय: ष्टान्त: *Madbyamakavṛtti* , p. 493.

48. प्रत्यात्मवेद्य ञ्रार्याणां सर्वपपञ्चातीत:। स नोपदिष्ठयते न चापि ज्ञायते *Madbyamakavṛtti*, p. 493.

प्रत्यात्माधिगमार्थोज्ञानगोचरलक्षणं बहिर्धा ते महामते असंकथ्या: *Laṅkāvatāra*, Nanjio edition, p. 61 आर्याणां स्वसंविदितस्वभावतया प्रत्यात्मवेद्यम्'' *Bodbicaryāvatārapañjikā*, p. 493.

49. नो हीदं भगवन् नास्ति स कश्चिद् धर्मो यस्तथागतेनभाज़ित: *Vajraccbedikāprajñāpāramitā*, p. 29 also अनक्षरस्य धर्मस्य श्रुति: का देष्ठाना च का quoted in Madhyamakavṛtti, p. 264

also in Bodbicaryāuatārapañjikā, p. 365. तत्वं ह्राक्षरवर्जितम् *Lankāuatāra*, p. 194.
निरक्षत्वाद्धर्मस्य *op. cit*. p. 48. also यतो वाचो निवर्त्तन्ते अप्राप्य मनसा सह *Katha Upaniṣad*, 2. 3. *Brahmasūtra* 3.2.17 with *Śaṅkarabhāṣya* a so मम तु महामते परमार्थनित्याचिन्त्यं परमार्थलक्षणहेतुयुक्तम् *Laṅkāvatāra*, p. 60. तस्यानित्याचिन्तयताया: सहेतुलक्षण न जानीते *op cit.*, p. 61.

50. श्रूयते देष्ठयते चापि समारापादनक्षर: *Madhoyamakavṛtti* p. 264 also *Bodhicaryāvatārapañjikā*, p. 365. ज्ञेयमेव समारोपितरूपत्वादावष्टति: *Bodhicaryāvatāra*, p. 447.

51. व्यवहारिकवस्तुत्वेनाभिमते रज्जौ अवस्तुभूतसर्पारोपो नाम रज्जववच्छिन्नचैतन्यस्थविद्या सर्पज्ञानाभासाकारेण परिणममाना *Vedāntaśarasubodhini*, p. 17. "असल्लक्षणसमारोपोऽसदष्टष्टिसमारोपोसद्धेतुसमारोपोऽसद्भावसमारोप: *Laṅkāvatāra*, p. 71 *et seq*.

52. असङ्गोदासीने परमात्मवस्तुनि तद्विवर्त्तभूताज्ञानादिमिथ्याप्रपञ्चस्य चिद्वस्तुमात्रावष्ठेज़तया. वस्थान भेवापवाद: *op. cit.*, p. 73. "कुदष्टष्टिसमारोपस्यानुपलब्धिप्रविचयाभवा. दपवादोभवति *Laṅkāvatāra*, p. 71.

53. यस्मात् प्रवर्तते भावस्तेनोच्छेदो न जायते। यस्मान् निवर्त्तते भावस्तेन नित्यो न जायते *Catuhśataka*, Viśvabhārati, 10.25 also *cf*. ष्ठून्यता च नोच्छेद: संसारश्च। कर्मणो विप्रनाष्ठाश्च धर्मो बुद्धेन देष्ठित: *Mūlamadhyamakakārikā*, 17.20.

54. न च वयं सर्वथैव निज़प्रपञ्चानां तथागतानां नास्तित्वं व्रुमो यदस्माकं तदपवादकष्टत: दोज़: स्यात् *Madhyamakavṛtti*, p. 443. श्रूयते देष्ठयते चापि समारोपादनक्षर: *Bodhicaryāvatārapañjikā*, Bi, p. 365.

55. समारोपापवादलक्षणं मे भगवान् देष्ठायतु *Laṅkavatāra*, p. 70.

56. स गुरूपरमकष्टपया अध्यारोपापवादन्यायेनैनमुपदिष्ठाति *Vedāntasāra*, p. 15 also अध्यारोपापवादाभ्यां प्रज्ञानं ब्रह्मादर्ष्ठितम् *Pañcadaśi*, 7.68.

57. ज्ञेयमेव समारोपितरूपत्वादावष्टति: *Bodhicaryāvatāra*, p. 447. also श्रुयते देष्ठयते चापि समारोपादनक्षर: *Madhyamadavṛtti*, p. 264 यदि खलु तदध्यारोपाद् भाववद्धिरस्तीत्युच्यते कीदष्टष्ठां तत् *op. cit.*, p. 264. *et. seq*.

58. केयं धर्माणां धर्मता धर्माणां स्वभावख़्कोऽयं स्वभाव:ख़्येयं ष्ठून्यता केयं ष्ठून्यता नि:स्वाभाव्यम् *Madhyamakavṛtti*, p. 264-65.

59. किमिदं नि:स्वाभाव्यम् तथता केयं तथता तथाभाव: *loc. cit*. For Tathatā see *MadhyāntavibHāgasūtrabhā2yaṭikā*, Calcutta, 1932, p. 41 (1.15-16). *Trimśika*, Levi's edition, p. 21.

60. तथाभावोऽविकारित्वं सदैव स्थायता *Madhyamakavṛtti,* p. 264-65.
61. यथैव गन्धर्व्वपुरं मरीचिका यथैव माया सुपिनं यथैवम्। स्वभावशून्या हि तु निमित्तभावना तथोपमान् जानथ सर्वधर्मान् *Samādhirājasūtra,* Buddhist Text Society, 9, p. 29. गन्धर्वनगराकारा मरीचिस्वप्रसन्निभा: *Mūlamadhyamadakārikā,* 17.33. also see *Vṛtti* thereunder. गन्धर्वनगरस्वप्नमायानिर्मायण-सदृशा: Laṅkāvatāra; p. 283. also *Subhāṣitasaṇgraha,* Bendall's edition, p. 14.
62. स्वकाये दृष्टिरात्मात्मीयदृष्टि: *Madhyamakavṛtti* on Kūrikā, 23.5.
63. सत्कायदृष्टिप्रभवान शेज्ञान्खआत्मानमस्य विज्ञयं च बुद्धा योगी करोत्यात्मानिज़ेध मेव *op. cit.,* p. 340, also see *tattvasaṇgraha,* 3489.
64. न शून्यवादी लोकधर्मे: संह्रियतेऽनाश्रितत्वात् न स लाभेन संहृज्यतैऽलाभेन वा विमना भवति यशसा न विस्मयतेऽयशसा न संकुचति।खशून्यवादिनो न क्वचिदनुरागो न विराग: quoted, *Śikṣāsamuccaya,* p. 264.
65. ममेति अहमिति क्षीणे बहिर्धाध्यात्ममेव च। निरूध्यत उपादानं तत्क्षयाज्जन्मन: क्षय: *Mūlamadhyamadakārikā,* 18.5.
66. स न च तेन समाधिना मन्यते अहं समाहित इति। अहं समाधि समापत्स्ये। अहं समाधि समापद्ये। सर्वे एते विकल्पा महासत्त्वस्य न विद्यन्ते नोपलभ्यस्ते *Pañcaviṃśatisāhasrikāprajñāpāramitā,* p. 144.
67. पुन: परमार्थेन प्राप्तिर्नाभिसमयो न स्रोतआपन्नो सकृदागमी नानागामी नार्हन्न प्रत्येक-बुद्धो न बोधिसत्वो न बुद्ध: *op. cit.,* p. 261.
68. सर्वाकारज्ञता अद्वया अद्वैधीकारा सर्वधर्माभवतामुपादाय *op. cit.,* p. 142.
69. आनन्दादिभिरस्थूलादिभिश्चात्मात्र लक्षित:। अखण्डैकरस: सोऽहमस्मीत्येवमुपासते *Pañcadaśi,* 9-73 also संसर्गो वा विशिष्टो वा वाक्यार्थो नात्र सम्मत: अखण्डैक-रसत्वेन वाक्यार्थे विदुज्ञां मत:।। प्रत्यग्बोधो य आभाति सोऽद्वयानन्दलक्षण:।। *op. cit.,* 7.75-76.
70. तस्माद्देहादिव्यतिरिक्तात्मास्तित्ववादिनां देहादावहंप्रत्यय: मिथ्यैव न गौण:। तस्मान्मिथ्या प्रत्ययनिमित्तत्वात् सशरीरत्वस्य सिद्धं जीवतोऽपि विदुज्ञोऽशरीरत्वम् *Śaṅkarabhāṣya,* (Samanvaya) p. 152.
71. मिथ्यात्मनोऽसत्वे देहेन्द्रियादिबाधनं श्रवणादिबाधनं च ततश्च न केवलं लोकयात्रा समुच्छेद: – *Bhāmati ; Adyar,* p. 243.
72. नापि संस्कार्यो मोक्ष: येन व्यापारमपैक्षते Śaṅkarbhāṣya (Samanvaya) p. 126.
73. अनाधेयातिशायब्रह्मस्वरूपत्वान्माक्षस्य *loc. cit.,* see also *Bhāmati,* thereunder.
74. तस्मादहं ब्रास्मीत्येतदवसाना एव सर्वे विधय: सर्वाणि चेतराणि प्रमाणानि *Śaṅkarbhāṣ*

ya, (Samanvaya), p. 154, also सगुणोपासनमपि चितैकाग्रथद्वारा निर्विष्ठोज़ ब्रह्मसाक्षात्कारहेतुः *Vedāntaparibhāṣā,* Nyayapañcānana edition, p. 355.

75. यस्तु साक्षात्कारो भाविकः, नासौ कार्यः तस्य ब्रह्मस्वरूपत्वात् *Bhāmati,* Adyar, p. 244.

76. ग्रप्रहीनमसंप्राप्तमनुच्छिन्नमष्ठाश्वतं। ग्रनिरूद्धमनुत्पन्नमेतन्निवांणमुच्यते *Madhyamakavṛtti,* chap. 25. यश्च धर्मधातुयां च तथता या च भूतकाटिः यश्चाचिन्त्यधा-तुर्यश्च निर्वाणम् सर्व एते धर्मा न संयुक्ता न विसंयुक्ता ग्ररूपिणोऽनिदर्ष्ठना एकलक्षणा यदुतालक्षणाः *Pañcaviṃsatisāhasrikāprajñāpāramitā,* p. 244 also see pp. 239-40.

77. तथागतो हि प्रतिबिम्बभूतः कुष्ठालस्य धर्मस्यानास्त्रवस्य *Madhyamakavṛtti,* pp. 449-50.

78. नित्यष्ठुद्धतां च ब्रह्मणो दर्ष्ठयतः ब्रह्मभावश्च मोक्षः। तस्मान्नसंस्कार्योऽपि मोक्ष : *Śaṅkarbhāṣya* (Samanvaya), p. 128.

79. *Śaṅdarabhāṣya, Brahmasūtra,* 3.2.17 also ग्रष्ठाब्दमस्पर्ष्ठमरूपमव्ययं तथा वसन्नित्यमगन्धवञ्च यत्। ग्रनाद्यानन्तं महतः परं ध्रुव। निचाय्य तन्मष्टत्युमुखात् प्रमुच्यते *Kaṭha Upaniṣad,* 3.15. also see 2.3.

80. ईज़द् भासमानाभासः प्रतिबिम्बस्तथाविधः विम्बलक्षणहीनः सन् बिम्बवत् भासते स हि *Pañcadaśi,* 8.31.

81. *advayajñāna* of the Mādhyamikas प्रज्ञापारमिताज्ञानमद्वयं स तथागतः। साध्या ताद्र्थ्ययोगेन तच्छब्द्यं ग्रन्थमार्गयोः quoted, *Abbisamayālaṅkāra,* Gaekward Oriental Series, p. 28. प्रत्यया प्रत्ययोत्पन्ना ग्रविद्यातथतादयः। ध र्मद्वयेन वर्तन्ते अद्वया तथता भवेत्।। *Laṅkavatāra,* p. 348. Saṅkara's explanation of *ādibuddhāb* in *Gauḍapadakārikā,* 4.92 as ग्रबुद्धाः नित्यबोधस्वरूपाः and of *kṣānti* as बोधकर्तव्यतानिरपेक्षता also नित्यष्ठुद्ध-बुद्धमुत्कसत्यस्वभावं प्रत्यक् चेतन्यमेव ग्रात्मतत्त्वमिति वेदान्तविदनुभवः *Vedāntasāra,* p. 72 ग्रात्मेति भदन्त ष्ठारद्वतीपुत्र बुद्धस्यैतदधिवचनम् *Saptaśatikāprajñāpāramitā,* Tucci edition, p. 124.

82. सर्वोपलम्भोपष्ठामः प्रपञ्चोपष्ठामः ष्ठिवः *Mūlamadbhyamadkakārikā,* 20.25 also निस्वाभावतयासिद्धा उत्तरोत्तरनिश्रयाम्। अनुत्पन्नानिरूद्धादिष्ठान्तप्रकृतिनिर्वताः *Mahāyānasūtrālaṅkarā.* 11.51. also Tibetan, gzod, ma. nas, shi. ba. meaning ग्रादितः ष्ठान्तः in Tibetan *Madhyamakaśāstra* of Nāgārjuna.

19

A RARE TYPE OF BODHISATTVA-IMAGES FROM SANCHI

In the exterior southern niche of Temple 45 at Sanchi, dating from the tenth-eleventh century, is a two-armed male deity : the head which had a circular halo around it is broken; the damaged right hand is in *varada-mūdrā* and the left, holding the stalk of a half-blown lotus, rests on the seat. Flanked by a female attendant on either side, he is seated in *lalitāsana* on a double-petalled lotus with a peacock below it, the pendant right leg resting on another lotus. He is richly bejewelled and is clad in an undergarment held by a girdle studded with gems; a pleated scarf encircles his body. But for the broken head the sculpture (pl. I)[1] would have been one of the best specimens of medieval art. Another image (pl. II), with almost identical features, again with its head broken, is exhibited in the local museum.

Sir John Marshall, probably thinking the sculpture as the representation of the male counterpart of Mahāmāyūrī, also known as Vidyārājñī, tentatively identified it with Mayūravidyārāja[2]. Such a deity, however, does not find mention in the extant texts on Buddhist iconography. Besides, there is hardly any similarity between this sculpture and the representation of Mahāmāyūrī, the personification of the Tantric text of that name. The peacock in the sculptures is the only point which might have led Marshall to associate them with the goddess of the Pañcarakṣāmaṇḍala. But the *dhyānas* of Mahāmāyūrī, as given in the *Sādhanamālā,* do not prescribe the peacock as her *vāhana* but lay down that she should hold peacock-tail or feather in one of her hands[3]. On the other hand the *varada* pose of the right hand and the lotus held by the left hand in the sculptures suggest their affiliation with some form of Avalokiteśvara.

Of all the deities of the later Buddhist pantheon, of whom *dhyānas* are available, that of Vajradharma Lokeśvara is the nearest approach to the sculptures under discussion. This form of Avalokiteśvara is thus described in the *Sādhanamālā:*

> *Tam sitaṁ rakta-varṇaṁ tu padmarāga-sama-dyutim*
> *Pañca-Buddha-makuṭa-dharaṁ harṣeṇotphulla-locanam*
> *Vāmato spardhayā nālaṁ dhṛtvā ṣoḍasa-patrakam*
> *Padmam vikāśayantaṁ ca bṛdi dakṣiṇa-pāṇinā*
> *Mayūropari madhyasthe niṣaṇṇaṁ candra-maṇḍale*
> *Sattvaparyaṅkam ābhujya sa-śṛṅgāra-rasotsavam*
> *Caityāntastha-mahākarma-kūṭāgāra-vihāriṇam*
> *Bhāvayed Vajradharmāgryaṁ nityaṁ bodhiṁ avāpnuyāt*[4]

'(The worshipper) should meditate on that supreme Vajradharma, who is of reddish white complexion, who has the brilliance of the *padmarāga* gem, who holds on his crown the five Buddhas, whose eyes beam with delight, who, while proudly holding in his left hand a lotus-stalk, causes a sixteen-petalled lotus to bloom on his chest with his right hand, who is seated in the centre of a lunar orb on a peacock while enjoying his animal-seat, who is festive with amorous sentiment and who lives in the sanctum inside a *caitya,* where great performances take place. (The worshipper meditating this form) obtains the *bodhi* eternally.'

The Sanchi sculptures agree in almost all the details with the above description of Vajradharma Lokeśvara, except that the right hand is in *varada*[5] and is not placed on the breast in the attitude of causing a lotus to blossom[6]. The *dhyāna* does not specify the ā*sana* of the deity but the *lalitāsana* of the sculptures is not unbecoming a god 'who is festive with amorous sentiment', with which is also consistent the rich ornamentation of the sculptures. As the crown along with the head is broken in both the images we cannot be sure whether it bore the effigies of the five Dhyāni Buddhas, as enjoined in the s*ādhana* of Vajradharma Lokeśvara.

It may be noted, however, that the images of Vajradharma Lokeśvara, truly answering to the description in the *Sādhanamālā,* are not unknown. In the gallery of the Indian Museum is exhibited an image, (p1. Ill)[7] of the deity, hailing from Bihar. Richly bejewelled he is seated in *paryaṅkāsana* on a *viśvapadma* (double-petalled lotus) resting on a throne suppor-ted by a pair of peacocks; he opens against his breast petals of a lotus, the stalk of which is held by his left hand. On his *karaṇḍamakuṭa* are shown five Dhyāni Buddhas in three rows of three, one and one each respectively. The oval halo is inscribed with the Buddhist creed and a donative record in characters of *circa* tenth century. In front of the throne is a dwarfish fierce-looking figure with bristling flame-like hair in *pratyālīḍha* attitude; with his right hand he brandishes a mace *(mudgara),* while his left hand is shown against his breast with the index finger raised and holding a noose *(tarjanīpāśahṛda-yastha vāmakaram).* This figure may stand for Kṛṣṇayamāri as described in one of the *sādhanas* quoted by B. Bhattacharyya in his *Indian Buddhist Iconography,* p. 71. The description tallies in most of the details with it except in the matter of the buffalo-mount which is absent here. A second representation of the deity (p1. IV) exists in the reserved collection of the said museum.[8] The main deity seated on a *viśvapadma* supported by a pair of peacocks is remarkably similar to the preceding, but here he is flanked by two goddesses seated in the same ā*sana,* the left one of whom holds *vajraghaṇṭ ās* in her both hands. She may be described as the goddess Vajraghaṇṭā,. one of the four 'guardians of the gates' associated with such Vajra-yāna deities as Lokanātha and Vajratārā. The sā*dhanas* describe her as one-faced and two-armed carrying a bell surmounted by *vajra.* The attributes in the hands of the right hand goddess are broken. Above these goddesses are the representations of a *viśvavajra* and *ratna(?)* on a stand, On the pedestal is a three headed six-armed dwarfish deity with terrible appearance, open mouths and bare fangs in *ālīḍha* attitude; in his right hand he carries a sword, a mace and a *padma;* of his left hands, one holds a *pāśa,* the second broken and the third is in *-kaṭihasta* pose. This deity may stand for another variety of Kṛṣṇayamāri as described in the *Sādhanamālā*[9] The absence of mounts in both the forms of Kṛṣṇayamāri, as represented in the pedestal of the two Vajradharma Lokeśvara images, may be due to their being attendant deities. On two sides of this figure on the pedestal are two goddesses, the left one of whom standing in *ālīḍha* pose and holding a *kartṛ* and a *kapāla* is equally awe-inspiring and dwarfish, corresponding in her iconographic details to Ekajaṭā; the right one holding a rosary and a *kamaṇḍalu(?)* stands in *pratyālīḍha* attitude. The sculpture, dating from *circa* tenth century, comes from Nalanda.

Debala Mitra

FOOTNOTES

1. Photographs reproduced on pls. I-IV are the copyright of the Department of Archaeology, Govt. of India.
2. J. Marshall, *Monuments of Sanchi,* vol. I, p. 74.
3. B. Bhattacharyya, *Indian Buddhist Iconography* (Oxford, 1924) p. 111.
4. *Sādhanamālā,* ed. B. Bhattacharyya, I (Gaekwad's Oriental Series, XXVI, Baroda, 1925), p. 33.
5. Of the two illustrations given by B. Bhattacharyya in his *Indian Buddhist Iconography,* one (p1. XXIV e), taken from the paintings of the modern Nepalese artists, has a manuscript in his right hand, while the other (p1. XLVIII), as found on the wooden panels of the Macchandar Vahal *vihāra* at Kathmandu, shows his right hand in *abhaya-mttdrā,* pp. 51 and 180.
6. The half-blown lotus in the left hand of the sculptures may possibly signify the 'causing of a lotus to bloom'. In the analogous case of Tārā as the attendant of Khasarpaṇa, the *sādhanas* say that she should cause to bloom a stalked lotus with her right hand *(sanālaṁ*

utpalaṁ dakṣiṇakareṇa vikāśayantī), Bhattacharyya, *ibid,* p. 37, but often in sculptures she holds a half-blown lotus in her left hand, the empty right hand being in some *mudrā* (cf. *ibid.*, pl. XXI).

7. No. 3784. The photograph has heen reproduced on pl. IX (a) of R, D. Banerji's *Eastern Indian School of Mediaeval Sculpture.* There it is labelled as Vajrapāni.
8. No. 3798. Both these sculptures are noticed in T, Bloch's *Supplementary Catalogue of the 'Archaeological Collection of the Indian Museum,* pp 61-62 where they are described as Padmapāni.
9. *Indian Buddhist Iconography,* pp. 72-73.

20

SCIENTIFIC BACKGROUND OF THE BUDDHIST TANTRAS

Usually, it is the habit with uninformed people to decry a thing because it is not understood. The rule applies with equal force to the science and practice of the Tantras. Many scholars have dubbed the Tantras as magic, black magic, necromancy, unscientific and psuedo-scientific, and decried the teachings and findings of the Tantras as being worthless and worthy of nothing but unqualified condemnation on this or that ground. It will, therefore, be a shock to many to learn that the Tantras are based on solid scientific facts, and that their followers derived and utilized cosmic power which is freely floating around.

The Tāntrics were conversant with the theory of tele-communication like radio and tele-vision, and that they could transmit sound and power through space without elaborate appliances. Durasravana (hearing distant sounds), Dūradarśana (seeing distant visions), Dūracikitsā (distant healing) and similar powers were listed as Siddhis (super-normal powers) as a direct outcome of Tantric Sādhana, In the Tantric works there is a clear indication that heat and cold could be transmitted through space to the desired object or person, and influence it or him from a distance. The process of Śānti (propitiation) could be performed from a distance, and thereby bring about the cure of a disease.

In the Tantras cosmic colour plays a most important part.

Every deity has an individual colour, every direction has a colour; the Dhyāni Buddhas were made up of one colour or another. The Tāntrics were conversant with the power of cosmic colours and employed them for multifarious purposes. The Tāntrics of the Buddhist faith considered Śunya as the creator of the universe, limitless, omnipotent and omni-present, and the repository of infinite wisdom, infinite knowledge, infinite sound and infinite light. The Tāntrics intuitively knew that the world of matter in its ultimate state is nothing but rays and radiations, and this knowledge is reflected in their writings and in their many and varied practices of bewildering intricacy.

The Tāntrics formulated that all letters, words and sentences, with or without meaning, are nothing but Śūnya in essence, that is to say, they are condensations of cosmic power, and therefore, these letters, words and sentences have certain definite vibrations, and these vibrations can be employed for good as well as evil. The deities are the beings of the invisible world just as we are the beings of the visible world. The deities have their definite vibrations because they are nothing but Śūnya in essence, that is to say, the deities are condensations of Śūnya, the ultimate cosmic force. The Mantras for the deities have the same vibrations as their presiding deities; they are able to attract the deities and make them visible to the mind's eye, and when Sādhana reaches its final point they become visible even to the naked eye. The worshiper and the deity become one by the process of complete identification, and the Sādhaka derives all the powers residing in the deity.

The Tāntrics knew the power of the mind which according to them was Śūnya in essence. The mind has one peculiar power, and with the help of this power the human mind could adjust itself to the different vibrations and become one with them. In modern scientific language the mind has the power to adjust itself to the same wavelength as that of the deity or anything, high or low. Low thoughts lower down the wave-length of the mind while higher thoughts raise its level. Even Śūnya can be conceived and realised if the mind is properly attuned to the highest wave-length of the Śūnya or the Absolute Limitless Cosmic Substratum.

Further, the Tāntrics were acquainted with the fact that certain syllables had the same wave-length as those of the five Skandhas (elements), and that the utterance of the syllables gave rise to the same set of vibrations as those of the five Skandhas (elements). The five Skandhas, it may be remarked, are the counterparts of the five *Tanmātras* or 'subtle substances' as formulated in the Sāṁkhya system of philosonhy. Behind the Skandhas are the five cosmic colours which by condensation give rise to the five Dhyāni Buddhas and their numerous offspring. The five Dhyāni Buddhas, their cosmic colours and the five Skandhas or cosmic principles represented by them are given in the Table below for ready reference :

Dhyāni Buddhas	*Skandhas*	*Colours*
Vairocana	Rūpa	White
Ratnasambhava	Vedanā	Yellow
Amitābha	Saṁjñā	Red
Amoghasiddhi	Saṁkāra	Green
Akṣobhya	Vijñāna	Blue

The Tāntrics recognised no difference between name and form, and believed rightly that the name is not different from form, and that even a syllable can represent the Skandhas, and all the power the Skandhas possess, is contained in the syllable itself. These syllables are known as the Bījamantras or Seed-syllables, usually consisting of one syllable with an anusvāra. There were syllables for the ultimate cosmic principles such as Earth, Air, Water and Fire. The seed LAṂ, for instance, stands for the Pṛthvī principle, VAṂ for the Ap principle, RAṂ for the Fire principle and YAṂ for the Air principle. This indicates that there is no difference between RAṂ and Fire, and that by constant meditation on the seed RAṂ the Fire principle can be brought under control, manifestly because the wave-length of the two happen to be the same.

In the same way, by patient research they found out the

germ syllables and the Mantras of the deities of the Vajrayāna system. The germ syllables were the deities themselves and the Mantras formed the call-signs for the different deities. In other words, the Tāntrics discovered the supreme truth that Bījamantras are endowed with the same vibrations as those of the deities, and by employing the Mantras the corresponding deities can be attracted, visualised and realised. In terms of modern science, the Mantras and the Bījamantras have the same set of vibrations or wave-length as the deities of the invisible world, and that the human mind was capable of changing and tuning its vibrations to the wave-length of the deity by constant meditation.

The difference between the Bīja and the Mantra is something like this: The Bīja represents the deity in a subtle form while the Mantra is for the gross form. The syllable TĀṂ, for instance, is the Bīja of the popular Vajrayāna deity, Tārā. This Mantra is required in the beginning of meditation, and the mind should concentrate on its Yellow Rays spreading out to the firmament and illumining the invisible worlds and there discover the form of the deity. The longer Mantra of Tārā is: OM TARE TUTTĀRE TURE SVĀHĀ which is to be constantly repeated and meditated upon in order to bring the deity nearer to the worshipper by the process of attraction. According to the Buddhist Tāntrics different Mantras have different powers although they may relate to the same deity. The different Mantras have to be utilized for different purposes. Everywhere it was conceded that the Bīja, Mantra and the rest had the same set of vibrations as the deity worshipped, because they recognised no difference between the deity and its various symbols—all having the same measure of vibrations.

The method of propitiation and realisation of the deities or the radiant beings of the invisible world was elaborated in the Sādhana which may be called the WHO's WHO of these radiant beings. But more interesting and instructive is the story of how the Tāntrics used to transmit power through space to distant objects either for good or for evil. In the Mahākāla

Sādhana at the end part of the famous Tāntric work, the *Sādhanamālā,*[1] this story is related in detail. The details of the process of distant influencing became the starting point of the unique and the most practical system of healing by Tele-Therapy or the Cosmic Ray Therapy which seeks to cure patients from a distance without medicine, personal attendance or examination. The process described in the Sādhana, therefore deserves special attention.

In the Mahākāla Sādhana, it is said that in order to influence a person at a distance an effigy of *Kuśa* grass should be made for the person aimed at, and thereon the Mahākāla Mantra should be repeated continuously. Then *Visarājikā* seeds and pungent condiments like black pepper, dry ginger and *Pippalī* should be powdered, mixed and prepared into a paste. This paste should be liberally applied to the effigy while repeating the Mantra already cited. Then on each and every limb thorns should be pierced. Thereafter, a fire should be made with *Khadira* wood, and on that fire the effigy should be baked while repeating the Mantra. When this is done, the person aimed at is suddenly overtaken by high temperature and his consciousness is lost.

When, however, it becomes necessary to counteract the effect of the process just described, the Sādhana adds that the effigy should be removed from fire, and milk should be poured on the effigy until fever subsides.

In terms of the present day science, it can be easily understood why Mantras have to be repeated in order to bring the effigy in tune with the vibrations of the victim aimed at. Mantras are repeated continuously in order to raise the wave-length of the inanimate effigy of *Kuśa* grass to the level of the person to be influenced by adding word vibrations. And unless the wave-lengths of both the effigy and the person are tuned to the same length, the cosmic forces will not recognise the person, just as a Radio set will not give any programme until it is tuned to the same wave-length as that of the station radiating the pragramme. When after continuous muttering of the Mantra the vibrations of the effigy and the person are brought to the same level, the Tāntric is able to transmit the fire principle through space by heating and baking the image. As the wave-lengths of the two ends are the same the heat applied to the effigy is immediately transmitted through space to the person at a distance. No wonder the heat of the fire-principle brings about fever and delirium.

To reverse the effect of the earlier process is to bring normalcy in the victim by sending out cold vibrations by the same wireless method. For this purpose the effigy is taken out from fire. By this, heat is first eliminated, and then when milk is poured incessantly on the effigy cold vibrations of milk is transmitted through space to the victim. Milk represents the Water (Ap) principle, and moreover, being white in colour, it is doubly cooling. The healing process takes effect almost immediately and in a short time the victim is well.

Taking the cue from the Mahākāla Sādhana, a new system of healing, called Tele-Therapy is developed which seeks to transmit hot and cold forces or the forces of the five elements (Earth, Air, Water, Ākāśa and Fire) through space to patients at a distance, and make them well without medicine and without examination or external applications. It is not possible to prepare effigies for particular persons and raise their wave-length, because that is a very cumbrous process now in the present century when photography is so well developed. It may be noticed that the photograph has the same set of vibrations as its owner, and therefore, the wave-lengths of both the photograph and its owner are the same. The cosmic forces recognise this identity of wave-length. On the photographs certain jewel vibrations produced from an electric motor are released for several hours a day, and this has yielded remarkable results in a number of acute and chronic diseases. The experience of the last three years in the line has shown great promise, and it is now possible for us to foresee a time when the work of healing will be done with the help of photographs from an office or a laboratory. Whether we like it or not, we are enveloped in cosmic rays, call them either Mahābhūtas or the planets as it pleases. They are not at a distance, they are right in the midst of our bodies and our sense-organs. This will be shown when a person is examined through a prism by any common inquirer. When the Rays become malefic, illness supervenes, and again when they are altered, that illness disappears. In spite of our researches into the subject of disease and medicine, we have progressed very little and have not been able to find out the true cause of even the principal diseases. Once the cause is known, eradication becomes easy and simple. Let us remember that the diseases are in their ultimate state, nothing but rays and radiations. The so-called *virus* of modern medicine is the Ray Malefic.

The doctrine of the Buddhist Tāntrics that everything in this world has for its substratum the limitless Śūnya, and wherever there is a manifestation of Śūnya, a colour is attached to it. This gives a clue to find out the true colours of all tangible objects through a prism. With the help of a prism true colours of gems have been ascertained, all the VIBGYOR rays have been individualised and their powers have been pretty well fixed. And what is important, all the seven cosmic colours have been produced with the help of gems and an electric motor, and transmitted through space to numerous patients over their photographs with gratifying results. The gems are cosmic colour concentrates, they are Śūnya in essence, and their brilliance shows that they are not only rich in cosmic colours but also can readily discharge their rays when under the influence of an electric motor. The Rays travel with the speed of thought, and they are omniscient, omnipresent and omnipotent like their substratum—the Śūnya. The gems release hot and cold vibrations, e.g. the Green rays discharged by Emeralds send out cold vibrations, and the Red rays released by brilliant Rubies transmit hot vibrations; and they know exactly their mission, and unerringly reach their destination and start their healing work. Their working ways are as mysterious as those of the Creator himself.

It is high time, in spite of what the uninitiated or the ignorant may think or write, to divert our close attention to the Tantras, the repositories of higher scientific knowledge. The Tantras should not only be studied and treated with respect they deserve, but also scientific facts should be gleaned from them, and put into practical use through scientific institutions. Still there is much for modern science to learn from the Tantras. When the knowledge of the scientific aspect of the Tantras becomes the general property of mankind, the scientists will come face to face with the real substratum of the Universe, the Śūnya or Brahman, as it may be called, and start playing with the Cosmic Rays even as the great creator, endearingly called The Grandfather, does. When that stage is reached, the latest scientific developments are likely to pale into insignificance, because we are as yet ignorant of the cosmic elements, the cosmic rays and the great cosmic powers that are freely floating around. When we come to know what the Tāntrics knew, the difference between Magic, Philosophy and Science will disappear.

It is ignorance that makes a person think that he can do sinful acts in secret without a chance of their being detected by any visible or invisible agency. When true knowledge dawns on mankind a person will think several times before doing any improper action, because he is surrounded and enveloped in the ever-vigilant, omniscient, omnipresent and omnipotent cosmic rays which are watching him by day and by night, limb by limb, and examining him thought by thought. True knowledge of a scientific nature may still lead mankind to the high principles of Right Living and Right Thinking, as Graciously formulated by Lord Buddha Two Thousand Five Hundred years ago !

B. Bhattacharya

FOOTNOTES

1. *Sādhanamālā, GOS*. Vol. II. p. 589.

21

BUDDHISM IN SOUTH-EAST ASIA

Beginning

According to a tradition preserved in the Ceylonese Chronicles. Buddhism was preached in Suvarṇabhūmi by the missionaries of Aśoka. Though the location of Suvarnabhūmi is uncertain, some having identified it with Burma, others with Siam (Thailand), there is no doubt that it refers to some part of Indo-China. But the authenticity of the tradition itself is open to question, as no early and reliable evidence has been obtained so far in support of it. Nor can we accept the view that the first two disciples of the Buddha named Trapuṣa and Bhallika, who built a sanctuary over his relics in their native land, belonged to Burma, for the Utkala country, which is referred to in the canonical texts as their native land, is certainly to be identified with Orissa.

There is, however, no doubt that Buddhism obtained a definite footing in South-east Asia during the early centuries of the Christian era. This is proved by the discovery of the images of Buddha of the Amarāvatī style in Thailand (Sum), Annam (Campā), Sumatra, Java and Celebes. The representation of the Buddha by a symbol, such as *dharmacakra* (wheel of law), rather than a human figure, in some of the sculptures in Thailand, also support the introduction of Buddhism in this region at an early date.

1. Thailand

The early sculptures discovered in Thailand prove conclusively that Buddhism was introduced in this region at the beginning of the Christian era. A Wheel of Law, associated with figures of crouching deer, was dug up at Pra Pathom. Another early site, Pong Tuk, has yielded bronze Buddha images of the Amarāvatī style, which may be dated in the second century A.D. Buddhist images of the Gupta style, both of earlier and later type, have also been discovered. As the inscriptions, engraved on the latter, may be referred to the fifth and sixth centuries A.D., those of the earlier type probably belong to the fourth century A.D.

From this early period we may trace the uninterrupted progress of Hīnayāna Buddhism in this country. The Thai conquest of the land in the thirteenth century A.D. gave a great impetus to this religion. The Thai rulers were ardent followers of Hīnayāna Buddhism. We learn from the inscription of Rām Kamheng, that this famous king was an ardent follower of Hīnayāna Buddhism and decorated his capital Sukhodaya with temples, monasteries and images of Buddha at the close of the thirteenth century A.D. The Hīnayāna Buddhism of the Thais was sustained and influenced by Burma and the island of Ceylon. The intercourse between Mons of Lower Burma and Thailand were of long standing. A Thai king sent a messenger to Ceylon in A.D. 1361 who brought back with him a senior monk who reformed the religion. The Hīnayāna Buddhism with its Pali canon flourishes even now in Thailand, Burma and Ceylon, and it is not therefore necessary to discuss its history in great detail.

2. Cambodia

Buddhism made its influence felt in Cambodia as early as the fifth century A.D., for king Jaya-varman of Fu-nan, who ruled towards the close of that century, sent an embassy to China in A.D. 503, with presents including an image of Buddha. An inscription of his son Rudravarman begins with an invocation to Buddha. From this time onward the prevalence of Buddhism is proved by inscriptions. But it had a set-back in the 7th century, and the epigraphic records indicate that Śaivism, not Buddhism, was the dominant religion of Cambodia. It is curious, in view of the present state of things, that very few kings of Cambodia, of whom we possess any epigraphic record, were followers of Buddhism. Sūryvarman I (11th century A.D.) was a Buddhist, for he had the posthumous title *Nirvāṇa-pada*. But his inscription on a temple at Prah Khaṇ[1] begins with an invocation to Śiva in the first verse, and to the Buddha in the second. Several inscriptions on the temple known as Prasat Ta Keo,[2] in honour of Yogiśvara Paṇḍita, the *guru* of king Sūryavarman, begin with invocations to Śiva and Viṣṇu, and refer to donations made to these gods. Jayavarman VII, perhaps the greatest king of Kambuja, was a Buddhist, and his Ta Prohm Inscription, dated A.D. 1186, gives a detailed list of his magnificent donations to this temple.[3] The merit of these pious works was to accrue to the king's mother so that she might obtain the state of Buddha (v. 141).[4] In addition to the kings mentioned above, high dignitaries like Kavīdrārimathana and Kīrtipaṇḍita, both belonging to the tenth century A.D., were ardent Buddhists, and the latter claimed to have lighted again the torch of the true law which the sins of the world had extinguished. The form of Buddhism referred to is clearly Mahāyāna.

But if we take the epigraphic data as a whole, there remains no doubt that Buddhism was never a dominant religion in Kambuja till the time of Jayavarman VII. But even the patronage of this great emperor did not establish Buddhism as a state religion, as it is now. It is interesting to note that during the reign of king Śrīndra-varmadeva, a later king, we find an inscription[5], dated A. D. 1308, written in Pāli and referring to Hīnayāna form of Buddhism. The next two kings, Śrīndra-Jayavarman and jayavarma-Parameśvara were followers respectively of Viṣṇu and Śiva.

The state of religion in Cambodia is described by Cheu Ta-kuan who visited the country in A.D. 1296. It appears that Hīnayāna Buddhism was in a flourishing state at this time. Yet the older inscriptions mostly refer to Mahayana doctrine. Taking everything into consideration, we are forced to the conclusion that it was the influence of Thailand (Siam) that gradually introduced a great change in the religion of Kambuja. On the whole Brahmanical religion, specially Śaivism, was dominant in Kambuja, though Mahayana Buddhism was also a powerful sect, up to the end of the thirteenth century A.D. But the political dominance of the Thais (of Siam) in Cambodia established the supremacy of Hīnayāna Buddhism which is now the only religion of the people.

3. Campā

The ancient Hindu colony of Campā corresponds, roughly, to the southern part of Annam. The early introduction of Buddhism in this region is indicated by an image of Buddha of the Amarāvatī style at Dong-Duong. But there is no epigraphic reference to Buddhism before the 9th century A.D.[6] The Bakul Stelae Inscription,[7] dated A.D. 829, refers to the construction of two temples and two monasteries for Jina and Śaṅkara. Jina may denote either the Buddha or Mahāvīra, but as there is no evidence for the existence of Jainism in south-east Asia, Jina may be taken to denote Buddha. The long inscription on the four faces of a stelae found at Dong-Duong[8] records the installation of an image of Buddha in A.D. 875, and the foundation of a Buddhist temple and a monastery by the Buddhist king Indra-varman. The remains of a Buddhist temple at this place, far greater in dimensions than the largest Brahmanical temple in Campa, prove that Dong-Duong (ancient Amaṛāvatī) in the province of Quang Nam was an important stronghold of Buddhism in Campā.

Many later kings patronised Buddhism, and monasteries and temples were built in different parts of the kingdom. Many Buddhist images have also been found in different parts of Campā.

I-tsing refers to the prevalence of Buddism in Campā and remarks that the "Buddhists generally belong to the Āryasammitāya-nikāya and there are also a few followers of the Sarvāstivādanikāya." Thus Hīnayāna prevailed at the end of the seventh century A.D. But the inscriptions and images leave no doubt that the Mahāyāna soon occupied the dominant position in Campā. Particular reference may be made to An-Thai Stelae Inscription[9] dated 824 Śaka (= A.D. 902) which records the erection of a statue of Lokanatha by *sthavira* Naga-puṣpa, the abbot of the monastery of Pramudita-Lokeśvara, and refers to Vajradhātu, Padmadhātu and Cakradhātu, Amitābha and Vairocana.

It is interesting to note that Buddhist and Śaiva temples and monasteries were often erected side by side, by the same donor, that the epithet Damareśvara (lord of the *Bhūtas),* originally belonging to Śiva, was applied to Buddha, and that figures of Śiva decorated the Buddhist temples of Dong-Duong.

4. Malay Peninsula

The well-known Buddhist formula *'ye dharmā hetupra-bhavā'* etc. followed by another verse beginning with *Ajñānāc = cīyate karma,* is engraved on a slab of stone found amid the ruins of an ancient brick building at Keddah. The second verse alone is engraved on a piece of stone, probably a part of an old shrine, in the northern part of province Wellesley. Both these inscriptions have been referred to the fourth or fifth century A.D.[10] Three Sanskrit verses are inscribed on a clay tablet found near Keddah. They inculcate Mahāyāna philosophical doctri-nes of Mādhyamika school, and have been traced to a text entitled *Sāgaramati-paripṛcchā,* which is known only from a Chinese translation."[11]

The inscriptions mentioned above also prove that Buddhist temples, both of brick and stone, were built in Wellesley Provi-nce and Keddah in the fourth or fifth century A.D. The great *stupa* of Nakhon Śrī Dhammarāt and a number of temples surrounding it indicate the existence of a flourishing Buddhist colony in this region. A number of terracotta votive tablets found in neighbouring caves also show that a large number of Buddhist monks resided therein.

5. Indonesia[12]

Buddhism did not obtain a secure footing in Indonesia till

after the fourth century A.D. At the time when Fa-Hien visited Java there was very little trace of Buddhism in that island. But Guṇavar-man, who belonged to the royal family of Kipin (Kashmir or Afghanistan) but had taken to religion, preached Buddhism in Java early in the fifth century A.D., and it soon took deep root in the soil. As Gunavarman translated a text of the Dharmagupta sect, he must have belonged to the Mūlasarv-āstivāda school, and it was evidently due to his influence that this sect became dominant in Java and the neighbouring islands.

The neighbouring island of Bali also came under the influence of Buddhism about the same time. For according to the *History of the Liang Dynasty* (A. D. 502-556), the earliest Chinese historical annals that give an account of this island, the king of Bali claimed that the wife of Śuddhodana was a daughter of his country.

By the seventh century A.D. Buddhism flourished all over Indonesia, and Śrī-Vijaya in Sumatra became a stronghold of this religion, We possess an inscription, dated Śaka 606 (A.D. 684), of a Buddhist king of this country named Jayanāśa. There was a regular trade and maritime intercourse between Śrī-Vijaya and India. On his way to India the Chinese pilgrim I-tsing halted at Śrī-Vijaya for six months, and he again visited the place, after his return to China, in order to copy and translate the voluminous Buddhist texts which he had brought with him from India.

It is evident from I-tsing's statement that although Hīnayāna was dominant in these regions there were in Srī-Vijaya a few who followed the Mahāyāna form of Buddhism. This is also proved by the inscription of Jayanāśa referred to above. It not only contains definite reference to the Mahāyāna doctrine, but the use of the word *vajra-śarīta* further indicates that this Mahā-yāna was of the Tantrik form known as Vajra-yāna, Mantra-yāna or Tantra-yāna.

Indonesia was visited by eminent Buddhist scholars from India such as Dharmapāla, a Professor of Nālandā in the seventh century A.D., and Vajrabodhi, a South Indian monk. The latter and his disciple Amoghavajra, who accompanied him, were teachers of Tantrik cult and are credited with its introduction to China. Both of them halted at Śrī-Vijaya for five months on their way from Ceylon to China, early in the eighth century A.D.

Towards the close of this century the Mahāyāna cult acquired great predominance owing to the patronage of the Śailendras who ruled over the greater part of Indonesia. Two inscriptions, dated A. D. 778 and 782, refer to the construction of a temple of Tārā at Kalasan, and setting up of an image of Mañjuśrī at Kelurak by the Śailendra emperors. The latter was inspired by their *guru* Kumāra-ghoṣa, an inhabitant of Gauḍa. The Śailendra emperors were in close touch with the Pala emperor Devapala of Bengal, and the Cola emperor Rajarāja, both of whom endowed the monasteries built by the Śailendras, respectively at Nālandā and Negapatam.

The Mahāyāna form of Buddhism has left permanent memorials in Java in the famous *śtupa* of Barabuḍur and a number of other magnificent temples erected during the Śailendra rule. The Javanese literature and the Buddhist images found in Java clearly indicate that all the essential features of Mahāyāna, even of its last phases, were fully developed in that island. As in India, a number of Hindu gods were adopted in the Buddhist pantheon, though they were relegated to an inferior position. New divinities were introduced, some of which, like Trailokyavijaya, Hevajra, Bhairava and Heruka, were of monstrous or terrifying appearance. The Tantra-yāna, including Kāla-cakratantra, prevailed both in Java and Sumatra. The famous king Kṛtanagara of Java was a devout follower of the Tantra-yāna or Vajra-yāna, and his drinking bout is approved in a Javanese historical text on the ground that he scrupulously followed the prescriptions of religion. King Ādityvaraman of Malayu in Sumatra, who was ruling as a vassal of Kṛtanagara in A.D. 1286, seems to have been a follower of the Bhairava cult.

As in India, there was a gradual rapprochement between Mahāyāna and Brahmanical religion. This was more clearly indicated in Indonesia by the fact that gradually Śiva, Viṣṇu and Buddha were regarded as identical and so were their Śaktis. A definite Śiva-Buddha cult existed in Java, and in modern Balinese theology Buddha is regarded as a younger brother of Śiva.

There are two Buddhist texts in Java which give an interesting insight into the developed form of Mahāyāna. The first, *Sang hyang Kamahāyānikan* is a free Javanese version of a Sanskrit original, interspersed with a number of original Sanskrit verses. It was probably composed iṇ the Śailendra period (8th century A. D.), but was modified, about a century or two later, in a manner which has been regarded as a Hinduised or Śaiva version of a Buddhist original. It contains an exposition of the leading principles of Mahāyāna and gives an account of its theology according to the Yogācāra system. It brings the Hindu Trinity in organic relation with the Buddhist pantheon. The picture of Mahāyāna in Java which it unfolds shows a close resemblance with, but also minor differences from, the form of religion current in India.

The second text *Kamahāyanan Mantranaya* contains forty-one Sanskrit verses with Javanese commentaries. It contains an exposition of the Tantra-yāna or Vajra-yāna both in its theoretical and practical aspects. The five kinds of sensual enjoyments *(pañca-ma-kāra)* are clearly prescribed, and the devotee is forbidden to communicate the secrets of *uajra, ghaṇṭa* and *mudrā* to those who do not belong to the *Maṇḍala*.

R. C. MAJUMDAR

FOOTNOTES

1. R. C. Majumdar, *Inscriptions of Kambuja,* p. 360
2. *Ibid.,* pp. 351 ff.
3. *Ibid.,* pp. 459 ff,
4. *Ibid., p.* 474.
5. *Ibid.,* p. 533

6. Many scholars find traces of Buddhism in Vocanh inscription, but I do not find anything definitely Buddhist in it. (For the inscription cf. R.C. Majumdar, *Champa,* Book III, p. 1). Coedes maintains that it is Buddhist— *Les Etats Hindouises d'Indo-Chine et d'Indonesie* (1948), p. 74.
7. *Champa,* Bk. III, p. 65
8. *Ibid.*, p. 74
9. *Ibid.*, p. 195
10. R. C. Majumdar, *Suvarnadvipa,* Part I, pp. 88ff.
11. *IGIS,* VIII, p. 2.
12. For the facts mentioned in this section of *Suvarṇadvipa,* part II.

22

PRINCIPLE OF THE KING'S RIGHTEOUSNESS

[IN THE PALI CANON AND THE JĀTAKA COMMENTARY]

The most important contribution of the Buddhist canonists of the *Theravāda* School to the store of our ancient political thought consists in their 'total' application of the principle of righteousness to the branches of the king's internal and external policy. Its importance is matched by that of the parallel early *Smṛti* conception of a fundamental law of the social order (indicated by the same term *dharma)* which is held to be based upon the twofold source of the Sacred Canon and custom (or convention). In the descriptions of good kings (1.260 II.118, III, 325, *ibid* 470, V. 378) in the *Jātaka* stories we are told that they ruled in righteousness, that they shunned the four wrong courses of life *(agatigamana)* [comprising excitement, malice, delusion and fear], that they practised the ten royal duties *(rājadhamma)* [namely, alms-giving, morality, liberality, straightforwardness, refraining from anger and from injury, forbearance, and refraining from opposition], that they won over the people by the four elements of popularity *(saṁgabhavatthu)* [namely, liberality, affability, beneficent rule and impartiality]. Cast in a distinctly sectarian mould are the descriptions of good kings (1.262, V.1, VI.96-97) in other stories to the effect that not only did they rule in righteousness, but they were zealous in the observance of the fast-day and keeping the ten items of good behaviour *(sīla)* [namely, abstinence from taking life, from taking what is not given, from adultery, from telling lies, from slander, from harsh speech, from frivolous talks, from covetousness, from malevolence, and from heretical views.] We have again a remarkable story (no. 276) of eleven persons with the king at their head in the Kuru kingdom who practised what was called 'Kuru-righteousness' *(Kumdhamma)* identified in the course of the story with the five *Sīlas* obligatory upon the Buddhist lay disciple. How a king's righteousness instead of its reverse benefits himself is told in a few stories. Thus we learn (nos. 51, 151, and 282) how a king who conquered wrath by mildness, and badness with goodness was adjudged superior to another who met the good with goodness and the bad with baldness and how kings allowed themselves to be captured and ill-treated by neighbouring kings only to gain back their freedom and their kingdom through their inherent goodness.

The most impressive lessons on the principle of righteousness occur in course of the admonitions addressed to kings by wise beings in the stories. When a monkey-king, we read in one story (no. 407), wore himself out by his effort to save his followers from certain death, his captor, a human king, asked him (III. 373) the question,—What he was to them and what they were to him, that he made himself a bridge for their safely passing through a river? He felt no pain of his bonds, replied the monkey-king, because of securing the happiness of those over whom he reigned. Asking the human king to learn the lesson by his example, the monkey-king admonished him to seek the happiness of his whole realm, his beasts of burden, his troops and the inhabitants of his cities. In a second story (no. 501) a wise king instructs another king in the so-called ten stanzas relating to the practice of righteousness *(dāsadhammacariyā gāthā)*. These comprise the observance of righteousness towards the mother and the father, the wife and the son, relatives and ministers, draught animals, the realm, recluses and Brāhmaṇas, birds and beasts. How a king is instructed in the duties of his office by three wise birds whom he had adopted as his children is told in a third story (no. 521). Asked by the king about the general duties of a ruler, the first speaker says at the outset (V. 112) that he should rule his kingdom with righteousness *(dhamma)* after abiding by the three truths *(dhamma)*. When the king puts to the third and the wisest speaker a specific question about the highest of all powers, the latter repeats the ten stanzas above quoted relating to the king's practice of righteousness. In a shorter and a longer version (nos. 533 and 534) of a dialogue between a wise swan and a king the question is asked by the bird whether his kingdom is ruled righteously and it is answered by the king in the affirmative (V. 348, ibid 377-78). To the above is added in the longer version the question whether the king observes the ten *rājadhammas* as well as the king's own affirmation of his observance of the virtues of liberality, good conduct, nonattachment, straightforwardness, mildness, austerity, suppression of anger, non-injury, patience and forbearance. How should a mortal (meaning himself), asks the king of a false ascetic in yet another story (no. 544), practise righteous-ness towards his parents, his teachers, his wife and children, the aged, the ascetics and the Brahmanas, the military forces and the countryfolk. With the answer of the ascetic who was a believer in the doctrine of annihilation we have no concern. The Great Being, being asked by the king to teach him the path of piety, admonished him by the example of the virtuous kings of old to shun unrighteousness and practise righteousness. The king, it is explained (VI. 251), should distribute every morning and evening by public proclamation food and drink, garlands and unguents, clothes, umbrellas and shoes to the needy; he should not put to labour old men and aged domestic animals, for when they were strong they gave him service. Following this instruction with an elaborate simile of the human body to a chariot, the speaker (ibid 252-53) impresses upon the king the lessons of abstinence from injury, liberality, circumspection, self-control and other virtues. In yet another story (no. 540) an ascetic's son admonishing a king asks him (VI 94) to practise the ten duties *(dhammas),* namely, those towards his mother and father, his wife and son, his friends and ministers, his townships and villages, the recluses and the Brahmanas, the birds and the beasts.

The above extracts indicate in the first place the authors' view of the relation of righteousness to kingship. Righteousness, we are told, is the essence of kingship as well as the king's best policy. Secondly, the authors clarify the principles and policies of government involved in the above concept. The king, we read, should avoid the specified groups of vices and practise the specified groups of virtues, the latter being identified in some instances with the precepts incumbent on the Buddhist lay disciple. Above all we are told that the king should apply himself to the promotion of universal happiness of his subjects so as to extend its benefit down to the dumb creation.

Nothing illustrates so well the belief of the early Buddhist canonists in the profound significance of the king's righteousness than their frequent references to the far-reaching consequences of the ruler's reaction to this fundamental principle. When kings become unrighteous, we are told in a canonical text *(Aṅguttara-Nikāya* II 74-76), the king's officers *(rāja-yutta)* also become unrighteous, this being so the Brahmanas and the mass of ordinary freemen *(gahapati),* the townsfolk and the villagers in their turn become unrighteous, this being so the Sun and the Moon, the stars and the constellations go wrong in their courses; days and nights, months, seasons, and years are out of joint; the winds blow wrong; the *devas* being annoyed do not bestow sufficient rain. This being so the crops ripen in the wrong season, and consequently men are short-lived, ill favoured, weak and sickly. Conversely, when kings become righteous all the reverse consequences follow.

The above view of the tremendous significance of the king's righteousness is repeated in the *Jataka* stories. How a king's violation of righteousness recoiled upon himself with tremendous force is vividly told in one story (no. 422). In an Age when the world spoke the truth and lying was unknown, a king, we are told (III 456-61), decided to make the appointment of his family priest by lying. An ascetic appearing in the king's presence warned him, but in vain, against the danger of this course by saying that the king by telling a lie destroys righteousness, and by destroying righteousness he destroys himself. When the king inspite of the warning told a lie, he was deserted by the four protecting deities, his body was befouled, he fell from the sky upon the earth, and all his four supernatural powers disappeared. Six times in succession the king's priest offered to restore his supernatural powers if he should speak the truth, but the king disregarding all these offers sank lower and lower in the earth till at last the earth opened up for him and he was consumed by the fires of hell.

The influence of the king's attitude towards righteousness upon the fortunes of his subjects and indeed upon their whole physical environment is told after the pattern of the canonical text quoted above in other series of the *Jātakas*. According to an oft-quoted passage in these stories (III III, V 222, ibid 242) the people follow the king as a herd of cattle follow the bull, and the whole realm enjoys weal or woe according as the king is righteous or otherwise. Turning to the stories themselves we have first the story (no. 527) of a virtuous king's self-admonition by way of escape from his sorest temptation. A king of the Śivis, we read having madly fallen in love with the wife of his commander-in-chief and being repeatedly and earnestly pressed by the latter to take her to himself, as often and passionately rejects the offer. The king ends (V 222.23) by teaching his most loyal officer the ways of righteousness as practised by good men. Blessed is a king, we read, who delights in righteousness, and happiness it is to eschew sin. Happily the subjects live as under a cold shade in the kingdom of a king who is free from anger and fixed in righteousness. The speaker next observes on the analogy of a herd of cattle following the bull that when the king becomes unrighteous, the common folk follow him and the whole realm comes to grief, and in the contrary case the common folk follow the king's example and the whole realm enjoys happiness. Declaring his intention not to win authority or conquest of the whole world by unrighteousness, the king concludes by expressing his determination to abide by the Śivi righteousness. The story ends *(ibid* 223) with a passionate admonition of the commander-in-chief to the king to practise righteousness after the text (V 223) quoted above.

When a householder, we read in a second story (no. 194), was about to be killed by the order of a wicked king on a trumped-up charge of theft, the cries and lamentations of his virtuous wife caused the God Sakka to descend from heaven and so use His supernatural powers that the wicked king was killed, and the honest householder became king in his place. Commending the new king to the people as one who would thenceforth rule righteously, the god pointed out the danger of the king's unrighteous rule. Should the king, he declared (II 124), be unrighteous, the gods would send down rain out of season and not in season, and the three 'fears' (those of pestilence, disease and the sword) would come down from heaven upon men. When the king, we read in a third story (no. 334), enquired of an ascetic why the ripe figs offered to him tasted sweet, he was told that it was because the king ruled his kingdom righteously. When kings rule unrighteously, it was explained, oil, honey, molasses and the like as well as wild roots and fruits lose their sweetness and strength and not only these but the whole realm lose their vigour, but should the kings be righteous, these would become strong. In the sequel the king found out by a practical test the truth of the ascetic's statement (III 110-11).

The above extracts indicate in impressive language the authors' view of the immense significance of the king's attitude towards righteousness in relation to his whole environment. In its simplest form it means that the king by his example influences for good or for evil the moral stature of his subjects and hence causes their happiness or misery. More complex than the above is the explanation that the king through his attitude towards righteousness influences for good or for evil the course of the climatic phenomena shaping man's agricultural production as well as the degree of productivity of his life-giving crops. According to the most complex interpretation the king through his attitude towards righteousness shapes by a regular chain of causation the moral stature of his subjects, the movements of heavenly bodies and the succession of time as well as the operation of the climatic factors governing agricultural production, and finally the physical type of the people. Political righteousness, as thus conceived, rises to the level of a cosmic principle of creation.

From the early Buddhist conception of righteousness in relation to the king let us now turn to the same concept in relation to the World-ruler (Pali, *Cakkavattī* = *Skt., Cakravartī)*. In the stock-description of the *Cakkavattī's* characteristics we are told that he is called the Emperor over the four quarters of the earth, righteous in himself, ruling righteously, triumphant abroad, enforcing law and order at home, possessed of the seven jewels. The process of the World-ruler's universal conquest is described in two canonical extracts *(Dīgha Nikāya* II 169*f* and III 62*f*). These deal respectively with the romantic biographies of the *Cakkavattī* Mahāsudassana and the son of the *Cakkavattī* Dalhanemi. The Emperor, we read, having discovered the wonderful Wheel and solemnly invoked it to roll onwards, followed it on its onward course successively towards the East, the South, the North and the West. As the mighty monarch appeared in each quarter with his fourfold army, the rival kings therein offered their submission. The *Cakkavattī* allowed them to retain their possessions on condition of their obser vance of the five moral precepts binding upon the Buddhist lay-man. "Ye shall", so goes his solemn admonition, "slay no living thing, ye shall not take that which has not been given, ye shall not act wrongly touching bodily desires, ye shall speak no lie, ye shall drink no maddening drink". The same stories illustrate the nature of the *Cakkavattī's* rule over his subjects as well as his vassals. Among the four gifts *(iddhis)* of Mahasudassana, we are told *(Digha-Nikaya* II 178) that he was popular with the Brāhmaṇas and the householders just as a father is near and dear to his own sons, while conversely the Brāhmaṇas and the householders were near and dear to him just as his sons are near and dear to a father. Of King Dalhanemi we read that he lived on this earth to its ocean-bounds, having conquered it not by the scourge, not by the sword, but by righteousness. In a third . extract *(Aṅguttara-Nikāya* III, 149) the Buddha referring to "the king, the world-ruler, the righteous one, the righteous king", observes that righteousness *(dhamma)* is his king. Such a king, he explains, honours, esteems and reveres *dhamma,* with *dhamma* as the standard he provides righteous safety, cover and prote-ction for folk within his realm, for Khattiyas and attendant army, for Brāhmaṇa and householder, for town-and country-folk, for recluses and Brāhmaṇas, for birds and beasts. "Thus verily by righteousness he sets the wheel in motion, of which the course cannot be resisted by any inimical king whatsoever".

Some further light is thrown upon the Buddhist conception of the World-ruler by the description in another canonical text *(Dīgha-Nikāya,* III 6o*f*) of the careers of the *Cakkavattīs* of Dalhanemi's line. When Dalhanemi we read left the throne to his eldest son and retired to a hermitage, the celestial wheel disappeared from view. Consoling the new king for his loss a hermit observes that the celestial wheel was not his paternal heritage, but it might manifest itself to him if he observed the Aryan duty of a *Cakkavattī (ariyaṁ cakkavatti-vaṭṭam).* What this means is explained in the following lines. "Thou should," says the sage, "provide right watch, ward and protection for thy own folk, for the army, for the nobles, for vassals, for Brahmanas and householders, for town-and country-folk, for recluses and Brāhmaṇas and for beasts and birds. Throughout thy kingdom let no wrong doing prevail. And whosoever in thy kingdom is poor, to him let wealth be given. Should recluses and Brahmanas ask thee for the proper line of action, thou should deter them from evil and bid them take up what is good".

Following this advice the king was rewarded with the reappearance of the celestial wheel. When a later king of Dalhanemi's line preferred to govern his people according to his own will, they failed to prosper as they had done under former kings observant of the way of life oi a *Cakkavattī*. Even when he was reminded of his duty by his ministers and courtiers, the king simply provided watch and ward and protection for his people but failed to give alms to the destitute. This led to poverty of the people and the progressive deterioration of their morals and shortening of their lives. At length the very extremity of the evil led the people on their own initiative to increase their performance of good deeds which resulted in the lengthening of their lives. The above extracts are of extreme significance as involving the extension of the principle of the king's righteousness to the concept of the World-ruler. The attributes of this ruler comprise not only universal supremacy and successful administration at home and abroad, but also and above all, righteousness. In the branch of the *Cakkavattī's* internal administration, this last principle connotes the reciprocal love and affection of the ruler and his subjects as well as the ruler's provision of universal security for his subjects down even to the dumb animals. In the sphere of foreign relations the *Cakkavattī's* conquest of the quarters is achieved not by force but by righteousness, while his rule over his vassals is founded upon the enforcement of the five precepts that are binding upon the Buddhist lay-man. Inrerpreting even the mystical wheel, the palladium of the World-ruler, in terms of righteousness, the canonist explains it to mean not the patrimony inherited by the ruler from his ancestors, but as the fulfilment of his characteristic attributes. These attributes comprise provision of universal security for the subjects, extensive poor-relief, prevention of wrong-doing, and instru-ction of the religieux in virtue. The concluding extract refers, after the pattern of the above-quoted text relating to kingship, to the profound repercussions of the World-ruler's attitude towards righteousness upon the fortunes of his subjects. For we are told that while a partial fulfilment of this principle by the ruler leads to the moral and physical decay of the people, its complete fulfilment by them even on their own initiative produces the contrary result.

We may consider in conclusion a remarkable view laid down by a well-known French Indologist of our time (Prof. Paul Masson Oursel in *Ancient India and Indian Civilization,* pp. 93-95) about a fundamental antithesis between the Brahmanical and the Buddhist ideas of *dharma* in their relation to political theory. The former, we are told, in maintaining a social order based upon the special constitution of each caste does not encourage the appearance of "a political spirit", while the latter by aiming at a law applicable to all mankind makes for unlimited imperialism. Expressing this contrast in another way the author argues that while the Brahmanical *dharma* falls "short of monarchy", its Buddhist counterpart leads to "world-empire".

Again he observes that while the king in the Brahmanical theory confines himself to the preservation of the eternal social order, the king according to the Buddhist theory not only causes the law to reign but starts and promotes the same. We have endeavoured to show in another place[1] that the true difference between the Brahmanical and the Buddhist concepts in relation to social and political theory lies elsewhere, and we can only repeat here some of our principal arguments. *Dharma* in the *Smṛitis* connotes above all the comprehensive law of the social order of which the king himself is the unit, while it signifies in the conception of the Buddhist cononists specially the principle of righteousness. In its political aspect the Brahmanical *dharma* stands particularly for the Whole Duty of the king *(rājadharma)* which from the first is conceived in sufficiently elastic terms to provide for the needs of the kingdom and to permit in Manu and still more in the *Mahābhārata* (after Bhīṣma) the wholesale incorporation of the *Arthaśāstra* categories and concepts relating to the branches of the king's internal and external administration. On the other hand the Buddhist *dharma* in its relation to the king involves the application of the universal ethics of Buddhism to the State administration, this principle being even extended to the somewhat idealistic concept of the World-ruler.

U. N. Ghoshal

FOOTNOTES

1. In chap. XIII of the author's forthcoming work, *A History of Indian Political Ideas,* in course of publication by the Oxford University Press.

23

BUDDHISM IN ANCIENT KAMBUJADESA

(AN EPIGRAPHIC STUDY)

Buddhism in ancient Kambujadeśa was characterised by two important features—its compatability with Brahmanism and its progress in the other way from Mahāyanism to Hīnayānism. In this respect it differed from Indian Buddhism which origina ted as a revolt against the existing socio-religious structure that recognised the hierarchy of the Brahmins, and stressed the conception of arhathood as the *summum bonum.* It is rather interesting to find that there is not a single record which could show the least sign of bitterness or antagonism between the two existing systems. On the other hand, we find Buddha being accorded a position in the Brahmanical trinity. The identification of Śaivism and Buddhism was complete and we find the trinity composed of Padmodbhava[1] (Brahmā), Ambhojanetra (Viṣṇu), and the Buddha *(Yaśca Padmodbhav = ambhojanetra-Buddham).* One has also to commend the catholic spirit of the emperors whose personal faith in no way affected their outlook. We find that some of the prominent Buddhists in the state service shared that catholic spirit. Kavindrānmathana, who had set up a statue of Prajñāpāramitā, was above suspicion *(Buddhānām-agraṇīr api)* so far as his loyalty to the Brahmanical emperor and his state religion was concerned.

The earliest reference to Buddhism in Kambujadeśa is noticed in a record dating from the end of the sixth or the beginning of the seventh century A. D.[2] It records dedications of male and female slaves by Pon Prajñā Candra to the three Bodhisattvas, Śāstā, Maitreya and Avalokiteśvara. The Bodhisattvas are accorded the Khmer title *Vrah Kamratā āñ* which is also borne by the Brahmanical deities. Avalokiteśvara is not noticed in any other record, but we notice the form Lokeśvara for the first time in the Prasat Ta Kam inscription[3] dated in the Śaka year 713. Buddhism, however, appears to have been introduced earlier than the seventh century A. D., as we find in the Vat Prei inscription (Ba Phnom Dist) of Jaya-varman, dated in the Śaka year 587[4], a reference to the two Bhikṣus Ratnabhānu and Ratna-siṁha whose sister's daughter was authorised and guaranteed the hereditary enjoyment of a religious property by king Jaya-varman in the year 587-565 A. D. There is no reference to any Brahmanical god, and the term Bhikṣu suggests that the family was Buddhist. In the Khmer text the donations by these two Bhikṣus were made in favour of *Vrāh* which is a vague term denoting Buddha, as well as Brahmanical gods, and also the King. We have, therefore, to take the character of the record from the reference to the Buddhist Bhiksus who are the donors.

There is no Buddhist record for a little over two hundred years, and here one has to believe the testimony of the Chinese pilgrim, I-tsing[5], who suggests that Buddhism flourished in Fu-nan in early times but was then subverted by a wicked king whose identity is not established, but it is suggested that he might be either Bhavavarman or Ī-Śana-varman or Jaya-varman. This state of stalemate seems to have continued. Although there is no reference to the persecution of Buddhists in Kambujadeśa, the absence of positive evidence throws some doubt on its flourishing nature. The Kok Samron inscription[6] (Siem Rap, Dist Battambang) records an invocation to Saṅgha, though Buddha and Dharma are also noticed in a subsequent verse *(namas Saṁghāya Sambuddharatnam praṇamāmi dharma).*

This invocation to Saṁgha, and the reference to Buddha and Dharma reveal the Buddhist character of the record. The eulogy of King Rajendra-varman makes the record contemporary with that ruler who became king in the Śaka year 883 = 961 A. D. It is interesting to find that in another inscription[7] of the time of Rajendra-varman, dated in the Śaka year 883 = 961 A, D. from Pre Rup (Angkor region), the Yogācāra system is mentioned.

It is equally interesting to find references to other divinities of the Buddhist pantheon whose statues were set up in Kambujadeśa in that period. An inscription from Thma Puok[8] (Svay Cek in Battambang) of the time of Jaya-varman V, and dated in the Saka Samvat 911 = 989 A.D. contains invocations to Buddha, Prajñapāramitā, Lokeśvara, Vajrin, Maitreya and Indra. The six divinities were installed by the sage Padma-Vairocana and some of them may be identified with the image of the deities round the miniature temple. A little earlier in the year 903-981 A.D., an image of the mother of the Buddha was set up by Tribhuvanarāja. The inscription found at Phnom Bantay[9] (South of Angkor Bauray to the west of Battambang) invokes the Buddhist Mahāyāna divinities including Lokeśvara and Prajñapāramitā. Installation of the images of other Brahmanical divinities like Jagadiśvara and Trailoyanātha is also mentioned. They were set up by other members probably of the same family.

The most important record is the Phimanaka inscription[10] of Jaya-varman VII in which Trikāya, Buddha and Lokeśvara are invoked. The two queens of the emperor were Buddhist. The second one, who was the elder sister of the first one, was very learned and taught the Buddhist nuns of the convents of Nagendratuṅga, Tilakttara and Narendrāśrama. This elder sister had initiated the younger one into Buddhism during the absence of her lord and she could see his image after the performance of certain ceremony. On the return of her lord, a dramatic performance, of which the plot was drawn from the Jātakas, was made by a body of nuns recruited from cast away girls. After the death of the younger sister, the elder sister won the favour of the king who asked her to teach the Buddhist doctrines in various convents. The importance of this record lies in serveral ways. First, it shows that Buddhism was active in its proselytising spirit and it freely drew its members from the Brahmanical and royal families, and there were a number of convents for cast away girls. The Buddhist literature was equally popular and the Jātaka stories could form the subjects of dramatic performances so as to impress upon the masses the importance and divine character of the Buddhist Lord.

The School of the lower vehicle, namely that of Sthāviras, also flourished in Kambujadeśa, though it arrived here much later than Mahāyāna. Unfortunately, there is only one record[11] of the time of Sūrya-varman I dated in the year 944–947 from Lopburi in the modern temple of Bang Pahin, but it was brought from Lopburi in Siam. The inscription contains an order of King Sūrya-varman laying down the regulation that in all sacred places, temples, monasteries and hermitages, the ascetics, the Sthāviras (monks of the little vehicle) and monks of the Grand vehicle were required to offer to the king the merit of their austerities.

From the findspots of these records certain conclusions might be drawn. The Mahāyāna Buddhist records are found (in chronological order) in Prasat Takham (Siem Rap), Vat Prei (Ba Phnom), Kok Saman (Siem Rap), Pre Rup (Angkor region), Thma Pook (Savay Cak in Battambang), Phnom Bantay (south of Angkor) and Phimanaka (Angkor Thom). They suggest that Mahayana Buddhism was introduced from the north west and it came probably by the land route. The earlier wave of Hīnāyānists probably followed the same route. The later influx of Hīnayānists from Ceylon seems to have come by the sea route. We learn from the Kok Svay Cek (two miles south of western Baray) inscription[12] of Śrīndra-varman that the king gave to *mahāthera* (the great monk) Sirindamoli a village, and a Vihāra was built in 1231 where an image of Buddha was installed. The king gave four villages to the monastery. This is the earliest epigraphic evidence for the introduction of Ceylonese Hīnayāna Buddhism in Kambuja. We might also consider here the evidence furnished by the Chinese sources on the state of Buddhism in ancient Fu-nan. We learn that a coral image of the Buddha was sent to the emperor Wu-ti (500-550) in 503 A. D., and the inhabitants of Fu-nan made bronze image of the heavenly genii with two or four heads and four arms. An image made of sandal wood was sent to the Chinese emperor by Liu-t'o-pa-mo (Rudra-varman) and in 539 he offered him a hair of the Buddha twelve feet long. The two monks who went to China to translate Chinese scriptures, namely Saṅghapāla and Mandra were also from Fu-nan. I-tsing while returning from India in 675 A. D. describes the country of Po-nan formerly called Fu-nan of which the people were originally worshippers of the devas, but later on Buddhism flourished there. A wicked king exterminated all members of the Buddhist brotherhood.[18] This suggests that Buddhism in its earlier phase flourished in the Ba Phnom region in the south-east. As the Chinese evidence is earlier than the epigraphic records noticed above, it may be presumed that Buddhism came to ancient Kambujadeśa at a fairly early date, probably synchronising with the time of the second Kauṇḍinya, and it had a set back probably in the time of Bhava-varman or his successors. It, however, flourished, but from the 10th to the 13th century it was at its peak because of the patronage of the Khmer rulers like Sūrya-varman, called *Nirvāṇapada* and Jaya-varman VII who was considerably influenced by his talented sister-in-law who later on became his wife. These rulers did not alienate their devotion to the family deity, and Śaivism continued to be the state religion, despite their adherence to Buddhism. Another ruler Yaśo-varman established a Sauga-taśrama like the Śaiva and Vaiṣ ṇava aśramas.

In the propagation of Buddhism some important state dignitaries also played a prominent part. These include Satya-varman[14] who was charged with the erection of the building known as Phimanakei, Kavindrārimathana[15] a minister under

Rajendra-varman V and Jaya-varman V who erected many statues including those of Buddha, Vajrapāṇi, Prajña-pāramita and Lokeśvara. Kīrti-Paṇḍita[16] was the minister of Jaya-varman V and it was due to his efforts that the pure doctrine of the Buddha reappeared like the moon from behind the clouds or the sun at dawn. This Kīrtipaṇḍita also introduced Buddhist books from abroad, and it is suggested that the *Śāstra Madhya Vibhāga* and the commentary on the *Tattva Saṅgraha*[17] were brought by him. These ministers were certainly Buddhists and they never let their personal religion interfere in their official duties and the state religion.

Another important point worth attention is that Buddhism was so much in line with Brahmanism that Buddha actually found a place in the Brahmanical trinity. In the Prasat Prah Khset inscription[18] of Udayārka-varman dated in the Śaka year 989 = 1067 A. D., there is a reference to the *liṅga,* formerly given to king Sūryavarman by his minister Sarāma and to this were added images of Brahma, Viṣṇu, and Buddha, and the entire group called *Caturmūrti* was consecrated to Siva. Buddha is associated with Rudra in another inscription. The Prah Put lo Rock inscription[19] (cave in Mt. Kulen) dated in the Śaka year 869 = 947 A. D. records in the Khmer text the installation of an image of Tathāgata (Buddha), Rudra and probably other gods in the holy cave. There is not the slightest doubt that Buddhism in ancient Kambujadeśa was not so violent against Brahmanism and the latter assimilated Buddha in its pantheon.

We also find charitable and missionary activities which were associated with Buddhism. Here one is reminded of the humanitarian activities of the Buddhist emperor, Aśoka. Jaya-varman VII issued an inscription from Ta Prohm near Angkor which opens with an invocation of the Buddha followed by Lokeśvara and probably Prajñā-pāramitā. It refers to an establishment with 18 principal priests *(adhi-kariṇah),* 2740 priests and 2232 assistants and dancing girls. This record also refers to 102 hospitals in his kingdom of which a detailed description is noticed in another record[20] found a Say-Fong in Laos. It opens with an invocation to the Buddha who in his three bodies transcends the distinction between existence and non-existence, and then to the healing Buddha and the two Bodhisattvas who drive away darkness and disease. The hospitals were open to everybody without any distinction of caste.

It would, thus, appear from a study of the Kambuja records that there were probably two or three waves of Buddhist immigrants in that country, and they experienced an initial set- back. From the tenth century onwards Mahlyanism flourished as an auxiliary to Brahmanism and not in a spirit of hostility. The assimilation of the Tathāgata in the Brahmanical trinity is a very important factor in the religious history of Kambuja, and it was one of the reasons for the rebuff given to Islam in Cam-bodia. Brahmanism did not stand in the prosperity of Buddhism and it flourished undisturbed and without any animosity from the State religion. In fact, we have cited instances of high dignitaries and even of kings patronising Buddhism. It seems that catholicity and toleration were the hallmarks in the history of Buddhism in ancient Kambujadeśa.

B.N. Puri

FOOTNOTES

1. Majumdar, *Kumbuja inscriptions,* No. 156, p. 399
2. Aymonier, *Le Cambodge,* vol. I, p. 442
3. Majumdar *op cit.,* No, 52 A, p. 571
4. *Ibid.,* No. 29, p. 37
5. Takakusu, p. 12
6. Majumdar, *op. cit,* No, 100 E, p. 583
7. *Ibid.,* No. 102, p. 233, v. 275
8. *Ibid.,* No. 113 A, p, 594
9. *Ibid.,* No. 113 p. 299
10. *Ibid.,* No. 182, p. 515
11. *Ibid.,* No. 139, p. 343
12. *Ibid.,* No. 188, p. 533
13. *Elliot, Hinduism & Buddhism,* vol. III, p. 106

14. Aymonier, vol. I, pp. 261 ff; *Ibid.*, p. 123.
15. Majumdar, *of. cit.*, p. 331; *Ibid.*
16. Elliot, *of cit.*
17. *Ibid.*, Nanjio, Catalogue 1244, 1248
18. Majumdar, *of cit.*, No. 156, p. 399
19. *Ibid.*, No. 90, p, 179
20. Elliot, *op cit.*, p. 124

24

HARIVARMAN'S THEORY OF COGNITION

Vasubandhu while expounding the eight-fold *dṛṣṭi* (view) brings in for discussions different theories of sensuous cognitions as entertained by earlier Buddhist authors. 'The question raised is, what is actually the agent for giving rise to our sensuous perceptions. There appear to have been different groups of philosophers pleading for theory peculiar to each one. The earliest of all is the Sarvāstivādin headed by Vasumitra. The next comes the Vijñānavādin led by Dharmatrāta. These two groups figure prominently in the discussions introduced by Vasubandhu. It will also be evident that Vasubandhu has favoured the Vijñānavādin (advocate of consciousness as the sole agent of perception).

Now we shall see in the following pages what Harivarman, one of the predecessors of Vasubandhu has to say about the subject. Harivarman was one of the profound and original thinkers of ancient India. He fought all his life for puritanic approach to Buddha's preaching, so much so that he had to take great pains to weed out the fungi that grew over the Master's teachings as found in the *Abhidharmas* of the Sarvāstivdins. It it unfortunate that his only treatise, the *Satyasiddhi Śāstra* has been lost to us in its original form now available in an imperfect translation in Chinese of Kumārajīva.[1] One of the most outstanding reforms he has introduced in his system was an absolute denial of any distinction between the primary elements *(bhūta)* and the secondary elements *(bhautika)* a theory which is attributed to Buddhadeva in the *Kośabhāṣya (ad.* 1,35) as well as in the *Vibhāṣā*. This theory again has been spoken of as one of the Sautrāntika tenets in the *Hetubinduṭīkā* (p. 355, 1. 19).

Therefore the five sense-organs which are reckoned as separate secondary atomic elements by the Sarvāstivādin-Vaibhāṣika, are no more than things of nominal existence *(prajñaptisat)* for Harivarman. They are the same as the four great elements that assumed such forms as the eye etc.

Now let us turn to see what Harivarman has to say in regard to epistemology. We may maintain that he was, in all probability, a fore-runner of Vasubandhu in pleading for the thesis of *Vijñānadarśana,* consciousness as the sole agent of cognition. Our author has employed for upholding his view almost all the arguments that were pressed for service by Vasubandhu. We may even say on comparison of these two authors that the former is more comprehensive in his arguments than the latter. It will not be without interest if we present here some of his arguments with a view of drawing attention of the scholars to the magnitude of his contribution to the development of Buddhist thought in India. As usual he presents his topic in the form of questions and answers.

(1) At the commencement of the discussion on the present subject *(Satyasiddhi,* sect. 48), Harivarman poses the question: Is it the sense-organ that effects cognition or the consciousness residing in it? His opponent, though not specified, is the Sarvāstivādin-Vaibhāṣika who entertain the former alternative.[2] Harivarman contends that in case the sense is cognizer, it will cognize all things simultaneously.

(2) The opponent strives to evade the difficulty by this reasoning: the function of the sense is to light up things and that of the consciousness to make them cognized. The author replies: the sense then that is not in the nature of light, i.e., ear, etç. cannot light up objects. Supposing even that the sense lights

up things, the power of cognizing can never be attributed to it. The lamp, for example, illumines its proximate objects but it never cognizes them. We must, therefore, attribute to the sense the function of giving support to the consciousness which is really the cognizer.

(3) The opponent argues that the passages like *cakṣuṣā rūpāni dṛṣṭvā,* etc. necessitate us to hold fast to the sense as sole cognizer. The author retorts by saying that there are still more authoritative passages, viz. *cakṣur brāhmaṇa dvāram yāvad eva rūpāṇām darśanāya,* etc. which prove unmistakably that the sense operates as an instrument whereas the consciousness residing in it is the agent in giving rise to the cognition. In the light of this unequivocal passage the sentence above cited by you must be explained figuratively, implying the same idea that the eye is the support, i.e., instrument and the consciousness the perceiver. There are also some sayings which attribute emotions to the eye, etc. e.g., *cakṣuh priyarū-paṇi kāmyati,* "the eye desires the pleasant objects." But no desire can be attributed to the eye. The mind alone desires. However people attributing the act of desiring to the eye, say that the eye desires. Similarly men in the world talk that the eye sees and the ear hears, etc. The Master, following their conventions employs similar expressions. He never quarrels with the worldlings. They call Viśākhā daughter-in-law of Mṛgāra as *Mṛgāramātā,* mother of Mṛgāra. Buddha also calls her *Mṛgāramātā.* The author has collected a number of such metaphorical expressions from the worldly usages which do not bear their sense. A typical example is when a man sitting on the cot is screaming, we say the cot is screaming *(mañcāḥ krośanti),* etc. It is evident therefore that these expressions should not be assessed at their face-value. Thus the author's conclusion stands that while the conciousness alone is peceiver, the sense is also spoken of so because the latter is related to the former as supporter.

(4) The opponent questions: if the sense is not cognizer, how can we account for the expressions like: eye-cognition, ear-cognition *(cakṣur-vijñānam,* etc.)? The author answers:

Though the sense and its object play the equally important role in bringing about their cognitions, the former excels the latter by virtue of its being support for the cognizing consciousness. In other words, the sense is the supporting cause *(āśrayahetu)* whereas the object is passive cause *ālambana-pratyaya*. So the sense does not stand on a par with the object. Since the sense plays a more active part in effecting a cognition, the people talk of cognitions as related to their senses, eyecognition, etc. The point is thus illustrated. The sound is produced when the drum is struck with a stick. The sound thus produced is the effect not only of the drum but of the stick and its act of striking. Nevertheless the people talk of it as the sound of a drum, *bherīśabda*. Similarly the expression like *yavāṅkura* should be explained. The sprout .is produced on account of several factors being put together, seed, earth, water, etc. we nevertheless call it *yavāṅkura* (sprout of millet-seeds) because the seeds are the material cause and excel other factors. We may note in passing that the examples above quoted, viz. *bheriśabda* and *yavāṅkura* are stock-phrases found in the *Kośabhāṣya* and the logical treatises of Diṅnāga school to illustrate the expression : *Pratyakṣa*.

(5) Then Harivarman considers the question whether the consciousness cognizes in a close proximity or otherwise. His answer here is as usual a qualified one, viz. the visual, auditory and mindformed consciousnesses are of non-contacted objects and the other three of proximate objects. It is probably the Vaiśeṣika who pleads that the eye cognizes the object after being contacted with it, and assumes for this purpose some sort of visual ray *(cakṣū-raṣmi)* which runs after the vicinity of cognizable things. The Vaiśesika contends that the eye operates only on the proximate object, because if it operates on the remote objects also, it could cognize in one stroke every thing in the world. Our author argues that even in his system the Ṭ said logical defect (i.e., the eye would be cognizant of remote things) cannot be raised because the scripture has laid down the rule that the visual consciousness will arise only when the

following three conditions are favourable : (i) the eye that is not defective ('/) the object that falls within the reach of light *(ābhāsagata)* and (3) the attention that is directed to the object. In the absence of any of these conditions the visual cognition will not arise. Yaśomitra has preserved this important quotation[3] from an unknown source (p. 94,12). This gives an oportunity for the author to elaborate what is *ābhāsagata* and what is *anabhāsagata;* what is the sense-defect and what is not and so on.

There is one more characteristic feature of Harivarman's system of thought. We have already seen that he has denied the distinction between the primary and secondary elements. Likewise he has also done away with the division of thought into mind and mental properties as postulated by the Sarvāstivādins, This division is illogical and apocryphal for Buddhadeva as well as Harivarman. Our author has on the authority of scriptures established that thoughts follow an order of sequence and never operate simultaneously, proving thereby that the so-called theory of *samprayoga* (i.e., one main thought is associated with several mental properties) of the Sarvāstivādins is not tenable. According to Harivarman, every sensuous consciousness in its first moment is absolutely pure and free from any *vikalpa,* discursive thought. The Sarvāstivādin, however, maintains that there is *vitarka* always present in every moment of consciousness, and hence *nirvikalpa* for him denotes that it is free from *vikalpa* other than the *vitarka* which is otherwise termed *svabhāvavikalpa,* (Kośa, I, 33). Vasubandhu has also criticised the Sarvāstivādin's view in this respect. It is evident that Harivarman was the earliest exponent of the theory of "pure sensation¿ later elaborated in the *Pramāṇasamuccaya* and other logical treatises of Dinnāga School.

N. Aiyaswami Sastri

FOOTNOTES

1. This translation contains 20 chuans, fasc. and the whole of the treatise has been translated into Sanskrit by me and will be shortly published.

2. The Sarvastivādin says: the pair of the eyes see *(Kośa, 1.* 43); the Yātsiputrīya: the single eye sees; the *Dārṣṭāntika:* the company, *sāmagrī (ho-ho)* sees, Ghoṣaka (Miao-yin) *prajñā* associated with the visual consciousness sees *(Vibhāṣā,* Taisho, vol. 27, p. 61c). Read also my *Abhidharma Problems, op. cit.* for Kwei-chi's summary of the eleven such theories of the Bu.ddhists and Hindus.
3. एवं हि विज्ञानकारणं पटयते। चक्षुरिन्द्रियमनुपहतं भवति। विषय ग्राभासगतो भवति। तज्जश्च मनसिकार: प्रत्युपस्थितो भवतीति।

25

THE NĀRĀYANPUR IMAGE OF VINĀYAKA

(DATED THE FOURTH REGNAL YEAR OF MAHĪPĀLA)

The village of Nārāyanpur, where this image was found, is about 15 miles to the north-east of the sub-divisional town of Chandpur in the Tippera district in Eastern Pakistan. The image has on it an inscription which is dated in the fourth year of the reign of King Mahīpāla. This inscription records the establishment of this image of the god Vināyaka by a merchant named Buddhamitra, son of Jambhalamira. This merchant is said to have been an inhabitant of a place called Bilikandhaka which was situated, in the country of Samatata, This image, however, is said to have been installed at a place called Bhasakāga. It may be noted in this connection that an image of Nārāyaṇa was discovered at Bāghāurā in the Brahmanbana sub-division of the district of Tippera in Eastern Pakistan. The Bāghāura image is said to have been installed in the third regnal year of King Mahīpāla by a Vaiṣṇava merchant named Lokadatta, an inhabitant of Bilakīndaka in the country of Samataṭa (Ṿide *Epigraphia Indica,* XVII, pp. 353ff). There can hardly be any doubt that the Nārāyanpur image and the Bāghāura image were installed during the reign of one and the same King Mahīpāla. There is reason to suppose that Bilikandhaka of the Nārāyanpur image inscription is identical with Bilakīndaka of the Bāghāura image inscription. Dr. N. K. Bhattasali has identified Bilakīndaka with the village Bilakendua, situated near Bāghāura. According to Dr. N. K. Bhattasali the kingdom of Samataṭa mentioned in these inscriptions corresponds to the tract of country bound by the Garo and the Khasi hills and the hills of Tippera on the north and east, by the Lauhitya or the Brahmaputra on the west and by the Bay of Bengal on the south. It comprised the eastern half of the Mymensingh and the Dacca districts lying east of the river Brahmaputra, the greater part of Sylhet, and the whole of the Tippera and Noakhali districts. According to Dr. D. C. Sircar Sarriatata apparently included the present Tippera Noakhali region.

Among the kings of the Pāla dynasty of Bengal there were two bearing the name Mahīpāla. According to some scholars Mahīpāla I ruled during the period circa 992 to 1040 A. D. and according to other scholars during the period circa 988 to 1038 A.D. Mahīpāla II reigned according to some scholars during the period circa 1081-82 A.D. and according to other scholars during the period A.D. 1070-75. According to Dr. D. C. Sircar it is possible to assign the Bāghāura and the Nārāyanpur images to the reign of any one of these two Mahīpālas, although the name of Mahīpāla I is usually suggested by many scholars. The king mentioned in the Bāghāura image inscription has been identified by some scholars with the Gurjara Pratīhāra king Mahīpāla I who seems to have reigned durihg the period A.D. 912-44. Dr. D. C. Sircar remarks in this connection: "This suggestion, however, cannot be accepted in the present state of our knowledge, as there is no evidence to prove Pratīhāra connection with south-east Bengal." (Vide *Indian Culture,* vol. IX., No. I., 1942).

The names Buddhamitra and Śambhalamitra seem to indicate Buddhist influence and hence one should naturally be inclined to suppose that the god Vināyaka installed by Buddhamitra, son of Jambhalamitra, is the Mahāyānic deity of that name. The image in question is about 3 feet in height and is in a seated posture. It is four-armed and wears bangles and a necklace and a crown. The left tusk of his elephant head is represented as broken. The image holds a radish in his right upper hand, rosary in his lower right hand, axe in his upper left hand and sweets in his lower left hand. The elephant-headed god Vināyaka is tasting the sweets in his lower left hand with his trunk. He has lotus symbols on his feet and bears a sacred thread to which a serpent is found tied. There is the representation of a rat, the god's *vāhana* or carrier on the pedestal.

According to Dr. D. C. Sircar (vide *Indian Culture,* vol. IX., No. I, July-September, 1942) the Narayanpur image of the god Vinayaka does not agree with the descriptions of the Mahāyāna Buddhist deity Vināyaka and the image in question agrees almost exactly with the description given in the *Viṣṇudharmottara* of the Brāhmaṇical deity of this name. In this text we find the following description of the Brāhmaṇical god Vināyaka: —

> Vināyakastu karttavyo gajavaktraścaturbhujaḥ/
> Mūlakaṁ cākṣamālā ca tasya dakṣiṇahastayoḥ//
>
> Pātraṁ modakapūrṇaṁ tu paraśuś caiva vāmataḥ/
> Dantaś cāsya na karttavyo vāme ripunisūdanaḥ//
>
> Pādapīthakṛtapāda eka āsanago bhavet/
> Pūrṇamoḍakapātre tu karāgraṁ tasya kārayet/ /
>
> Lambodaras tathā kāryaḥ........./
> Vyāghracarmāmbaraḍharaṁ sarpayajño-pavītavān//

Jambhalamitra's son Buddhamitra who installed the image in question thus seems to have been a Brāhmaṇical Hindu. The personal names of Jambhalamitra and of his son Buddhamitra, however, show Buddhist influence. In fact, there was, as Dr. D. C. Sircar aptly argues, hardly any appreciable gulf of difference between a Brāhmaṇical Hindu and a Buddhist householder in Bengal in or about the eleventh century A.D. In manners and customs a Buddhist lay worshipper differed very little from a common Brāhmaṇical Hindu householder of that age in Bengal. The later form of Mahāyāna Buddhism or Tāntric Buddhism, which was in vogue in certain parts of Bengal during this period, had in its pantheon many gods and goddesses, which were alike worshipped by Brāhmaṇical Hindu householders in Bengal at that age. Thus Brāhmansm and later Budddhism in Bengal had many common gods and goddesses. A lay Buddhist and an ordinary Brāhmaṇical Hindu householder in Bengal had in consequence during this period many common beliefs and religious practices. The distinction between Brāhmanism and Buddhism in Bengal seems during this later period to have been exhibited only in the debates of the philosophers of these two rival schools of thought. Thus the Bhuvaneśvar inscriptions (verse 20) of Bhaṭṭa Bhavadeva informs us that Bhavadeva II, who is the hero of this *praśasti* or eulogistic account, was prominent among the exponents of the Brahmādvaita system of Hindu philosophy and was conversant with the writings of Bhaṭṭa (i.e. the great philosopher Kumārila Bhaṭṭa). He was an antagonist of the philosophers of the Buddhist school and he refuted with ease the opinions of the heretic dialecticians

(cf. "Brahmādvaitavidāmudāharaṇabhūrudbhūtavidyād-bhūtasraṣṭā

Bhaṭṭagirāṁ gabhīrimaguṇapratyakṣadṛśvā kavih/

Bauddhāmbhonidhikumbhasambhavamuniḥ pāṣaṇda-vaitaṇḍikaprajñākhañḍana

pañḍitoyamavanau Sarvvajña līlāyate//).

According to verse 23 of this inscription by following Kumārila Bhaṭṭa Bhavadeva wrote a guide to Mīmāṁsa philosophy,

According to the description given in the Bhuvaneśvar inscription Bhavadeva's forefathers were inhabitants of the village of Siddhala in Rāḍhā (i.e. Western Bengal). On palaeographic evidence Prof. Kielhorn *(Epigraphia Indica,* vol. 6, p. 198ff) assigned the Bhuvaneśvar inscription of Bhaṭṭa Bhavadeva to about 1200 A.D. and observed that "its interest lives in the fact that it treats, not of kings and princes, but of a scholar". Depending on literary sources Monmohan Chakravarti (Vide *Journal of the Asiatic Society of Bengal,* New Series, vol. 8, pp. 342-45) came to the conclusion that the date of Bhavadeva must be somewhere between circa 1025 and 1150 A.D. According to N. G. Majumdar (Vide *Inscriptions of Bengal,* vol. 3, p. 32) the date of Bhavadeva should be taken as being earlier than the first quarter of the 12th century A.D. and even earlier than the last quarter of the 11th century A.D. Whatever differences there might have been in religious doctrines and philosophical thoughts between Brāhmaṇical Hinduism and Buddhism, the lay Buddhist householders may be said to have differed very little from ordinary Brāhmaṇical Hindu householders even in the early period. So far as the common householders or the ordinary people were concerned, the feeling of separatism among the lay Buddhists and lay Hindu householders in Bengal gradually died out during the eleventh, twelfth and thirteenth centuries A.D. The emperors of the Pāla dynasty of Bengal are mostly known to have been Saugatas or followers of Sugata (i.e. Buddha). But they claim in their records (cf. Verse 5 of the Monghyr Copper-plate inscription of Devapāla) to have been upholders of the Varṇāṣrama order or of Brāhmaṇical Hinduism as well. The grant of villages by Nārāyaṇavarmā during the reign of the Pāla emperor Dharmapāla (cf. the Khālimpur copper-plate inscription of Dharmapāla) for the continuance of the worship of an image of the god Nanna-Nārāyaṇa and the grant of land as fee by the Pāla emperor Madanapāla (cf. the Manahali copper-plate inscription of Madanapāla) to a Brāhmaṇa who recited and explained the text of the *Mahābhārata* to his chief queen Citramatikādevī may be pointed out in this connection.

This shows that in spite of differences in religious beliefs and practices there was no ill feeling of communal rivalry between Brāhmaṇical Hindus, Buddhists and Jains in Bengal during the tenth, eleventh and twelfth centures A. D. The Pāhrpur copper-plate inscription dated in the year 159 of the Gupta era (corresponding to A.D. 478-79) thus records that a Brāhmaṇa named Nāthaśarmmā and his wife Rāmī deposited three dīnāras or three gold coins in the city council (*adhiṣṭ hānādhikaraṇa*) for purchasing one *kulyavāpa* and four *droṇavāpas* of land situated in four different places for meeting the cost incurred for the maintenance of worship with sandal, incense, flowers, lamps, etc. of the divine Arhats in the monastery at Vaṭa-Gohali. The donation of a Brāhmaṇa couple for the worship of Jinas, as recorded here, is noteworthy for it shows the spirit of toleration during this period (vide *Epigraphia Indica,* vol. 20, pp. 59ff.). Gautama Buddha gradually came to be regarded in Hindu society in India as an incarnation of Viṣṇu and with the growth of later Vajrayāna and Sahajayāna phases of Mahāyāna Buddhism in Bengal the religious differences which originally existed between ordinary Buddhist and Hindu householders in Bengal gradually ceased to exist with the result that both became fused together as members of one community. That is the reason why Buddhism gradually disappeared from the land of its birth during the medieval period. The fact is that ordinary Buddhist householders had by this time no touch with the writings of philosophers of the Buddhist school.

Tapo Nath Chakravarti

26

ZEN BUDDHISM AND BODHIDHARMA

In the Far East, there is no Buddhist influence so profound and penetrating as that of the Ch'an (Dhyāna) School, popularly known as Zen Buddhism. It has effected a change in the cultural life as well as the general outlook towards the method of attaining Enlightenment. Not merely that; from the beginning of the 10th century A. D. this School has gained supremacy over all other Schools in China, so much so that the monks in the monasteries throughout the country claimed in one way or the other the patriarchal lineage of celebrated Dhyāna masters. This phenomenon may be ascribed to the fact that the Dhyāna School has been the life and soul of Buddhism for over a thousand years in China. As a result of its important position, voluminous works have been produced by various writers. Some of them are compositions containing the sayings of Dhyāna masters, mystical and paradoxical in nature, and others are historical records concerning the patriarchal genealogy, eapecially that of the various branches of the disciples of Hui Neng, the 6th Patriarch. However, all of them unanimously claim that Bodhidharma, the sage from India, was the 28th Patriarch of the Indian tradition and the First Patriarch of the Chinese Dhyāna School. To substantiate this claim, various fabulous tales or legends have been popularized and linked with his life. We give below a few of them as an illustration ; —

1. When the Emperor Wu Ti of the Liang Dynasty (502-549 A. D.) could not understand and appreciate unusual answers given by him, he went across the Yangtse River by means of a piece of reed. He then entered the Shao Lin Monastery in Ho Nan province and practised deep meditation facing the wall for nine long years. As a sequel, it is said, he imprinted his image on the wall.

2. He is said to have attained the hoary age of 150 years, and passed away after that. However, a Chinese envoy, while returning from India, saw Bodhidharma with one shoe dangling from his monk's staff in the Pamirs (Ts'ung Ling). When he reported this to the Emperor, his tomb was unearthed and, to their surprise, they could not find anything else in the coffin, except a broken shoe!

The stories mentioned above appear to indicate that he was a person possessing supernatural powers, or, in the derogatory sense, that he was some sort of a magician. This, indeed, is unfortunate. We shall endeavour, in the following pages, to bring out the truth about this great sage. Special attention will be paid to the conditions of this School prior to his arrival in China and after his demise.

I. Was he the founder of the Chinese Zen Buddhism?

The answer to this question may be divided into two different categories. In one case, we may say 'No,' and in the other, 'Yes, but partially.'

It is a well-known fact that when Buddhism was introduced into China, it embraced all the three aspects of that religion viz., disciplinary observance, meditation and philosophy (Śīla, Samādhi and Prajñā). As such, we find a large number of works on Dhyāna or meditation in the Chinese Tripiṭaka. The earliest ones are probably those translated by An Shih-Kao in 148-170 A. D. Take for instance: —

1. The Sūtra spoken by the Buddha on keeping thought in the manner of great Ānāpana. Nanjio No. 682;

2. The Sūtra on perception in the law of practice of meditation. Nanjio No. 683.

and the works on the same topic translated by Chih Yao in 185 A.D. (Nanjio Nos. 724, 1338), by Buddhabhadra in A. D. 398-421 (Nanjio No. 1341), and many other important texts translated by *Kumārajīva* in 402-412 A. D. This would show clearly that the theory and practice of Dhyana had been known to the Chinese Buddhists quite early. Further, we find that there are 21 Dhyāna masters in the Buddhist Biographies[1] (completed in 519 A.D.) by Hui Chiao, in which the name of Bodhidharma is not included, while in the second series of the Buddhist Biographies[2] (completed in 645 A.D.) by Tao Hsuan, the names of 135 Dhyāna experts are found including a few of the immediate disciples of Bodhidharma. These facts clearly show how popular and well-known was Dhyāna Buddhism among the Buddhists at that time. They also show that Bodhidharma, who came to China round about 480 A. D., was the founder of the Dhyāna practices would not accord with truth.

This, however, concerns only the early phase of the Dhyāna School in China which had already a firm footing before the arrival of Bodhidharma, and, therefore, he is not entitled to the honour of being its founder, as is usually supposed. We must make it clear, nevertheless that the later developed Zen School has much to do with him, though the honour seemed to have been forced on him.

When we say the later developed Zen School, we mean the particular form of Zen Buddhism which flourished during the T'ang and the Sung Dynasties (618-905 and 960-1278 A.D. respectively), and was greatly popularized by Hui Neng, the 6th Patriarch who succeeded the Bodhidharma lineage. It was during the early portion of this period that the Japanese Buddhists came to China for higher studies and later took back with them the various Buddhist Schools including the Zen (Zen is the Japanese term for 'Ch'an' which in turn is derived from the Sanskrit word 'Dhyāna'). It is this form of Zen Buddhism that has been widely known to the West. It may be said of Bodhidharma that he was in some way associated with this School, though indirectly.

II. The truth of his being the 28 Patriarch.

Several Chinese records[3] of the Biographies of the Patriarchs of the Zen School claim that Bodhidharma was the 28th Patriarch of the Indian tradition starting from Mahākāśyapa. Ch'i Sung, author of two of these records, asserted that he was really the 28th Patriarch in India and refuted the authority of Fu-fa-tsang-yin-yuan-ching or 'sūtra on the Nidāna of transmitting the Dharmapiṭaka' (Nanjio No. 1340), a Sanskrit text translated into Chinese in 427 A. D. by Chi-chia-eh. This work gives us a list of the 'Parampara' tradition of 23 Indian patriarchs, beginning with Mahākāśyapa and ending with Siṁha Bhikṣu. In between we have Aśvaghosa as the 11th, Nāgārjuna the 13th, Vasubandhu the 20th and so forth. In the biographical sketch of the last Patriarch, Siṁha Bhikṣu, we are told that he was killed by Mirakutsu (Mihirakula?), a king belonging to the heretic faith, known for his destruction caused to Buddhist establishments and the massacre of the Buddhist monks in Kashmir. As a sequel, the line of 'Parampara' was discontinued after his death, because he could not find a suitable person to succeed him while he was alive. On the evidence of this document, it is very difficult for us to believe the claim that Bodhidharma was the 28th Patriarch of the Indian tradition. Moreover, as this claim was first made only in the 11th century A. D. by a staunch supporter of the Zen School in China, viz., Ch'i Sung, it can hardly convince us. We know that the motive behind this claim was to enhance the prestige of the said School.

III. The date of Bodhidharma's arrival in China

The popular tradition[4] recorded in the literature of the Zen School tells us that Bodhidharma reached Canton in 527 A. D. (or 520 A.D. in another version) in the reign of Emperor Wu Ti of the Liang Dynasty (502-549 A.D.). It is stated in the same source that he met the Emperor. As this Emperor chiefly devoted his attention towards the building of monasteries, giving alms to the monks and so forth, he could not understand the mystical teachings of Bodhidharma and, therefore, the latter left him without being appreciated. However, other earlier and more reliable sources present us with quite a different picture. The following cases may be cited : —

1. Tao Hsuan (595-667 A.D.), author of the second series of Buddhist Biographies gives us a life-sketch of Bodhidharma where he says: 'He first reached the territory of the Sung Dynasty (420-479 A.D.) and then proceeded towards the North'. This Sung Dynasty came to an end in 479 A.D. Moreover, he does not mention anything about his interview with the Emperor of the Liang Dynasty. If we accept this version, we may safely place the date of his arrival somewhere between 420-479 A.D.

2. One of the chief disciples of Bodhidharma was Sheng Fu who met the Master sometime about 480 A.D. when he was about 17 years of age. Sheng Fu passed away in 524 A.D. at the age of 61 years.

3. Hui Sheng,[5] another pupil of Bodhidharma learnt all the meditational methods from him and observed strictly the ascetic practices. He enjoyed the mature age of 70 years and died sometime between 502-519 A.D.

All the foregoing evidence leads us to the same conclusion, that is, that Bodhidharma reached China sometime round 480 A.D. If that is so, then the popular tradition about his arrival in 527 A.D. and about his meeting in the same year the Emperor of the Liang Dynasty, falls to the ground.

IV. His teaching and relation with the later Zen Buddhism

According to the general belief, it is said that the way of teaching adopted by Bodhidharma differed substantially from that of all the Buddhist missionaries who found their way into China. He seemed to have been a bad linguist because he never translated any Sanskrit text into Chinese, nor did he compose any literary piece. What was worse, judging by conventional standards, was that he preached an ultra-modern doctrine which seemed to harbour a profound hatred towards the traditional Buddhism as contained in the books. We quote below an outline of the fundamental principles of Zen Buddhism: —

"A special tradition outside the Scriptures;
Not to depend on books or letters;
To point direct to the heart of man;
To see (one's own) nature and become Buddha."

These lines tell us of the Dhyāna School of the developed form. We believe they have been strictly observed by most of the Zen followers in the Far East. However, to have a glimpse of its early simple teachings and practices, we have to go back to the sayings and the mode of life of Bodhidharma and his immediate disciples.

In his short life-sketch we find that he used to instruct Hui K'e, later on known as the Second Patriarch, the following twofold doctrine: One is 'reasoning' or the basic principle, and the other 'practice'. As regards 'reasoning' he says: —

"I firmly believe that all living beings possess the same Real Nature (Svabhāva). But in most cases it has been covered by the external dust of obstruction. I now ask them to give up falsehood and return to reality by gazing at the wall and meditating. They should not try to make any distinction between the self and others, between the saintly and the profane, but to stand firmly on these foundations and not to follow any other teachings. This, indeed, will be in concordance with the 'Tao' which is silent and devoid of activities".

Among the 'practices' there are four in number: —

1. The attitude towards one's enemy:—

"During the course of religious training, calamity may fall on the practitioner. Under such circumstances, he should think that in the previous Kalpas he had been led astray and had many ties of attachment and hatred. In the present life he might have been freed from them, but the suffering should be regarded as the effect of the deeds performed in one's former births. Therefore, one should willingly face all the sorrows and should not harbour any enmity towards the wrong-doer.... When this occurs in one's mind, it is in accordance with the 'Tao', because trying to understand what is the nature of enmity is to enter into the path of 'Tao'.

2. To be content with one's lot:—

"There is no Ātmā (soul) in living beings. Happiness and misery should be received calmly as they came. Even if one is treated with honour, it is due to his previous deeds; when their effect is over, it would not come again. Therefore there is no occasion for rejoicing. In the case of gain or loss, there should not be any difference in the tranquillity of the mind. If the Wind is calm and gentle with regard to success or failure, then, it is said to be in fitting accordance with the Dharma".

3. The avoidance of hankering:—

"The ordinary folk have for a long time lost themselves in greed—that means hankering. A seeker after the Truth should be different from them. He ought to rest his mind on inactivities and let him face squarely whatever is his lot. Indeed, all the Three Worlds are full of sufferings and nobody is secure. The Sūtra says:

'Whatever you hanker after,
The sequel is suffering.
There will be happiness
When one is devoid of greed."

4. To be in accordance with the Dharma:—

This is meant that the Svabhāva or Real Nature is inherently pure.

As Bodhidharma never composed anything himself, this sums up the total output of his teachings. In addition to this, we are told that he recommended to his disciples the study of the Lankāvatārasūtra. This is the only Mahāyāna text which had some connection with the Dhyāna School in its early stages.

Judging by the rather curt outlines of his teaching and the ascetic way of life of his immediate disciples, it appears to us that theoretically he had more or less based his philosophy on the interpretation of Buddha-nature in sentient beings as found in the Nirvāṇa Sūtra. Therefore, he regarded the saintly and the profane as on the same level, because intrinsically there would not be any difference between them. However, there is not the slightest hint of the theory of 'sudden Enlightenment' here, though it is very prominent in the teachings of the later patriarchs and their disciples. Moreover, the apparently eccentric ways of teaching, such as giving a blow, a kick or a tweak of the nose, drawing a circle in the air, saying paradoxical things, ' answering questions with incoherency and all kinds of absurdities—adopted by the patriarchs after Hui Neng, the 6th Patriarch (639-713 A.D.) cannot be said to have originated with Bodhidharma, because he had nothing to do with them. On the contrary, the emphasis laid on austerity, selfcontentment, self-mortification, the curb of desire, the belief in the effect of Karma, the insistence on concentration of mind by gazing at the blank wall, and other ascetic trends appear more akin to the early 'Arhat' ideal than the Mahāyāna Dhyāna practices seen after the 7th century A.D. To substantiate our statement, we cite a few examples in order to show what kind of austere life Bodhidharma's disciples used to lead: —

(i) Hui K'e, his chief disciple and in later generations known as the Second Patriarch, used to practise the teachings of Bodhidharma very strictly. During the period of persecution of Buddhism started by Emperor Wu Ti of the Northern Chow Dynasty (561-578 A.D.) one of his arms was cut off by an assassin. As he took it calmly by adhering to his master's instructions, he did not feel any pain. To stop bleeding, he cauterized the wound with fire and bandaged it with a piece of cloth. He went on begging his alms as if nothing had happened.

(ii) Na Ch'an-shih, or Na, the Dhyāna master, was a disciple of Hui K'e. Before his renunciation he was a renowned Confucian scholar. From the time of his becoming a monk, he gave up reading non-Buddhist literature and never touched a pen. Regarding his personal possessions, he had only a robe, and a begging bowl. He ate only one meal a day and observed the practice of 'Dhūta' very strictly.

(iii) Hui Man, a disciple of Na Ch'an-shih and a great-grand-disciple of Bodhidharma, devoted himself to the practice of non-attachment. He had only a robe and ate once a day. There was no other property belonging to him except two needles. He needed them for mending his rug in the winter, but would discard them during the summer. Once he was meditating in an open ground which was covered by snow over five feet deep. Some one saw him and offered him free board and temporary lodging. He refused that kind offer and said:

"I would accept your invitation only when no one else in the whole world is alive!"

Besides, the lives led by his other immediate disciples like Sheng Fu (who died in 524 A. D.) and Hui Sheng (who died during 502-519 A. D.) are more or less like the ones described above. If we compare their spirit of self-mortification and quiet contemplation with the boisterous daring of burning a wooden image of the Buddha (by Tan Hsia) and the killing of a cat (by Nan Chuan) and other strange acts performed by later Dhyāna masters—supposed to contain the mystery of Dhyāna ideals—we would come to the conclusion that there is hardly any common ground between them. Thus, it would appear to be an irony of Fate that Bodhidharma was placed as the First Patriarch of the Zen School.

From the foregoing evidence we are led to believe firstly, that historically speaking Bodhidharma was very sober, simple-living and comparatively less known than most of his contemporaries. The story of his meeting with the Emperor of the Liang Dynasty and other fabulous tales associated with his life cannot stand critical enquiry. Secondly, Bodhidharma's theories and practices concerning Dhyāna differed a good deal from those of the later patriarchs and their numerous disciples. If that is so, why was he regarded as the First Patriarch of the Zen School? Thirdly, the list of the six Patriarchs,

1. Bodhidharma
2. Hui K'e
3. Sheng Tsan
4. Tao Hsin
5. Hung Jen
6. Hui Neng (or Shen[6] Hsiu)

popularly known from the beginning of the 8th century A. D. and later on recorded in the Dhyāna literature written by Ch'i Sung in the 11th century A. D. was not found in early Buddhist historical records. Sheng Tsan, the Third Patriarch in our list, was not known to any author of the Buddhist Biographies (The second series completed in 645 A. D. and the third series in 988 A. D.). Tao Hsuan mentioned very briefly in his 'Biographies' the names of Tao Hsin and Hung Jen as teacher and pupil, but he did not say anything about their being the 4th and the 5th Patriarchs in the Bodhidharma line. Naturally, he could not, because he had already recorded the life-sketch of Hui Man, the great-grand-disciple of Bodhidharma.

On the face of all this, we would suggest that it is high time to correct wrong but popular traditions and beliefs concerning Bodhidharma and the patriarchs.

W. Pachow

FOOTNOTES

1. Kao-sheng-chuan or Biographies of eminent Buddhist masters. Nanjio No. 1490.
2. Shu-kao-sheng-chuan or the second series of the Biographies of eminent Buddhist masters by Tao Hsuan. Nanjio No. 1493.
3. i. Ch'i Sung: A treatise on the right School of transmitting the Law. Nanjio No. 1528,
   ii. Ch'i Sung: Records of the right School of transmitting the Law. Nanjio No. 1529.

iii. Tao Yuan: Records of the transmission of the lamp upto the Ching Teh Periodṭ1004-1007 A.D. Nanjio No. 1524.

4. See Nanjio Nos 1528, 1529 and 1524.
5. See Nanjio No. 1493. Ch. 6. 29
6. Shen Hsiu died in 706 A.D. The inscription on his tomb contains the above-mentioned list. It is claimed that he was the 6th Patriarch.

27

THE BUDDHIST VIEW RE-ETERNITY OF THE VEDAS

Śantarakṣita in his *Tattvasaṁgraha* has refuted the 'nitya-tva' (permanence) of the *Vedas,* which are regarded as eternal by the Mīmāṁsakas, according to whom words, meanings and their relationship are all eternal. The Vedas are without any condition before their existence nor have they any condition after them—they are authorless and eternal. The Mīmāṁsakas urge that the Vedas have unquestionable authority[1] as they are not human creations. As the five kinds of proof fail to establish the author of the Vedas, it is by the sixth proof i.e. proof of absence, the contention is established. Further, the Vedas being eternal are neither produced nor destroyed.[2]

Śāntarakṣita argues that the authority of the Vedas cannot be recognised in view of the fact that as the Vedas have got no author whose excellent qualifications would make him say the truth, knowledge derived from them is bound to be invalid. Again if the eternity of the Vedas is established on the ground of the absence of proof then the sky-flower should also be held as eternal.[3]

The Mīmāṁsakas argue that knowledge derived from the Vedas cannot be proved as invalid by inference, because inference is much inferior in authority to the proof of the revealed literature.[4] The Buddhists reply that inference is certainly of a superior authority to the Vedas which are nothing but sounds. If the sounds however are taken as proved by perception, then there is no justification as to why the words uttered by human beings should not be regarded so.

Again when Mīmāṁsakas argue that sound is eternal and omnipresent, because it is always and everywhere known like the Sun, the Buddhists reply that sound should not be accepted as omnipresent for the reason that sounds are produced in different places and at different times. The Sun on the other hand is seen at all places by all persons. Experience *(pratya-bhijñā)* not being a valid proof like perception cannot establish the eternity of sounds. Experience expresses' — 'same as that' and hence cannot represent perception which isfreefrom reflection *(kalpanāpoḍham)*.[5]

The words, according to the Mīmāṁsakas, are treated as eternal inasmuch as they express their meanings. In the *Śabdārthaparīkṣā* it has been shown that there is no relation between the word and its meaning,[6]

Again it has been contended that words and letters being eternal, the sentences should also be accepted as eternal. Though some sentences and words like *guṇa, vṛddhi* etc. may be used to express the wishes of their authors, yet that does not go against the eternity of the Vedas for they have got no authors and again for the reason that things described in the Vedas ate beyond the power of human beings to witness.[7] The Buddhists in this connection argue that eternity of sentences need not be proved in the light of the fact that there is no connection between the objects and the sentences. If the sentences are merely combination of words, then the letters so combined have no meanings to express. If the letters arranged one after another are to be considered as a sentence then how can eternal letters have arrangement as they are for ever existent and omnipresent?

Thus the Buddhists conclude by stating that the Vedas cannot be regarded as eternal and divine for the reason that they contain many unpleasant things as *kāma, mithyā, prāṇihiṁsā* etc.[8] Inasmuch as the theory of momentariness is established by Śugata the question of eternity of the Vedas should be dropped by all means.[9] Therefore as the Vedas have no authority on points of Dharma,[10] one should try to learn it from a person who is pure and who possesses pure knowledge of the universe in order to obtain truth and emancipation.[11]

Heramba Chatterjee

FOOTNOTES

1. सा हि प्रमाणं सर्वेषां नराकृततया स्थिता।
   वैतथ्यं प्रतिपद्यन्ते पोरूषेय्यो गिरो यतः।। *Tattvasamgraha,* sl. 2086
2. ग्रकृततत्वाविनाष्ठाभ्यां नित्यत्वं हि विवक्षितम्।
   तौ चाभावात्मकत्वेन नापेक्षेते स्वसाधानम्।। Ibid., sl. 2105.
3. Vide *Tattvasamgraha* sl. 2432: ग्रतो गगनराजीव नित्यता ऽस्ति न वास्तवी।
4. प्रत्यक्षपक्षनिक्षिप्तं शास्त्रमेव यतः स्थितम्।
   बलवत्तरमित्येतदनुमानस्य बाधकम्।। Ibid., sl. 2108.
5. प्रत्यक्षप्रत्यभिज्ञा तु प्रागेव विनिवारिता।
   भ्रान्तेः सकल्पनत्वाच्च नातो नित्यत्वनिश्चयः।। Ibid., sl. 2448.
6. वस्तुतस्तु न सम्बन्धः शब्दस्याथेन विद्यते। Ibid., 2470
7. न ह्येवं वैदिके शब्दे स स्वयम्प्रत्ययो यतः Ibid., sl. 2775.
8. स्म्भाव्यते च वेदस्य विस्पष्टं पौरूषेयता।
   काममिथ्याक्रियाप्राणिहिंसाऽसत्याभिधा तथा।। Ibid., sl. 2787.
9. ततश्चापौरूज़ेयेषु सत्याष्ठा त्यज्यतामियम्। Ibid., sl. 2795.
10. धर्म्मं प्रति न सिद्धाऽतश्चोदनानां प्रमाणता। Ibid., sl. 2809
11. ज्ञानालोकव्यपास्तान्तस्तमोराशिः पुमानतः।
    श्रुत्यार्थानां विविक्तानामुपदेशकृदिज़्यताम्।। Ibid., 2810.

28

PĀṬALIPUTRA : ITS IMPORTANCE IN THE HISTORY OF BUDDHISM

Name and Location—Pāṭaliputra, the later capital of the Magadhan empire, was recognised as one of the six great cities of ancient India. The various forms of the name Pataliputra are Pāṭaliputta (Pāli); Pāḍaliputta (Prakrit), Palibothra[1] or Palimbothra;[2] Palien-fu (Chinese.)[3] The city was otherwise known as Puṣpapura or Kusumapura.[4]

All the sources of information about the city of Pāṭaliputra suggest its location to the southern bank of the Ganges near the ancient site of modern Patna. The village Pāṭaligāma (earlier name of the place) lay opposite to Koṭigāma on the northern bank of the Ganges which formed the boundary between Magadha and the territory of the Licchavis of Vaiśalī.[5]

According to the Jaina *Vividha-tīrthakalpa* the city was built on the bank of the Ganges near the confluence of the great rivers of Mid-India, the Ganges, the Sone and the Gaṇḍak. Patañjali locates the city just on the bank of the Sone *(anuśonaṃ Pāṭaliputram)*[6] while in *Mudrārākṣasa* (IV. 16) Malayaketu is said to have crossed the river Sone to reach Pāṭaliputra. These accounts indicate that formerly the river Sone met the Ganges at the ancient site of Pāṭaliputra but later receded westwards.

Fa-Hien coming from Vaiśālī crossed the river Ganges and walked southwards for a *yojana* along the river and reached Pāṭaliputra.[7] Prolonged excavations carried out by the Archaeological Department have led to the exact location of the city of Pāṭaliputra, the remains of which have been found in the villages of Kumrāhār, Bulandi-Bāgh and other outskirts of the city of Patna.[8]

Buddhist Heritages of the City

Pre-Maurya Period: At the time of Buddha, Pāṭaliputra was merely a village named Pāṭaligama *(op. cit)*. During his last visit to the village while he was passing from Rajagṛha to Vaiśalī, shortly before his death, Buddha prophesied about the future greatness of the village and its ultimate destruction by fire, innundation and internal dissensions. At this time King Ajātaśatru employed two brāhmin ministers Vassakāra and Sunīdha to build a fortress at Pāṭaligāma as a precaution against the Vajjian attack. In honour of Buddha the people of Pāṭaliputra called the gate, Gotamadvāra, through which he left the city and the ferry ghat, Gotamatittha, at which he crossed the Ganges.[9]

The *Udāna*[10] relates that a large hall was constructed in the middle of the village of Pāṭali for the officers of Ajātaśatru. At the reguest of the villagers, Buddha passed a night in the hall. On the following day, he delivered a sermon to the people on the five kinds of reward of observance of precepts and the five kinds of disadvantages of an evil doer.[11] At a later date a brāhmin householder of Aṅga built an assembly hall for the Saṅgha of Pāṭaliputra.[12]

After the demise of Buddha, the waterpot and the girdle used by him were deposited in the city of Pāṭaliputra.[13]

According to the Buddhist traditions Ajātaśatru in his later life became an earnest and enthusiastic devotee of Buddha. After Ajātasātru, his son, Udāyībhadra reigned for 16 years. Udāyībhadra was succeeded by Anuruddha and then by Muṇḍa. Muṇḍa, it seems, had leanings towards Buddhism, because, just after the death of his queen Bhadrā he approached Bhikkhu Nārada at Pāṭaliputra and listened to a discourse on the impermanence of worldly objects.[14]

One hundred years after the demise of Buddha, the Second Buddhist Council was held for the purpose of settling disputes over certain Vinaya rules. Due to the difference of opinions, the Buddhist Church was split into two and afterwards into more than eighteen schools. The seceders were known as the Mahāsāṅghikas and the orthodox party as the Theravādins.

According to Hiuen Tsang, Khujjasobhita, a prominent member of the Second Council belonged to Pāṭaliputra.[15]

The Mahāsāṅghikas had great influence at Pāṭaliputra and though the Theravādins lived side by side with the other school they could not live with the Mahāsāṅghikas and finally receded westwards.[16]

After Kālāśoka and his descendants another new dynasty headed by Nanda came to the throne of Magadha. According to the *Mañjuśrimūlakalpa,* a Sanskrit Buddhist text, Nanda was a great patron of Buddhism. King Nanda, at the advice of his spiritual teacher, offered several gifts to the Caityas which were built on the deposited relics of Buddha.[17] Mahāpadma Nanda, son and successor of Nanda, was also devoted to Buddhism and provided the monks at Kusumapura with all their requisites.[18]

Bu-ston quotes from the *Mahākaruṇapuṇḍarika* Buddha's prediction of a list of successive guardians of his doctrine after his death and cites the names of two monks Aśvagupta and Uttara, both of whom belonged to Pāṭaliputra.[19]

All the facts stated above show that within a century after Buddha's demise the main centre of Buddhism along with the capital of Magadha was shifted from Rājagṛha to Pāṭaliputra, which also became the stronghold of the Mahāsāṅghikas.[20]

Maurya Period : Pāṭaliputra attained pre-eminence during the rule of the Mauryas. The first two emperors of this dynasty Candragupta and Bindusāra, were not so much in favour of Buddhism as were their remote ancestors, the Moriyas of Pipphalivana, who took a share of the relics of Buddha and erected a stūpa over them.[21]

Aśoka surpassed all of his ancestors by his outstanding system of administration and by his broad religious outlook. Though Aśoka showed sympathy and favour to all religious creeds, there are clear evidences which reveal his sṭrong faith and leanings towards the doctrine of Buddha and his Order.

As the accounts of the Chinese travellers testify, Pāṭaliputra was the first place where Aśoka commenced his activities for the benefit of Buddhism. He took out the relics preserved in the seven stūpas (vide *Mahāparinibbāna Sutta),* distributed them all over his dominion and erected on them stūpas of which the very first was constructed at Pāṭaliputra.[22] Aśoka it is said did this pious act at the advice of Upagupta, the spiritual teacher of the emperor.[23]

Huen Tsang furnishes us with the information that there was a miraculous stone with Buddha's fodt-print, placed in a temple near the relic tope at Pāṭaliputra. Buddha stood on this stone before his departure from Magadha towards Kuśīnagara.[24] Near that temple there was an Aśokan pillar, more than thirty feet in height with an inscription recording Aśoka's deep faith and his offer of the whole of Jambudvīpa (his empire) to the Buddhist Saṅgha.[25]

About two hundred yards north from the stūpa Aśoka built a new palace called Ne-le and erected another stone pillar known by the same name with a lion capital on the top of it and an inscription.

Both Dr. Spooner and Col. Waddell, who carried on excavations at the ancient site of Pāṭaliputra, support the statements of the Chinese travellers that Aśoka erected two pillars, some fragments of polished sandstone of which were traced by Col. Waddell.[26]

During the excavations at the site, a well, known as Agam Kuāñ (unfathomable well) was discovered. It was a large circular well (20 feet and 2 inches in diameter), the walls of which were raised-about 10 feet above the ground level and had eight windows. Huen Tsang perhaps witnessed this well and identified it with Aśoka's Prison. He is supported by Waddell. The tradition about the prison is as follows:[27] Aśoka, when he was very cruel (before his conversion to Buddhism) constructed a prison called 'Hell' which accomodated one thousand inhabitants within a walled city in order to punish the unruly citizens. But one day the king was overwhelmed at the sight of the magical power of a Buddhist Śramaṇa who was thrown into the Prison, and since then he destroyed the 'Prison' and made the penal code liberal.[28]

Among other objects noticed by Huen Tsang, there are, (i) a large stone vessel, which Aśoka said to have kept to hold the food for monks;[29] (ii) a large cave excavated at the instance of Aśoka at Pāṭaliputra for the use of Mahendra who joined the Buddhist order and attained the state of Arhathood;[30] (iii) caves for the use of Upagupta and other Arhats on a small hill to the south west of the city. By the hill side there were stone foundations of an old terrace and holy tanks[31] and (iv) five topes to the south-west of this very hill in a dilapidated condition. In later period some other smaller topes were built upon this main tope.

Col. Waddell identified the above cave-dwelling of Upagupta with the Chota-Pahari site of Pañch Pahari now known as Bara Pahan in the village of Nirandanpur Kharuma. The Panch Pahari was a group of five mounds containing five stūpas constructed by Aśoka. The Bara Pahari mound was the largest and highest of all in the area. Dr. Spooner discovered a few fragments of Chunar stone probably of the Mauryan period and remains of two brick stūpas. Dr. Spooner supposes that all the fives stūpas which Aśoka built were in this single mound. In one of the stūpas Dr. Spooner found an empty relic chamber and a small very early type of a Triratna symbol.[32]

The Monastery of Kukkuṭārāma

Kukkuṭārāma was a park at Pāṭaliputra The Kukkuṭārāma vihāra was situated in a garden named Upakaṇthakarāma on the right bank of the Ganges[33]. Originally the monastery was built by Kukkuṭāseṭṭhī[34]. It became an *āvāsa* of monks and a favourite resort of Āṇanda[35]. A monk named Bhadda, also a resident of the monastery, had conversation with Ānanda on the subjects of true religion, objects of recollection etc[36]. The Elders Nitavāsi, Sānavāsi, Gopaka, Bhagu, Phalikasandana lived here[37]. At a later date here resided Bhikkhu Nārada who delivered a discourse to king Muṇḍa[38]. Soṇaka, the preceptor of Siggava, Thera Caṇḍavajji, the teacher of Moggaliputta Tissa lived in this monastery[39]. Upagupta also resided in this monastery[40].

According to Tāranātha and *Divyāvadāna,* Puṣyamitra made an attempt to destroy the monastery but was obstructed, as the legend goes, by the roar of a lion which appeared miraculously.[41]

Huen Tsang located the Kukkuṭārāma to the south-east of the old city of Pāṭaliputra. Perhaps the old shrine of Kukkuṭ-ārāma fell into decay before Aśoka. Asoka built another monastery over the ruins of the old one which at a later date was known as Aśokārāma. Tissa, the younger brother of Aśoka, was ordained in this monastery and he lived here.

In the Pāli commentaries and Ceylonese Chronicles it is stated that the Third Buddhist Council of the Theravada School was convened in this monastery under the patronage of Aśoka, Huen Tsang also mentioned an assembly of one thousand Buddhist monks in this monastery.[42] In the *Divyāvadāna* the number of monks is given 30000 but they did not come to hold a council but only to attend Aśoka's first 'quinquennial festival of the holy priesthood.' The senior among them was the great Piṇḍola Bhāradvāja who had seen the Buddha.[43]

Aśoka used to provide daily food for all monks residing at the Aśokārāma.[44] A large number of monks from Aśokārāma headed by *Miṭṭhina* went to Anurādhapura of Ceylon to celebrate the foundations of the Mahāthūpa.[45] From this monastery Mahinda set out on his mission to Ceylon.[46]

Thera Dhammarakkhita, teacher of Nāgasena, lived in this

monastery.[47] Indagutta Thera (date unknown) was appointed by the king of the country to superintend the building of the Vihāra of Aśokārāma.[48]

The Āmalaka, and the Gong Tope

Huen Tsang found a large tope called Āmalaka stūpa just by the side of Kukkuṭārāma. He records that when Samprati ascended the throne after Aśoka's retirement he stopped the Asoka's largesses to the Buddhist church and reduced gradually his allowance which was given away by him to the Sangha. At last Samprati gave him half an ā*malaka* fruit in an earthen pot. Aśoka sent- even this half to the bhikkhus of Kukkuṭārāma. Yaśa, the abbot of the monastery, had the fruit cooked "to keep the kernal and have a tope raised" over it.[49] This mound was situated to the east of modern Ranipura within the Kukkuṭ-ārāma.[50]

Huen Tsang witnessed another tope called Gong-Call Tope in an old monastery to the north-west of the Āmalaka Tope. He narrates the legend of the foundation of this tope also. Formerly there were in the city about one hundred monasteries with the "Brethren of high character and the Tirthikas (heretics) were silenced. The Buddhist clergy gradually died and there was a great falling off in their successors." The Tirthikas assembled in the city and defeated the Buddhists in discussion and as a result occupied the Buddhist monastery and gained royal favour. After twelve years Deva Pusa (Āryadeva) a disciple of Nāgārjuna (Pusa Bodhisattva) of South India came to Pāṭaliputra and defeated them in an open meeting. "The king and his minister's were greatly pleased and raised this sacred structure as a memorial". But according to Fang-Chih it was not Āryadeva but Nāgārjuna himself who defeated the Tīrthikas[51].

After Aśoka

The successors of Asoka were not in favour of Buddhism and so the traditions are silent on the condition of Buddhism in Pāṭaliputra during their reigns. But there is no doubt that Pāṭ-aliputra still continued to be a centre of Buddhist learning for several centuries.

Though Puṣyamitra Suṅga, the usurper of the Maurya throne was an adherent of Brahmanism, he was not so antagonistic towards Buddhist monks as stated in the *Divyāvadāna* and the *Aśokāvadāna*[52]. According to these texts, Puṣyamitra attempted to destroy the monastery of Pāṭaliputra[53] and declared the reward of one hundred dinaras to one who would bring the head of a Buddhist monk. Buddhism however was in flourishing condition within the boundary of the Magadhan empire under the Suṅgas. Besides the massive construction of the Sānchi Stūpa, archaeological antiquities of this period have been traced from Pāṭaliputra[54].

According to the *Petavatthu commentary* (pp.244 ff) the general of King Piñgala of Saurāṣtra came to Pāṭaliputra and embraced Buddhism. King Paṇḍu of Pāṭaliputra (date not mentioned), his vassal Guhasiva and his subordinate King Cittāyana were converted to Buddhism[65]. Two Brahmins of Pāṭaliputra set out for Ceylon to meet Mahānāga Thera, a famous monk of the Island[56].

Tāranātha relates that during the reign of Kaṇiṣka, a brahmin named Vidu was making one thousand copies of the sacred Buddhist texts at Pāṭaliputra, while Huen Tsang states that the great Buddhist poet Aśvaghoṣa lived in a house at Pāṭaliputra[57].

As archaeological evidence of the presence of Buddhism, a large Bodhisattva image of Mathurā school of the Kuṣāṇa period, was found at the site of Pāṭaliputra[58].

Period of the Guptas and Kanauj King Harṣavardhana

Fa-Hien (or Fa-hsien) visited the city during the reign of Candragupta II. At the time of his visit there resided in the city a great learned Brāhmaṇa named Rādhasvāmi, a professor of Mahāyāna doctrine. The king of the country honoured and showed reverence to him. He might be more than fifty years old and all the kingdom looked up to him as a great teacher[59].

According to the traveller[60], the cities and towns of Magadha were the greatest of all in the Middle Kingdom (Central

India). The inhabitants were rich and prosperous and vied with each other in the practice of benevolence and religious ceremonies. Every year on the eighth day of the second month they used to take out a procession of images.

By the side of the tope of Aśoka there was a Mahāyāna monastary, a very grand and beautiful structure and there was also a Hīnayāna one, two together containing six or seven hundred monks. A brāhmin teacher, Mañjuśrī of the greatest virtue to whom the Samaṇas and the Mahāyāna Bhikṣus in the country showed honour, lived in this monastery.

A Bodhisattva image brought from Mathurā of early Gupta period was found in the ruins of a building at Pāṭaliputra.[61]

Dr. Spooner discovered a maze of ruined brick walls of the late Gupta period extending over the entire area of excavations.

Numerous clay sealings of which one or two were old but the majority belonged to the Gupta period had been found at the site.[62]

Buddhism had already begun to decline before the visit of Huen Tsang who travelled over this country for 16 years during the reign of Kanauj King Harṣavardhana. Huen Tsang witnessed Buddhism in a gradually decaying condition in many places of India. In the places like Malava, Mahārāṣṭra, Kanauj and Jalandhara where once Buddhism overshadowed all other religions, the traveller found Buddhists and non-Buddhists in equal number. But still in Pāṭaliputra along with Ayodhyā and Sind, Buddhist establishments and the monks of both the Vehicles were of far greater number in comparison to the Devas and the Heretics.[63] In the view of the traveller there were fifty monasteries with ten thousands monks but only ten Deva temples in Pāṭaliputra.[64]

Ou-Kong, who came after Huen Tsang, found Buddhism in a flourishing condition in Magadha. He stayed in a monastery of the Chinese which was probably situated at Pāṭaliputra. This was a rich monastery frequented by the monks and their disciples.[85]

Our history of Buddhism in Pāṭaliputra ends here on account of the final destruction of the city. Though the exact causes and the time of destruction are hithereto unknown to us yet the discovery of burnt wooden structures and the masses of alluvial soil over the site suggest that the first two of the three dangers if not the third one predicted by Buddha were the main catastrophes and it occurred long before the rise of the Pālas of Bengal. But the fame of Pāṭaliputra lasted even at the time of Alberuni in the tenth or at the commencement of the eleventh century A.D.[66]

Archeological finds

Archaeological finds which were discovered during the prolonged excavations testify that Pāṭaliputra was a great centre of Buddhism for more than one thousand years. Interesting discoveries bearing Buddhist antiquities (besides those which are mentioned above) found out by the Archaeological Survey of India are as follows ;[67]

1. Fragment of sandstone polished on both sides and with one face decorated with very narrow flutings (Mauryan).

2. A smooth slab of stone bearing in low incision an admirable figure of the Triratna symbol, the conventional trident representing the Buddhist Trinity with the Wheel of Law underneath.

3. Inscribed stone fragment possibly from the Triratna slab (Maurya or Sunga period).

4. A matrix bearing a trio of a very archaic symbols probably of 3td century B.C.

5. Ovel terracotta plaque bearing apparently, a picture of Bodh-Gayā temple in the centre with a figure of Buddha seated inside.

6. Head of a small Buddha figure in terracotta (probably from the plaque).

7. Matrix of baked clay bearing the legend ("seal of Buddharakṣita) in Brahmi character of the most primitive form.

8. Seal bearing the Buddhist creed in the lower half of a complete stūpa containing a figure of Buddha and flanked by two Bodhisattvas above.

9. A hoard of 52 Kuṣāna copper coins, containing coins of Kadphises II, Kaṇiṣka and Huviṣka.

10. Two gold coins of Kuṣāṇa type.

Binayendranath Chaudhuri

FOOTNOTES

1. McCrindle, *Anciet India as described by Megasthanes and Arrian,* p. 65.
2. McCrindle, *Ancient India as described by Ptolemy* (N. G. Mazumdar edition), p. 169.
3. Beak, *Records of the Western World,* I. iv.
4. *Allahabad Stone Pillar Inscription of Samudragupta* (C.I.I.); *Mahāvaṁsa,* ch. 18, 5; *Mahāvastu,* III, p. 89.
5. *Digha Nikāya,* II, p. 89.
6. *Mahābhāṣya,* 2.1.2. p. 510.
7. Legge, p. 77, *Nothern India According to the Shui-Ching-Chu* by L. Petech, p. 42.
8. *Annual Reports* (A.S.I.) 1912-13, pp. 54-59.
9. *Vinaya, I,* pp. 226-230; *Dtgha,* II, 86 ff.
10. *Udāna,* VIII. 6; *Ud. A.*, 407 ff.
11. *Digha,* H, pp. 85-86.
12. *Majjhima,* II, 57 ff.
13. *Buddhavaṁsa,* ch. XXVIII.
14. *Aṅguttara Nikāya, III,* pp. 57 ff.
15. Dutt, *Early Monastic Buddhism,* vol. II, p. 28,
16. *Buddhist Sects* by N. Dutt, in B. C. Law Volume I, pp. 285-286.
17. *Mañjuśrimūlakalpa,* pp. 611-612.
18. *Tāranātha's Geschichte des Buddhismus* by Scheifner, p. 55.
19. Bu-ston's *History of Buddhism,* vol. 2, p. 109.
20. *Early Monastic Buddhism,* vol. II, p. 30.
21. *Mahāparinibbāna Suttanita of the Dīgha Nikāya.*
22. Watters, *On Yuan Chwang,* vol. II, p. 91; Legge, *Travels of Fa-Hien,* p. 79; *Samanta-pāṣdikā,* Introduction; *Sumaṅgalavilāsinī.*
23. Watters, vol. II, p. 91.

24. Watters, II p. 92, Legge p. 79.
25. Watters, II, p. 93, Legge p. 79.
26. *Ancient Monuments of Bihar and Orissa, by* H, Quereshi, A.S.I., 1931, p. 102. Henceforth shortened as *Ancient Monuments.*
27. *Ancient Monuments,* p. 96.
28. Watters, vol. II, p. 88.
29. Watters, vol. II, p. 93.
30. *Ibid.,* p. 93.
31. *Ancient Monuments,* p. 96.
32. *Ibid.,* p. 98.
33. *Aśokāvadāna* in R. L. Mitra's *Sanskrit Buddhist Literature,* 6f. vide, N. L. De's *Dictionary,* p. 152.
34. *Majjhima Aṭṭhakatha,* II, 571; *Aṅguttara Aṭṭhakathā,* II, 866,
35. *Aṅguttara,* v. 342; *Majjhima,* I. 349.
36. *Saṁyutta,* v. pp. 15-16; 171-172,
37. *Vinaya,* I. 300, vide, Malalasekara's *Dictionary of Pali Proper Names,* vol, I. p. 615
38. *op cit.*
39. *Mahavaṁsa,* v. 122; *Dictionary of Pali Preper Name,* by G. P. Malalasekara, I, p. 615.
40. *Svayambhū Purāṇa,* ch. I.
41 . D*ivya.,* pp. 381 ff; 430 ff.
42. Watters, vol. II, p. 98.
43. *Dtvyā.,* p. 398 ff. v. 80; 163, 174, 234, 276.
44. *Mahavaṁsa,*
45. *Ibid.,* xxix, 36. '
46. *Samantapāsādikā,* I. 69.
47. *Milinda,* pp. 16-18.
48. *Samantapāsādikā,* 1. pp. 48-49.
49. Watters, vol. II. pp. 99-100; *Dtvya.,* p. 430.
50. N. L. De, *Geographical Dictionary of Ancient and Mediaeval India,* p, 152.
51. *Watters,* vol.. II, pp. 100-102.
52. *Early Monastic Buddhism,* vol. 2. p, 256.
53. *Op cit.*
54. A beautiful Triratna slab of high artistic value of the Suṅga period was found in Pāṭaliputra.—Annual Reports of 10,12-13, *A.S. I* (1916), p. 77.
55. *Dāṭhāvaṁsa,* by B.C. Law, pp XII-XIV. .
56. *Aṅguttara Nikāya Aṭṭhakathā,* 1. 384.
57. Watters, vol, 2, p. 102. p. 107.

58. *Ancient Monuments.*
59. Legge, p. 78, .
60. *I bid.,* pp. 78-79.
61. *Annual Reports,* op cit, p. 26.
62. *Ancient Monuments,* p. 102,
63. Vide *Decline of Buddhism in India,* by R. C. Mitra, p. 3.
64. Watters, II. pp. 86, 165.
65. *Decline of Buddhism,* p. 18.
66. *Alberuni's India,* vol. I, p. 200 Vide N. L. De's *Dictionary of Geography of Ancient India,* p. 151
67. *Ancient Monument,* pp. 107-110.

29

AN EARLY BUDDHA STATUE FROM YŪNNAN

The statue reproduced on plates 1-3 hails from Yūnnan province. In another paper.[1] it is described as follows:

Bronze-statue of Kuan-yin P'u-sa. Originally gilded. Height about seven inches including pedestal. This is considerably damaged, the lower and some of the upper part having broken away. The remainder of the halo and three pegs which fixed it to the body are still visible on plate 3. The Bodhisattva whose chinese name corresponds to Sanskrit Avalokiteśvara, is standing upright, the left hand carrying an alms-bowl, the right hand a willow-wisp.

The following story went with the statue. Originally it had been in the *garbha* to the great pagoda of Ch'ung-sheng Ssu near Tali city[2] but had dropped down during an earthquake. The military, stationed in the monastery, found it and sold it. Thus it got into the market. As Chinese curio-dealers usually collect all possible kowledge with regard to the origin of their curious in the interst of their foreign customers this legend might be true though it is unverifiable. The heavy damage which the precious piece has suffered is otherwise unexplainable.

The Chinese origin of the statue cannot be doubted. But it is not impossible that it was cast by Chinese artisans in Yūnnan. As much as we know now, the first bronze figures were cast there in the year 810 A.D. The style of the statue suggests rather an earlier date. During the period of the T'sang Dynasty (618-907) the folds of garments began to come off from the body and float freely while on our sample the drop stiffly and perpendicularly. Early Chinese Buddhist brozes were copies from stone-Budhas and follow the rules valid for stone sculpture. Besides, the halo seems to have been pointed.

If the statue was not cast in Yūnnan, it might have got there with an embassy. Embassies plied between Ch'ang-an, the Chinese capital, and Tali, the capital of the Tali Kingdom, since the middle of the seventh century, but the intercourse was interrupted between 751 and 788. As the pagoda was begun in A.D. 833, the statue might have been brought to Tali between 788 and 833 A.D.

Whatever that may be, it is one of the most charming Chinese Buddhas I know of and deserves well to be published for the first time in this volume in honour of Lord Buddha.

Walter Liebenthal

FOOTNOTES

1. *Sino-Indian Studies,* vol. V. I (1955) p. 67 p. 4.
2. *Monumenta Serica,* XII (1947) pp. 6-16.

30

A NOTE ON THE ĀRYADHARMADHĀTU-GARBHAVIVARAṆA

The *Āryadharmadhātugarbhavivaraṇa,* 'Discussion on the root of Dharmadhātu' (phags pa chos kyi dbyins kyi sñiṅ po'i rnam par 'grel), which is not available in Sanskrit and Chinese sources, is preserved in its Tibetan version in the Bstan 'gyur collection (mdo, nu, pp. 244b : 7-245b : 4). It is mainly an interpreatation of the famous verse

ye dharmāḥ hetuprabhavāḥ hetuṃ teṣām Tathāgato hyavadat/

teṣāṃ ca yo nirodha evamvādī Mahāśramaṇaḥ//[1]

The author attempts to comment upon the technical terms, such as, *dharma, hetuprabhava, Tathāgata* and *Mahāśramaṇa.* He classifies *dharmas* into seven nidānas A *Vijñāna* (consciousness), *nāma-rūpa* (mental and physical elements), *saḍāyatana* (six senses), *sparśa* (touch), *vedanā* (feeling), *jati* (birth) and *jarāmaraṇa* (old age and death). These seven dharmas originate from the five *hetuprabhava.* The five hetus are: *Avidyā* (Ignorance), *tṛṣṇā* (thirst), *upādāna* (grasping), *saṁskāra* (impulses) and *bhava* (becoming). The cessation of the above-mentioned dharmas and of the five *hetus* is itself *Nirvāṇa* or *Vimukti* (freedom).

According to the author, Tathāgata is one, who teaches others the true nature of things without any error. He fares in the same way which reveals truth to others. He speaks what he sees (lit. hears), so he is *evamvādī*. Then the author explains the meaning of the term *mahā* (in *mahāśramaṇa*) by referring to various synonyms, such as: *paṇḍita* (wise), *śūra* (brave), *tāpasa* (recluse) etc. Tathāgata is spoken of as *paṇḍita,* because he knows everything knowable; Tathāgata is *śūra*, because he destroys all sufferings; Tathāgata is *tāpasa,* because he practices *śīla* (moral conduct) strictly.

The atrributes of a *Brāhmaṇa* and those of a *Śramaṇa* becomes free from vices, a *Śramaṇa* totally removal the fetters of sufferings, so he possesses no vice. He is ordained (*pravrajita*) for he has removed all his defilements.

At the end of the text, the author opens a short discussion on the Four Noble Truths. He adds that, while suffering, its causal factors, and the cessation of those causal factors are explicitly mentioned in this verse '*ye dharmāḥ* etc', the *mārgasatya* (the way to cessation) is also necessarily implied here, though not explicitly stated. By the *anuloma* order the *hetus* (i.e. *avidyā* and others) lead to the effects (*jarāmaraṇa* etc.) On the other hand, reversely, the cessation of *avidyā* and others will lead to the cessation of the *jarāmaraṇa* etc. by the *pratiloma* order. If there be no *avidyā* there will be no *saṁskāra* and so on.

Regarding the critical estimation of the small text, it may be said that, the text shows the attempt made by Mahāyāna thinkers to comment on the above-mentioned verse, which has been explained by the Pali commentators. The Pali commentary, *Samantapāsādikā*[2], interprets the verse more briefly. It mentions *hetuppabhava* the five *khandas* (the constituent elements), but it does not attempt to explain the *meaning* of '*dhamma.*'

Nāgārjuna has his own method of interpreting the *Pratītyasamutpāda* doctrine. For example, in the *pratītyasamutpāda-hṛdayakārikā* (rten ciṅ' brel par byuṅ ba'i sñin po'i tshigs le'ur byas pa) preserved in Tibetan and Chinese sources (Tai-So No.

1654) of Nāgārjuna, he divides the tweleve nidānas into three groups[3], such as, *kleśa* (defilement), *karma* (action) and *duḥkha* (pain). *Avidyā, tṛṣṇā* and *upādāna* belong to *kleśa* group; *saṁskara* and *bhava* belong to karma group, and, the rest are of *duḥkha* group. But in our text, Nāgārjuna takes *avidyā, tṛṣ ṇā* and *upādāna*—which make up the *kleśa* group, and *samskara* and *bhava* which make up the *karma* group of the *Pratītya-samutpadahrdaya* together, and puts all the five under *betu.* The remaining seven are together placed under *dharma*[4].

Secondly, it is to be noted that the acceptance of the *margasatya* as implied in this verse is found also in the Pali Commentary[5] as well as in the *Mahaprajnaparamita "astra* (Chinese version)[6] of Nagarjuna. Nagarjuna quotes the verse '*ye dharmah* etc' in the *Mahaprajnaparamita "astra* with reference to the discussion on *anuloma* and *pratiloma* orders of Buddha's teaching. He says "It is evident that, when the first three out of the Four Noble Truths are mentioned, necessarily the fourth one, Noble Eightfold Path, i.e. *margasatya,* is also implied".

As regards the authorship of the *Aryadharmadhatugarbhavivarana,* the Dkar chag (of snar than edition Bstan'gyur) and the Colophon of the Tibetan version oŚ the text mention the name of *klu grub* i. e. *Nagarjuna* as the author. But, the Dkar chag also mentions the title of *Dhrmadhatugarbhavivarana* (chos kyi dbyiiis kyi "nin po'i mam par 'grel) as the work oŚ Dul ba'i go cha or *Vinitavarman*[7]- without giving any corresponding text.

However, from the internal evidences, it may by inferred that Nagarjuna, the auchor of the *Pratttya-samutpada-hrdaya* as well as of the *Mahaprajnaparamitasastra,* in all probability wrote the commentary the verse "*ye dharmah* etc" in order to explain the dharmadhatu essential nature of the dharmas and their causal factors), which constitute the theme of the doctrine of *Pratityasamutpada.* It may be that Vinayavarma (Vinītavarman) made another commentary, *Dharmadhātugarbhavivaraṇ*, which was evidently translated into tibetan but the translated has not come down to us.

आर्यधर्मधातुगर्भविवरणं नाम।।

रत्नत्रयाय तम:।।

ये धर्मा हेतु प्रभवा हेतुं तेषां तथागतो ह्यवदत्।
तेषां च यो निरोध एवंवादी महाश्रमण:।। इत्युत्कम्।

तत्र 'ये धर्मा' इति सप्ताविधा ज्ञेया:। विज्ञानं नामरूपं षड़ायतनं स्पर्शो वेदना जातिर्जरामरणं च। ते धर्मा: पञ्चधासमुत्पन्ना इति 'हेतुप्रभवा:'। पञ्चहेतव: कतमे? अविद्या तृष्णोपादानं संस्कारो भवश्चेति ते पञ्चहेतव:। ये च सप्तविधा धर्मास्तेषां ये च पञ्चहेतप–'स्तेषां च यो निरोध:'[8]। स एव उच्यते उपशमो विमुक्तिर्निर्वाणम्। स तथागतस्य देशितो भाषित: स्वाख्यातोऽर्थ:।

यथार्थस्तिष्ठति तथव[9] गच्छतीति तथागतोह्यवदत्। यो हि भावान् यथावदभ्रन्तेनान्येंषां तथावदवगमयतीति[10] स तथागत:। यथामार्गभ्वगमयति खयमेव तथा चर तीति। यथा श्रतं तथैव वदतीति 'एवंवादी'।

'महान्' इति प्रधान: श्रेष्ठ: परम उतमोऽर्थ:। तस्य वादी। य: पणिडत: शूरस्तापसो महोत्साहो वीर्यवान् अद्भतमुदावार: स हि महान्। ज्ञेयमशेषं वेत्तीति पंणिडत:। सर्वान् क्लेशान् हन्तीति शूर:। शीलं सम्यग्भावयतीति तापस:। न गुणादिपु निर्विद्यते महोत्साह:। शीर्षोष्णीषेऽग्निना लग्न इव वीर्यवान्। अद्भुतं ध र्ममभिमुखं करोतीति अद्भुतसमुदाचार:। एवं हि 'महान्'।

'श्रमण' इति पापक्लेशोपशमयतीति श्रमण:। सर्वपापविमुक्त इति ब्रामण:। (सर्व) संक्लेशजटाविमुक्त: श्रमण:। आत्ममलनिराकरणात् प्रव्रजित इति। आत्ममलनिकरणत् प्रव्रजित इति। अद्यशगुणयुक्तो भगवान् एवंवदतीति योज्यम्।

तथा दु:खं समुदयो निरोधश्च। मार्गसत्यमपि संग्रहीतव्यम्। तत्र अविद्याहेतो: संस्कारादि जरामरणान्तं कर्तारं विना प्रवर्तमातोऽनुलोभ:। अविद्यादि हेतुनां निरोधो ह्यस्य प्रतिलोभ:। अविद्या–वैपरीत्येन संस्कारादयो भवस्ति। एवंवादी महाश्रमण इति।।

इत्यार्यनागार्जुमकृतमार्यधर्मधातुगर्भविवरणं नाम।

Suniti Kumar Pathak

FOOTNOTES

1. Cf. Mahāvastu (Senart's edn.) III, p. 62; Vinayapiṭaka Mahāvagga, I, p. 146.

2. Mahākhandakavaṇṇanā, p. 728 (Colombo Hewavitaraṇa edn.)
3. Yaṅ lag bye brag' bcu gñis gaṅ/
thub pas rten 'byuṅ gsuṅs te dag/
ñon moṅs las daṅ sdug bsṅal daṅ/
gsum po dag tu zad par 'dus//
dṅ po brgyad daṅ dgu ñon moṅs/
gñis da..........pa las yin te/
lhag .... du sdug bsṅal yin/
bcu gñis ** ni gsum du 'dus// (mdo, tsa, fol. 158—Bstan gyur)
Cf. Mahāprajñāpāramitā Śāstra (Chiese Version) Tai So edn. 1509 f. 100b
4. See Compendium of philosophy (by Aung) p. 259-264 for different divisions of nidanas,
Cp. Nāgārjuna on the Buddhist theory of Causation by N, Aiyaswami Sastii (K. V. Rangaswanji Aiyanger dommemoration Volume)
5. ..... Maggasaccam panittha sarūpato adassitamapi/ nayato dassitam hoti/nirodha hi utte tassa sampāpako maggo utta va hoti/ ....(Samantapāsādika p. 108 Colombo edn.)
6. Nanji 1169; Tai-so edn. vol. 25, 1509 192b
7. Catalogue (vol. II, p 399), mdo 'grel LXXII:........ not give the page number of the text. Tohoku Impeual University catalogue mentions only the text of Nāgārjuna (No. 4101)
8. Tib. 'rgu daṅ' seems redundant
9. Tib. rtog pas na
10. Tib ....

Plate 1.1 Decent of Bodhisattva and Māyā's Dream, Amarāvati

Plate 1.2 Dream of Maya Bharhut

Plate 1.3 The Birth, Gandharā

Plate 1.4 The First Bath and Return, Gandhāra

Plate 1.5 Prediction, Gandharā

Plate 1.6 At School, Gandharā

Plate 1.7 The Midnight Scene, Gandharā

Plate 1.8 The Great Renunciation, Gandharā

Plate 1.9 Worship of Buddhas hair lock, Bharhūt

Plate 1.10 Buddha's Skelton

Plate 1.11 Approaching the Seat, Gandhara

Plate 1.12 Māra's Defeat, Gandhara

Plate 1.13 The First Sermon, Gandhāra

Plate 1.14 Miracle of the Fire Temple, Sānchi

Plate 1.15 Miracle of the Sacrifice, Sānchi

Plate 1.16 Miracle of Kapilavāstu, Sānchi

Plate 1.17 Division of the relics of Buddha

Plate 1.18 Miracle of Srāvastī, Gandhāra

Plate 1.19 Descent from Trayastriṁśa Heaven, Bharhūt

Plate 1.20 Offering of Honey, Sānchi

Plate 1.21 Śakra's visit to Indraśāla Cave, Mathurā

Plate 1.22 Submission of Devadatta's Hirelings, Gandhara

Plate 1.23 Mahāparinirvāṇa, Gandhāra

Plate 1.24 The Coffin, Gandhāra

Plate 1.25 Parinirvāṇa & Cremation of Budha, Gandhāra

Plate 1.26 Worship of Stūpa, Bharhūt

Plate 19.1 Vajradharma Lokeśvara (?), Temple 45, Sānchi, ht, 2′ 4″

Plate 19.2 Vajradharma Lokeśvara (?), Sānchi Museum, ht, 2′ 3 $\frac{3}{4}$″

Plate 19.3 Vajradharma Lokeśvara, Indian Museum (No. 3784), ht, 1′ 10″

Plate 19.4 Vajradharma Lokeśvara, Indian Museum (No. 3798), ht, 1′ 8″